# Engaging China

## How Australia can lead the way again

# PUBLIC AND SOCIAL POLICY SERIES

## Gaby Ramia, Series Editor

---

The Public and Social Policy series publishes books that pose challenging questions about policy from national, comparative and international perspectives. The series explores policy design, implementation and evaluation; the politics of policy making; and analyses of particular areas of public and social policy.

# Engaging China

## How Australia can lead the way again

Edited by Jamie Reilly
and Jingdong Yuan

SYDNEY UNIVERSITY PRESS

First published by Sydney University Press
© Individual authors 2023
© Sydney University Press 2023

Sydney University Press
Gadigal Country
Fisher Library F03
University of Sydney NSW 2006
Australia
sup.info@sydney.edu.au
sydneyuniversitypress.com.au

A catalogue record for this book is available
from the National Library of Australia.

ISBN 9781743329221 paperback
ISBN 9781743329238 epub
ISBN 9781743328835 pdf

Cover design by Naomi van Groll
Cover image: DniproDD/Shutterstock.com

We acknowledge the traditional owners of the lands on which Sydney University Press is
located, the Gadigal people of the Eora Nation, and we pay our respects to the knowledge
embedded forever within the Aboriginal Custodianship of Country.

# Contents

# List of Abbreviations

| | |
|---|---|
| ACC | Australia-China Council |
| ALP | Australian Labor Party |
| ANZUS | Australia, New Zealand, and the United States Security Treaty |
| APEC | Asia-Pacific Economic Co-operation |
| ASEAN | Association of Southeast Asian Nations |
| ASIO | Australian Security Intelligence Organisation |
| AUSMIN | Australia-US Ministerial Consultation |
| AUKUS | A trilateral defence co-operation arrangement between Australia, the United Kingdom and the United States |
| BRI | Belt and Road Initiative |
| CCP | Chinese Communist Party |
| ChAFTA | China–Australia Free Trade Agreement |
| CPTPP | Comprehensive and Progressive Trans-Pacific Partnership |
| GDP | gross domestic product |
| GFC | Global Financial Crisis 2008 |
| PLA | People's Liberation Army (China) |
| PRC | People's Republic of China |
| Quad | Quadrilateral Security Dialogue |
| RAA | Reciprocal Access Agreement (Japan and Australia) |
| RCEP | Regional Comprehensive Economic Partnership |

# Acknowledgements

We first conceived of this project back in September 2021, when the outlook for Australia's diplomatic relations with China looked grim. Seeking to follow on our 2012 co-edited volume, *Australia and China at 40*, we wanted to mark the 50th anniversary of diplomatic ties by producing a collaborative book bringing together a diverse group of leading China experts in foreign policy, security, economics, business, media, education, and cultural diplomacy.

Inspired by Gough Whitlam's bold China visit of July 1971, we embarked on this project in hopes of recapturing Whitlam's vision and courage by calling for Australians to renew their confidence in a robust engagement strategy. We began seeking out Sydney-based scholars, diplomats, and journalists who shared both our concerns over the surge of fear and misinformation that has undermined thoughtful public deliberations over Australia's complex relationship with China and our vision for how we could collectively contribute to a more stable, productive, and successful relationship with China.

The contributors to this volume have realised this vision by offering practical advice for how the Australian government and Australian firms, institutions, and individuals can confidently, proactively, productively and securely engage with China in ways that best benefit Australia and Australians today.

Throughout this project, we have received enthusiastic support from numerous individuals and institutions; it is our pleasure to acknowledge them herein. We are grateful for the administrative and financial support from the University of Sydney's China Studies Centre and its Centre for International Security Studies and their directors, David S.G. Goodman and James Der Derian. Stu Rollo and Yanping Zhang provided superb support for our book workshop. Workshop participants who generously offered valuable feedback on the draft chapters included David Brophy, Peter Cai, and James Curran, among others.

We would also like to thank Susan Murray and Naomi Van Groll of Sydney University Press for their professionalism, understanding, and enthusiastic support throughout the long and often challenging process of producing this book, and to Gaby Ramia for his encouragement and advice along the way.

Most importantly, our deep appreciation goes out to all of the chapter authors. Your generous contributions of time, wisdom, energy, patience, and good cheer – along with some much-needed encouragement over a cold beer from time to time – has sustained and inspired us. Thank you.

Jamie Reilly & Jingdong Yuan
Sydney, June 2023

# Foreword

*Gareth Evans\**

For Australia, navigating a course between China and the United States is not a task for the diplomatically or politically faint-hearted. The stakes could hardly be higher. We are hugely economically dependent on trade with China. We are highly vulnerable in security terms if drawn into any outright conflict. We are increasingly enmeshed in, and dependent upon, an alliance relationship with America – the longevity and protective value of which can, in the age of Trump, no longer be assumed. And we have a domestic environment where these issues are increasingly salient, and have assumed an ideological and potentially divisive cast, not least for the 1.4 million Australians with Chinese ancestry whose political voice is increasingly being heard.

There has never been a greater need, under these circumstances, for informed, rational and measured debate about how we can best position ourselves to meet the challenges presented by our relationship with China. The primary responsibility for conducting that debate, and steering the future national course, unquestionably lies with our political leadership, and in that context the election of the Albanese government in 2022 has brought some welcome respite from the stridency and superficiality of its recent Coalition predecessors. Foreign Minister Penny Wong has been properly applauded for the calm, measured and thoughtful tone that she, with strong support from the Prime Minister and key ministerial colleagues, has brought to stabilising and rebuilding our relationship with China, as well as repairing fractured or fraught relationships in the Pacific and elsewhere around the region.

The current government, although not without its critics from both left and right, has also been reasonably successful in communicating to the wider Australian community what it is doing and why, perhaps most notably and comprehensively, at the time of this writing, with the Foreign Minister's widely reported speech to the National Press Club in April 2023. She was clear-headed in saying that we should "not waste energy with shock or outrage" at China using its great and growing strength and international influence to advance its national interests, but rather "co-operate where we can, disagree where we must, [and] manage our differences wisely". And she was equally right in being very explicit that Australia's national interest lay, above all, in our living in a *multipolar* region, one "where no country dominates, and no country is dominated ... and all countries benefit from strategic equilibrium".

Some of the force of that latter message was diluted, however, by Wong spelling out China's various manifest challenges to that equilibrium, with its coercive trade behaviour, over-reach in the South China Sea, sabre-rattling over Taiwan and the like, but without also calling out specifically America's own contributions to putting that equilibrium at risk. Not least with its demand – supported publicly, if not always privately, across the political spectrum in Washington – for recognition of the continued *primacy* of the USA both regionally and globally. This may not have been a bad time to revisit a line from Bill Clinton that I have often quoted, in which he stated in my hearing soon after he left the presidency, off the record then and never subsequently on it, that the right choice for America was not to use its great and (then) unrivalled military power "to try to stay top dog on the global block in perpetuity", but rather "to create a world in which we will be comfortable living when no longer top dog on the global block".

But even the most competent and principled Australian governments tend to be excessively nervous about doing or saying anything that we think might conceivably put at risk our long-standing alliance love affair with the United States, and the security insurance that we like to believe flows from it. Although I would argue that our record was less timid than most, I don't exclude the Hawke-Keating governments from that assessment. Caution comes with the territory.

That is why it is so critical that public debate about our foreign policy choices – and all the defence, trade, investment, industry, immigration, education and other international policy choices that impact upon our national interests – be not just left to government, and to the media barons who have always tried, with some success, to influence its decisions. It is critical that the wise and well-informed voices be heard: leading scholars in the field, think-tank analysts and advocates with a long record of perspicacity, and highly experienced former diplomatic and business practitioners. That is exactly the task that Jamie Reilly and Jingdong Yuan have performed in bringing together their stellar cast of contributors to this volume.

There is an achingly long list of issues bearing on Australia's engagement with China that our policymakers are going to have to wrestle with for decades to come, all of them systematically addressed in these chapters. They include how to strike a balance, with AUKUS, the Quad and all the rest, between military prudence and provocation; judging whether and when US alliance demands, not least over Taiwan, will involve more risks than rewards; deciding how far to take the securitisation of trade, investment, and technology transfer; determining the point at which legitimate risk mitigation in research collaboration descends into counterproductive paranoia; and working out how best to turn on, not turn off, the massive contribution Chinese-Australians can make to the development of a safe and productive bilateral relationship.

All of these issues are going to require incisive decisive decision-making: upholding and advancing the universal values we embrace, including civil and political as well as economic and social rights; not being shy about using, as we have in the past, such creative middle power influence as we have to advance global and regional public good; and recognising that for the most part we have to take the world – and our biggest neighbours – as we find them, not as we might like them to be, and that we have no choice but to balance our idealism with pragmatic realism.

That is the flavour of all the contributions to this admirably well-researched, well-argued and timely book. It is, as the editors say, "a full-throated defence of engagement" with China – but intelligent, principled engagement, not engagement at any cost. If Australian policymakers, now and into the future, carefully read and take to heart this volume's analysis and prescriptions, our national interest will be well served indeed.

* Professor the Hon Gareth Evans AC KC FASSA FAIIA was Australian Foreign Minister from 1988–96, President & CEO of the International Crisis Group from 2000–09, and Chancellor of the Australian National University from 2010–19, where he is now Distinguished Honorary Professor.

# 1
# Engaging China: how Australia can lead the way again

*Jingdong Yuan and Jamie Reilly*

In July 1971, Gough Whitlam's bold visit to Beijing as Leader of the Opposition inaugurated Australia's engagement strategy. Within three weeks of winning the December 1972 federal elections, Whitlam had secured an agreement to establish diplomatic relations with China. The Australian embassy in Beijing opened on 12 January 1973. In October 1973, Whitlam fulfilled his promise to Chinese Premier Zhou Enlai by making the first official visit to the People's Republic by an Australian prime minister. At a banquet hosted by Zhou, Whitlam's brief speech laid out Australia's logic of engagement:

> China is our close neighbour ... capable of exerting profound influence in the world. Close co-operation and association between our two peoples is both natural and beneficial ... the different social systems of the countries in the region should not inhibit the flow of ideas. Greater consultation and dialogue ... may remove the barriers of misunderstanding and lessen the possibility of international conflict.

"The continuing importance of expanding trade", Whitlam added, "will be balanced by the development of close contact over a broad range of political issues". He concluded:

We believe that there are great benefits for all in putting aside
the rigidities and animosities of the cold war era and grasping
the opportunities inherent in the more open framework of
relationships now developing in the world, to build a structure of
co-operation based on mutual respect and mutual trust.[1]

Over the past five decades, Australia's engagement of China has
facilitated a deepening economic relationship alongside expanded
cultural, educational and people-to-people exchanges, fostering greater
understanding between the two countries and populations. Guided, for
the most part, by pragmatic approaches to navigating and managing
bilateral differences, Canberra's engagement strategy has yielded
numerous benefits for Australia and Australians. Yet, as the strategic
rivalry between the United States and China rapidly deepens, growing
distrust and fears of China are once again shaping Australian media
coverage and public discourse, with potent implications for Australia's
China policy.

In response, *Engaging China* offers a full-throated defence of
engagement. At this crucial historical moment, we seek to provide a
collective counter to the worrisome "China panic" that has swept across
Australia in recent years.[2] For all the different perspectives reflected in
the following pages, the contributors to this volume share a common
vision: Australia and Australians should continue to engage with China.
In explaining how and why an engagement strategy continues to serve
Australian interests, *Engaging China* offers a timely alternative to the
prevailing public and policy discourses on Australia's most challenging
bilateral relationship.

Our 2012 book, *Australia and China at 40*, brought together
Chinese and Australian experts to engage the most pressing issue of the
day: the tensions between Australia's security alliance with the United
States and its economic relationship with China. A decade later,
*Engaging China* calls on a diverse set of Australia's leading experts
on China to assess the current state of Australia–China relations and
offer pragmatic advice for how Australia can restore a healthy and

---

1   Whitlam 1973.
2   Brophy 2021.

stable relationship with China, one informed by a broader assessment of Australian national interests and guided by clearly defined objectives and pragmatic approaches.

Reaching the fiftieth anniversary of diplomatic relations between Australia and China also offers an opportune moment for this volume's contributors to step back and provide a broader set of reflections on this complex, crucial relationship. Collectively, the enclosed chapters capture the richness of Australia's relationship with China, reflecting the diverse perspectives of the numerous stakeholders across this broad relationship. In the following pages, the authors take stock of past achievements, identify recent challenges, and offer practical suggestions for how the Australian government and Australian firms, institutions, and individuals can proactively, productively and securely engage with China in ways that best benefit Australia and Australians today.

In recent years, Australia–China relations have been marked by growing estrangement, with tensions and animosity rising in both bilateral and regional settings. By 2022, as Geoff Raby, a former Australian ambassador to the People's Republic of China ( PRC) and the lead author in this volume, warns, the bilateral relationship had sunk to its "lowest ebb". While the change of government following the May 2022 federal election offers some hope for a restoration of normal diplomatic interactions, significant obstacles remain, informed by both sides' fundamentally differing perspectives on global and regional orders, and shaped by numerous contentious issues affecting both countries' core interests. Despite formally retaining their "comprehensive strategic partnership", in fact the Australia–China relationship is characterised today by a sense of drift and uncertainty, seeking an elusive anchor and a stable balance between coexistence, co-operation and contestation.[3] To ensure a return to normalcy and pragmatism, both sides will need to make serious efforts. *Engaging China* represents our collective contribution.

In this introductory chapter, we aim to denote key structural constraints, challenges and opportunities for Australia's engagement strategy. After briefly providing some historical context, we discuss the

---

3    Curran 2022.

descent into diplomatic acrimony over the past decade. The second section compares variations in China policy across Australia's two major political parties; the third section describes how deepening security tensions are affecting the broader economic relationship. We conclude by briefly previewing the remaining chapters. Throughout, we aim to highlight two crucial challenges for Australian policymakers: how to "right-size" the role of the United States within the Australia–China relationship, and the importance of restoring a bipartisan, socially embedded consensus in support of a robust engagement strategy.

## The US alliance and Canberra's China policy

Since federation in 1901, Australia has always sought "a great and powerful friend" to rely on for its security. For more than 70 years, the Australia, New Zealand and the United States Security (ANZUS) Treaty has served as the anchor of Australia's foreign and security policy, which in turn has affected how Australia conducts its China policy, thereby affecting its relations with Beijing. Formed during the early years of the Cold War, the alliance has endured major changes in international politics and regional geopolitical shifts, and remains a key pillar for Australian security and prosperity.[4] Australia's vulnerability to security threats due to its geographic location – a continent-sized territory that is thinly populated but with an extensive coastline and vast areas to defend – has had a major impact on its strategic culture, statecraft and diplomacy. Most important has been the courting of "great and powerful friends," namely since 1945, the United States.[5] Australia has lent its unswerving support for all major US foreign policy actions by dispatching troops to the Korean War, Vietnam War and US invasions of Afghanistan and Iraq, and the fight against the Islamic State of Iraq and Syria (ISIS) in northern Iraq.

As long as Washington remained committed to engaging Beijing, Australia–China relations generally developed smoothly. Up through

---

4    Dean, Frühling and Taylor 2016. See also United States Studies Centre 2021.
5    Fernandes 2022; Gyngell 2017.

the second Obama administration, engaging China had remained the United States's guiding principle for managing China's rise, under expectations that China would become a stakeholder in the US-led postwar rules-based liberal international order. Australia, for its part, played an important role through the 1990s by helping to integrate China into the regional networks of economic institutions, in particular the Asia-Pacific Economic co-operation (APEC), and by supporting Beijing's inclusion in the region's emerging security institutions such as the Association of Southeast Asian Nations (ASEAN) Regional Forum (ARF). But even during this period, serious disruptions in Sino-US relations, most prominently the 1995–96 Taiwan Strait crisis and the 1999 US/NATO bombing of the Chinese embassy in Belgrade, led Canberra to adopt similar positions and, as a result, caused crises in Australia's relations with Beijing.

During periods of relatively stable and even improving US–China relations, Australia has been able to expand its economic ties with China while continuing to strengthen its security relationship with the United States. Maintaining this delicate balance, which has been characterised as "riding two horses", has never been easy, yet Australian policymakers generally managed to avoid costly tensions with Beijing. A decade ago, Canberra's balancing act began to experience greater pressure, as the Obama administration launched its "Pivot to Asia" strategy while China was becoming more assertive in its foreign policy. Initially, both Labor and then Coalition governments sought to retain their engagement strategy by signing up to a "comprehensive strategic partnership" with China, concluding a bilateral free trade agreement, and joining the China-led Asian Infrastructure Investment Bank (AIIB), despite Washington's admonitions. Broader structural shifts at both the global and regional levels have subsequently forced Canberra to become more "realistic" about China and embark upon major policy reassessments.[6]

Since the Trump administration came to power in 2017, US–China relations have rapidly deteriorated. Australia responded by adjusting its China policy, at times even going further than Washington in what

---

6    This changing perspective and subsequent shift in Australia's China policy is
     discussed in detail in Curran 2022, chapters 6–7.

the Coalition government under Turnbull characterised as "standing up" to Beijing. Canberra joined forces with Washington, Tokyo and New Delhi in reviving the Quadrilateral Security Dialogue (the Quad), a regional mini-lateral security arrangement. Indeed, not only did the Turnbull government fully embrace the Free and Open Indo-Pacific concept that calls for the maintenance of the rules-based regional order, the succeeding Morrison government went out of its way in discarding Australia's long-held "strategic ambiguity" of managing its relations with China, replacing it with a decidedly "strategic clarity" approach by firmly aligning with Washington's positions.[7]

The Morrison government's hardened policy stance on China aligned with and to a large extent responded to the Trump administration's confrontational approach towards Beijing, including but not limited to an across-the-board trade war, increasing restrictions on technology transfers, and greater efforts in strengthening alliances and expanding security partnerships in the Indo–Pacific region. Canberra's policy shift not only saw enhanced alliance coordination such as the annual Australia-US Ministerial Consultation (AUSMIN) meetings but also in the areas of increased defence spending, major procurement of US weapons systems, and more frequent joint military exercises. In addition to the Quad, Canberra's participation in the recently launched AUKUS, a trilateral defence co-operation arrangement between Australia, the United Kingdom and the United States, has raised serious concerns whether the loss of autonomy under the structural pressure would be truly beneficial to Australia's national interests, including its security.[8]

## (Bi)partisan approaches to Australia–China relations

Up until the 2010s, Whitlam's China engagement policy had received bipartisan endorsement by successive Australian governments, albeit with different rationales and applied with variation.[9] The Australian

---

7   Medcalf 2021.
8   White 2022. See also Fraser and Roberts 2014.
9   For a historic review, see Fitzsimmons 2023.

Labor Party (ALP) has generally embedded its preferred China policy within the broader regional context, relying upon a combination of regional institutions as well as US leadership to address the myriad challenges arising from China's rise in power and prosperity. The Liberal–National Coalition (Coalition or LNP), on the other hand, has consistently identified the US alliance as the anchor of its overall foreign policy, including towards China. While diverging in emphases, both parties generally shared a faith that a pragmatic approach towards China could be found and sustained – one that ensured that Australia continued to accrue economic benefits by engaging China while relying upon US leadership in the region alongside expanding networks of US-led alliances and partnerships to address the security risks associated with a stronger and more assertive China.[10]

At the same time, Labor governments have been particularly wary of being portrayed as less than totally committed to the US alliance, and therefore often have made extra efforts to reassure their American counterparts. This consideration helps explain behviour such as Prime Minister Julia Gillard's remark that America "has a true friend Down Under" to the joint session of US Congress and her government's ready endorsement of the rotation of US Marines in Darwin, Kevin Rudd's confessed "realism" about the China threat and Anthony Albanese's attendance of the Quad meeting the day after his swearing-in as Australia's prime minister.

Towards the end of the previous federal Labor government (Gillard/Rudd), Canberra held a relatively cautious but optimistic view of China as a major trading partner, a rising power in the region that was still amenable to the overall framework of multilateralism and rules-based order. The 2012 *Australia in the Asian Century* White Paper is indicative of this general assessment. The government was also adopting a hedging strategy as it welcomed and embraced the Obama administration's "Pivot to Asia" policy, including agreement to hosting the rotation of US Marines in Darwin. In fact, President Obama gave a speech at a joint session of the Australian parliament announcing the US decision to shift its focus to Asia. Prime Minister Gillard, for her part, praised the US–Australia alliance during her speech at the

---

10   Cohen 2020; Matthews and Ravenhill 1988, 9–20.

US Congress, telling her hosts that America has a trusted friend in Australia. The ALP government also banned Huawei from participating in Australia's national broadband network construction, although the decision was not widely publicised. The general public also held the view that China played an important role in Australia's economic growth and prosperity. According to the Lowy polls during this period, China was even ranked higher than other Asian countries and the United States as the "more liked" country. But during this period, Australian experts also raised the question of whether the United States had the staying power of China, which, having surpassed Japan as the world's second-largest economy, would challenge American primacy in the region. Professor Hugh White, in a prescient *Quarterly Essay*, cautioned Australia against ignoring this fact as he drew attention to the significant "power shift" taking place in the region.[11]

This relatively optimistic view of China continued under the Coalition government, which took power after the 2013 federal election. Between 2013 and 2016, the Abbott and Turnbull governments welcomed Chinese President Xi Jinping to give a speech at the Australian parliament (2014), signed the Australia–China Free Trade Agreement (2015), and, despite US objections, joined the China-sponsored AIIB (2016). But major shifts were taking place in 2016, when Canberra was beginning to take another hard look at its relations with China. Several factors informed this reassessment. The first was a recognition that Australia's relationship with China, up to that point one that had been driven by – based on Prime Minister Abbott's confession – "greed and fear", was confronting new realities. As China's power continued to expand, together with a more assertive foreign policy, a new reality was sinking in: that China could be a major force that would undermine and challenge the postwar rules-based order upon which regional peace and prosperity had depended for over seven decades. Several events pointed to this major shift: China's artificial island building in the South China Sea and its outright rejection of the Hague-based Permanent Court of Arbitration's verdict on the South China Sea disputes; the People's Liberation Army's (PLA's) frequent encounters with the US military in western Pacific, raising

---

11   White 2022.

the risks of accidents; and the growing Chinese influence activities in Australia, both widely covered by the media and reported by the intelligence agency. These developments played a critical role in hardening Australia's views of China, which were spelled out in the 2016 defence White Paper and the 2017 foreign policy White Paper. Australia subsequently passed legislation regulating foreign political influence in Australia, refused to conclude a bilateral extradition agreement with China that had been negotiated for a decade, and formally and more publicly banned Huawei. During this period, the Australian government also tightened its scrutiny of foreign investment.

By 2017, bilateral relations had deteriorated sharply, as Canberra's growing concerns over Chinese political interference in Australian politics triggered heated policy and public debates, leading ultimately to the passage of a major new foreign interference law in late 2018.[12] Meanwhile, the Turnbull government banned Chinese communications providers Huawei and ZTE from participating in Australia's fifth-generation (5G) broadband network development, the first country from the Five Eyes alliance to do so. Australia also tightened its scrutiny of Chinese investments in what are considered national security-sensitive sectors and critical infrastructure. Canberra further infuriated Beijing by calling for an independent international inquiry into the origins of the COVID-19 pandemic. In retaliation, China imposed bans on various Australian exports ranging from barley, beef and coal to wine and lobsters.[13] The outbreak of the COVID-19 pandemic and Canberra's proposal for an international investigation reflected an inflection point where a much more hardened view of China was taking shape and formed the basis of Australia's policy towards China.

Clearly, over the past decade, what has generally been a bipartisan consensus in support of engaging China has steadily eroded.[14] While the Abbott government sought to retain what it portrayed as a reasonable balance between China and the United States, the

---

12   For an excellent analysis, see Chubb (forthcoming).
13   Strangio 2020.
14   Galloway 2022.

subsequent Turnbull and Morrison governments increasingly emphasised the need to stand up to Beijing's aggressive foreign policy. This shift has been justified through an emphasis on normative principles such as human rights, rule of law, and democracy, augmented by deepening concerns over China's alleged influence operations in Australia (for example, through efforts to co-opt Chinese-language media and civic groups in the Chinese–Australian community), its foreign policy direction and the resulting challenges to regional stability and to Australia's own national security.[15]

The ALP criticised the Coalition for its unnecessary, provocative and so-called "warmongering" rhetoric in its China policy, and for failing to engage countries in the region to strengthen multilateral institutions, which ALP leaders insisted could provide valuable counterweights to China's growing influence and assertive behaviours.[16] While in opposition, the ALP also warned against viewing China's rise as inevitably threatening and so requiring direct confrontation with Beijing. Instead, ALP policymakers called for Australia to retain its autonomy, agency and pragmatism within the context of the US–Australia alliance while sustaining diplomatic engagement with Beijing.[17]

The Coalition government responded by doubling down on its hardline approach. In April 2021, the Morrison government used the *Foreign Relations Act* to cancel the memorandums of understanding on the Belt and Road Initiative that the state government of Victoria had signed with China's National Development and Reform Commission. Canberra also conducted a review of the Port of Darwin lease with the Chinese state-owned Landbridge Group, but eventually allowed the deal to stay.[18]

During the May 2022 federal election, Australia's China policy became the subject of sharp partisan debate, as the Morrison government

---

15  These concerns and assessments are encapsulated in a series of foreign policy (Department of Foreign Affairs and Trade 2017) and defence white papers (Department of Defence 2016, 2020) during the reign of the Coalition governments (2013–22).
16  McHugh 2021.
17  Burgess and Li 2022.
18  Coorey 2021; Galloway and Bagshaw 2021.

sought to depict the ALP as Beijing's preferred party. Anthony Albanese, then Leader of the Opposition, rejected the allegation and argued that it was difficult to discern the difference between the ALP and the Coalition on national security issues. Instead, he highlighted the three pillars of the ALP's proposed foreign policy: Australia's alliance with the United States; engagement with regional partners; and engagement in multilateral forums such as the United Nations.[19]

Upon assuming power, the Labor government began to face up to the significant challenges of managing Australia's relations with China. Prime Minister Albanese and his team have chosen continuity rather than change, while at the same time placing more emphasis on diplomacy rather than solely relying on the US alliance. With the Biden administration increasing its focus on strengthening regional alliances and partnerships to counter China, the new ALP government has reaffirmed its continued commitment to the Quad and AUKUS. Canberra continues to strengthen its military alliance with the USA, including the reported future deployment of B-52 strategic bombers south of Darwin in northern Australia.[20] It has also expanded and deepened its security and economic ties with its regional partners with the signing of a landmark Australia–Japan Joint Declaration on Security Co-operation (JDSC) and the Australia-India Economic Co-operation and Trade Agreement (ECTA).[21]

At the same time, the Albanese government has also renewed official engagement with China at the ministerial level, culminating in the Albanese–Xi summit on the sideline of the November 2022 Group of Twenty (G20) meeting in Bali, Indonesia. While these are welcome developments, a real reset in bilateral relations will take time and much more effort than simply the restoration of high-level meetings.[22] The ALP's China policy will likely be marked by principled pragmatism, with a focus on policy deliberation rather than rhetoric, and a pursuit of reciprocity in diplomatic ties.[23] Meanwhile, the new government is

---

19   Albanese 2022. See also Collinson 2022.
20   Grigg, Robinson and Bali 2022.
21   Kaul 2022; Reuters 2022.
22   *Australian* 2022; Gunia 2022.
23   SBS 2022.

shifting its focus towards the South Pacific to repair the damage done through years of negligence by the Coalition governments. Indeed, the Labor government has placed the Pacific island states front and centre of its diplomacy, with additional resources (although in absolute terms still small) dedicated to addressing the more urgent issues of climate change. The growing importance of these small states has been reflected in Foreign Minister Penny Wong's frequent visits to the region. A major effort has been focused on the Solomon Islands, whose recent agreement with China had caused great concern in Australia. Canberra has sought clarification from and also conveyed reassurance to the Solomon Islands government.

## Managing economic ties despite diplomatic alienation

Amidst these turbulent political ebbs and flows, economic ties have proven the most resilient dimension of an increasingly complex relationship. China remains Australia's largest trading partner, playing a central role across multiple key sectors of the Australian economy. The scope, speed and scale of these developments were unimaginable in 1972. Most significant has been the growing bilateral trade over the past 15 years, particularly during the 2007–08 Global Financial Crisis (GFC) when China's unprecedented economic stimulus helped Australia avert a potential economic downturn. The resulting economic interdependence helps explain why, amid escalating diplomatic tensions over the past few years, bilateral trade remains strong, despite China's economic sanctions against several Australian exports.[24]

The phenomenal growth in Australia–China economic ties over the past 15 years has been attributed to two key drivers: China's post-GFC growth model of capital- and resource-intensive infrastructure developments, growing urbanisation, and the booming property market on the one hand; and the success of the country's poverty alleviation program on the other. Lifting hundreds of millions of Chinese people out of poverty, with resulting demands by the new middle class for housing and automobiles, has generated China's need for the minerals and energy

---

24   Wickes, Adams and Brown 2021.

supplies that Australia is well positioned to provide. Iron ore has been one of the essential commodities (others being crude oil and natural gas) that has enabled China to transform its economy, including a strong steel industry that accounted for 57 per cent of global output in 2020, with 88 per cent of the iron ore for steel production sourced from the global seaborne market. Australia alone meets 60 per cent of Chinese overseas imports.[25]

These economic realities help explain why, despite the diplomatic difficulties, Australia–China trade ties remain strong. Even amidst the onset of the COVID-19 pandemic, Australian exports to China in 2020 registered a new record high at A$159 billion, with bilateral trade totalling A$245 billion, thanks largely to rising commodity prices and China's continued strong demand for iron ore. While Australia's global trade as of July 2021 declined by 13 per cent over 2020, its trade with China fell only 3 per cent.[26] Bilateral trade continued to grow in 2021 to A$282 billion, although Australia's exports experienced decline.[27] But Chinese investments in Australia have experienced significant declines in recent years after years of steady growth, dropping from a record high at US$16.2 billion in 2008 to only US$585 million in 2021 due largely to Canberra's closer scrutiny of foreign investments and the COVID-19 pandemic.[28]

While the economic dimension of the bilateral relationship appears to have weathered the diplomatic storms, Beijing's increasing use of economic coercion and the vulnerability of Australia's economic reliance on China led many in Canberra to seriously consider trade diversification away from China. Chinese investment in Australia has raised concerns over the risk of Beijing using its economic might to gain access to and exert influence over Australian politicians and politics. The degree to which Australia is able to quickly find alternative export destinations and import sources remains subject to market realities as well as political considerations. Yet despite the considerable challenges facing any government-guided trade diversification

25   Uren 2021.
26   Department of Foreign Affairs and Trade 2022.
27   Bloomberg 2022.
28   KPMG and the University of Sydney 2022.

initiative, Canberra's efforts may be yielding some modest results. Recent statistics suggest that Asian countries collectively, apart from Japan, have now overtaken China as both the most important destinations for Australia's exports and sources of Australia's imports.[29]

Like Australia, Japan has enmeshed extensive economic interdependence with China, yet Japan's approach in China policy differs sharply from that of Australia. Tokyo and Canberra share similar views about the growing China challenge strategically and diplomatically; the two countries have strengthened their security ties through the Quad and the Reciprocal Access Agreement (RAA) that Tokyo and Canberra signed recently. The RAA is a co-operative agreement between the two countries' defence forces to train in each other's territories in addition to joint military exercises, access to facilities and transfers of military equipment and technologies. But the Japanese business community remains vocal about the importance of maintaining economic ties with China and it has been more involved, including through back channels with Japanese politicians, to influence the government's policy.[30]

By contrast, the Australian business community and sub-national actors, most importantly states and territories, appear to be less vocal – at least publicly, with rare exceptions – in expressing their concerns over the potential economic consequences of gradual deterioration of Australia–China relations at the politico-diplomatic level. To some extent, big business players, typically in the resources sectors, have not perceived the need to intervene, given that the bilateral diplomatic tension has not severely affected their bottom line since soaring commodity prices have continued to deliver handsome payoffs.[31]

There is no guarantee that bilateral political tensions will not spill over to the economic realm. The spectre of Australian firms losing reliable access to their most important export market is a harsh reality that cannot be ruled out. Several factors could undermine Australia's economic ties with China. China's slowing economy, due partly to COVID-19 and partly to Beijing's efforts in economic restructuring,

---

29   Uren 2022.
30   Ueda 2021.
31   Korporaal 2021. See also her contribution to this volume.

could result in lesser demand for natural resources from Australia. China could also choose to further punish Australia by restricting imports from an expanded list of Australian products while discouraging Chinese students and tourists from travelling to Australia. Like Australia, China is also exploring how it can diversify supply sources for its commodity imports. Furthermore, the temptation to place education, science and technology exchanges under greater scrutiny to mitigate foreign influence threats risks spilling over some of Australia's more profitable and, so far, mutually beneficial areas of co-operation, with serious implications. These sectors also remain subject to broader structural conditions, including the ongoing US attempts at decoupling from China across a range of high-tech sectors.[32]

The past decade, particularly the nine years 2013–22 when the Coalition governments were in power, have witnessed a steady deterioration in Australia–China relations. While Australia's engagement policy as advocated by Whitlam suggested a pragmatic approach for managing ties with China, the intensity and style of Australia's approach to engagement have been most powerfully shaped by broader structural factors – most importantly US–China relations. Australia's foreign and security policies continue to be predicated upon the close security alliance with Washington. As a result, the growing US–China strategic rivalry over the past decade has imposed significant constraints on Australia's policy towards China, with alliance solidarity increasingly providing the justification for a more confrontational posture towards Beijing.

The US–China strategic rivalry and Australia's increasing hawkish – and even with the current ALP government, firm and uncompromising – positions on China have both fed and in turn taken their cue from the media depiction of the bilateral relationship, which has been largely negative in its discourse.[33] Canberra would do well to uphold its independent foreign policy, which may sometimes be different from US positions in terms of priorities and approaches. While acknowledging that the regional order is undergoing fundamental changes, Australian

---

32    Bateman 2022.
33    Brophy 2021.

policymakers should seek a more active role in regional diplomacy, promoting an emerging new order based on multilateralism and regional institutions, with binding norms and rules on all players, including both the United States and the People's Republic of China (PRC). At the same time, when US policy strengthens multilateralism, rather than just promotes its unilateral agenda, Canberra should work with Washington. Likewise, Beijing could also go beyond goodwill in rhetoric only by seriously evaluating and acting on Australia's concerns, seeking to resolve diplomatic and political differences without resorting to punitive actions.

Perhaps the least subject to structural constraints and partisan debates on China policy are the myriad grassroots interactions between Chinese and Australian people, and especially involving Chinese Australians. These cultural and historical dimensions of bilateral relations can generate deeper and more candid conversations, while offering opportunities for non-governmental organisations and foundations to play more prominent roles.[34] The Australian business community could play a more central role. The few voices in Australia's business community calling for stable bilateral relations have faced strident criticism for being driven by self-interest and been advised against stepping into the foreign policy debate. Academic and think tank discussions exploring areas of common interests and co-operation have also been limited, due in part to perceived vulnerability to PRC political influence in Australia and the impact of COVID controls, as well as ideological and security constraints within China.

## Our contributions

Engagement begins with nuanced and thoughtful diplomacy – as does *Engaging China*. The first chapter, by former ambassador Geoff Raby, draws upon his extensive diplomatic experience to explore the contours, challenges and potential contributions of diplomacy to a robust Australian approach to engagement. Raby is followed by Bates Gill, whose chapter warns of the danger of intensifying military tensions between Australia and China. In response, Gill identifies

---

34   Such an approach is reflected in Walker, Li and Walker 2022.

common ground and suggests several potential constructive pathways that could help stabilise bilateral security relations. This first section – on foreign and security relations – is rounded out by Brendon O'Connor, Lloyd Cox and Danny Cooper's chapter examining the history of the US role in Australia's relations with China. Warning of the risks of the present Canberra consensus in support of being "all the way with the USA", they call for an alternative Australian foreign policy that avoids the pitfalls of over-reliance on the United States.

The second section tackles economic issues. While warning that trade with China does not offer a magic bullet for stabilising bilateral relations, James Laurenceson and Weihuan Zhou highlight clear opportunities for greater co-operation, particularly through multilateral institutions such as the World Trade Organization, where disputes can be managed through established procedures. Chinese investment into Australia has become one of the most politicised elements of the relationship, as Wei Li and Hans Hendrischke explain. They draw upon their extensive empirical research to identify recent trends, point to issues of concern and explain how and why Australia might attract more Chinese investment. The final chapter in this section tackles the sensitive topic of Australian businesses in the China relationship. Recalling the rich history of bilateral co-operation while spotlighting similarities and shared interests, Glenda Korporaal explains how and why Australian businesses could provide a breakthrough to a more stable relationship.

The final section of the book considers experiences, challenges and future opportunities for engagement in the realms of media, education, culture and society. Wanning Sun leads off by exploring how Australian news coverage of China has changed over the past few decades, with particular attention to the politics of voice and truth-claiming in China coverage. Anthony Welch then documents the substantial intellectual and financial capital Chinese students have made to Australian universities, alongside beneficial research collaboration. He warns against a climate of growing securitisation and polarisation, including the passage of restrictive foreign interference legislation and the tendency to see China as more threat than opportunity.

In the penultimate chapter, Ien Ang explains how cultural diplomacy can help bridge the increasingly toxic divide between

Australia and China, offering pragmatic examples of on-the-ground cultural-diplomatic work taking place in Australia, as local cultural institutions engage with Chinese immigrant communities and artists to generate more expansive, less oppositional and less mutually exclusive understandings of nation and belonging. Australia's first ambassador to China, Stephen FitzGerald, concludes the volume by recalling the initial Whitlam visit, which he participated in, in urging a new opening of the Australian mind:

> What Australia needs, for the good of our society and social cohesion, is for the Labor government to find a dramatic circuit-breaker, comparable in effect to Whitlam's in 1971, to open our minds, jolt us out of our complacency and self-referencing, confront our attitudes to race, and demonstrate the great contribution of Chinese Australians to the Australian story in our history and today, and the benefits of talking seriously and productively with China.

## References

Albanese, Anthony (2022). Australia's best days are ahead. Address to the National Press Club. Transcript Q&A. 25 January. https://bit.ly/3BcFe8p.

*Australian* (2022). Albanese-Xi talks should help stabilise relationship. Editorial, 17 November. https://bit.ly/3ptR4sl.

Bateman, Jon (2022). *U.S.–China technological "decoupling": a strategy and policy framework*. Carnegie Endowment for International Peace, April. https://bit.ly/3NY7yTA.

Bloomberg (2022). China remains Australia's "important trading partner" despite tensions, decrease seen as "unimaginable". *South China Morning Post*, 19 October. https://bit.ly/42p59pe.

Brophy, David (2021). *The China panic*. Melbourne: La Trobe University Press/ Black Inc.

Burgess, Annika and Michael Li (2022). How will the Labor government shape foreign policy on China? *ABC News*, 25 May. https://ab.co/43vVcGt.

Chubb, Andrew (forthcoming). The securitization of "Chinese influence" in Australia. *Journal of Contemporary China* 32(139): 17–34. https://doi.org/10.1080/10670564.2022.2052437.

Cohen, Michael D. (2020). Political parties, Australia and US alliance, 1946–2016. *Asian Security* 16(3): 323–42.

Collinson, Elena (2022). The China consensus. Australia–China Relations Institute, University of Technology Sydney, 14 March, https://bit.ly/3Bw69wh.

Coorey, Phillip (2021). PM opens door to reviewing Darwin port lease. *Australian Financial Review*, 28 April. https://bit.ly/42j7Dpc.

Curran, James (2022). *Australia's China odyssey: from euphoria to fear*. Sydney: NewSouth Books.

Dean, Peter J., Stephan Frühling, and Brendan Taylor (eds) (2016). *Australia's American alliance*. Melbourne: Melbourne University Press.

Department of Defence, Australian Government (2020). *2020 Defence Strategic Update*. https://bit.ly/3Bio9do.

Department of Defence, Australian Government (2016). *2016 Defence White Paper*. https://bit.ly/3I0IK9U.

Department of Foreign Affairs and Trade, Australian Government (2017). 2017 Foreign Policy White Paper. https://bit.ly/41vCzRQ.

Department of Foreign Affairs and Trade, Australian Government (2022). China country brief. https://bit.ly/3BmEnBX.

Fernandes, Clinton (2022). *Subimperial power: Australia in the international arena*. Melbourne: Melbourne University Press.

Fitzsimmons, David (2023). *Australia's relations with China: The illusion of choices, 1972–2022*. Abingdon, UK: Routledge.

Fraser, Malcolm and Cain Roberts (2014). *Dangerous allies*. Melbourne: Melbourne University Press.

Galloway, Anthony (2022). Has Australia lost its bipartisan consensus on standing up to China? *Sydney Morning Herald*, 18 February. https://bit.ly/3Mjmlqr.

Galloway, Anthony and Eryk Bagshaw (2021). Victoria's Belt and Road deal with China torn up. *Sydney Morning Herald*. 21 April. https://bit.ly/3O2gCac.

Grigg, Angus, Lesley Robinson and Meghna Bali (2022). US Air Force to deploy nuclear-capable B-52 bombers to Australia as tensions with China grow. *ABC News*, 31 October. https://ab.co/3I0xFWc.

Gunia, Amy (2022). Why Australia–China tensions are here to stay, despite a diplomatic reset. *Time*, 15 November. https://bit.ly/44LCVpB.

Gyngell, Allan (2017). *Fear of abandonment: Australia in the world since 1942*. Melbourne: La Trobe University Press.

Kaul, Natasha 2022. India-Australia trade deal takes effect this month; work visas for chefs, yoga teachers, backpackers. *SBS*, 1 December. https://bit.ly/3Q1nWDW.

Korporaal, Glenda (2021). *Behind the headlines: why Australian companies are still doing business with China.* Research report. Sydney: Australia–China Relations Institute, University of Technology Sydney, December. https://bit.ly/3O07OBl.

KPMG and the University of Sydney (2022). Demystifying Chinese Investment in Australia. April. https://bit.ly/42FscvG.

Matthews, Trevor and John Ravenhill (1988). Bipartisanship in the Australian foreign policy elite. *Australian Journal of International Affairs.* 42(1): 9–20.

McHugh, Finn (2021). Penny Wong accuses Peter Dutton of warmongering with China for federal election votes. *Canberra Times,* 23 November. https://bit.ly/42IPG3h.

Medcalf, Rory (2021). *Indo–Pacific empire: China, America and the contest for the world's pivotal region.* Manchester, UK: Manchester University Press.

Reuters (2022). Australia's Albanese, Japan's Kishida agree to strengthen security ties. *Canberra Times,* 22 October. https://reut.rs/3puzQei.

SBS (2022). "Co-operate where we can, disagree where we must": Penny Wong outlines plans on China relations. 13 November. https://bit.ly/42vVuxh.

Strangio, Sebastian (2020). Australian import bans show the sharp edge of China's economic power. *Diplomat,* 5 November. https://bit.ly/44QD8YO.

Ueda, Michio (2021). Japan's challenge in the age of China–US rivalry. *Diplomat,* 2 August. https://bit.ly/3ptt7kT.

United States Studies Centre, the University of Sydney (2021). *The alliance at 70: the story of the alliance between Australia and the United States.* Sydney: United States Studies Centre. https://bit.ly/44OJU1I.

Uren, David (2021). *Iron ore futures: possible paths for Australia's biggest trade with China.* Canberra. Australian Strategic Policy Institute. September. https://bit.ly/3MeLBOK.

Uren, David (2022). Australia's trade diversification away from China picks up pace. *Strategist,* 13 October. https://bit.ly/3MeNvxV.

Walker, David, Li Yao, and Karen Walker (2022). *Happy together: bridging the Australia–China divide.* Melbourne: Melbourne University Press.

White, Hugh (2022). *Sleepwalk to war: Australia's unthinking alliance with America.* Quarterly Essay 86. Melbourne: Black Inc.

Whitlam, E.G. (1973). Speech by the Prime Minister, the Hon EG Whitlam QC MP, at Premier Chou En-Lai's Banquet at Peking on 31 October 1973. PM Transcripts. https://bit.ly/3W0ZpQf

Wickes, Ron, Mike Adams and Nicholas Brown (2021). *Economic coercion by China: the impact on Australia's merchandise exports.* Working paper no. 4. Institute for International Trade, the University of Adelaide. https://bit.ly/41vUp7k.

# Part One – Foreign and security relations

## Introduction to Part One

The first section of this volume engages the most contentious aspects of Australia's relationship with China: security challenges and diplomatic tensions. Charting a path towards a more robust and enduring engagement strategy on China requires a clear-eyed assessment of the reasons for the rising tensions and realistic suggestions for a path forward. All three chapters tackle these challenging issues head on, albeit with varying assessments and prognoses.

Geoff Raby's chapter begins by tracing the sharp decline in Australia's relations with China since 2017, detailing how the two sides fell into a destructive tit-for-tat dynamic before reaching rock bottom in 2020. Beijing's aggressive foreign policy and its bullying behaviour, exacerbated by tightening authoritarianism and a "hyper-sensitivity to criticism", are partly to blame. Yet for Raby, the primary problem has been the security, intelligence and defence establishment's weaponisation of Australia's China policy. Consumed by fears of abandonment by the United States, Australia became the leading advocate of a range of groupings such as the Quad and AUKUS intended to constrain and challenge China. Warning that depending solely upon the US alliance is a highly risky strategy, Raby calls for a return to a more independent foreign policy grounded in a clearer sense of Australia's own self-interest. He urges creative solutions that avoid gratuitously confronting Beijing while seeking cooperation in areas of common interests. Raby concludes by praising the Labor government's more restrained diplomacy as offering hope for relations to return to a more stable footing.

Bates Gill, in contrast, attributes the deteriorating relationship over the past few years to a combination of deep-seated structural factors and secondary ripple effects. Driven by a perceived worsening regional security environment in which each feels compelled to develop defence and war-fighting capabilities with the other in mind, exacerbated by deepening normative and ideological divisions, China and Australia are falling into a dangerous security dilemma in which both sides spend ever more on their militaries and yet end up being less secure. On the Australian side, perhaps the most significant has been the AUKUS partnership, which, if fully realised, Gill argues will result in one of the most sweeping transformations of Australia's defence posture since the 1950s. These structural factors have fed a worsening domestic political environment in both countries, shaped by accusations of domestic political interference, and contributing to sharply declining public sentiments on both sides – particularly in Australian attitudes towards China.

Gill thus expects that, at best, the two sides might maintain bounded engagement, with positive effects from economic cooperation constrained by greater uncertainties, deepening mistrust, restricted diplomatic relations, punitive sparring and heightened security concerns. Nonetheless, he concludes by praising the arrival of new leaders and restrained rhetoric, urging both sides to deepen channels of communication and enlarge a sense of common interests by jointly dealing with common challenges such as climate change, global health and economic development.

The contribution by O'Connor, Cox and Cooper rounds out this first section. While echoing Raby's criticism of Australian policymakers for relying too heavily upon the US military alliance, they see less hope for a shift away from this posture. They acknowledge the serious challenges posed by China's burgeoning military and economic power, augmented by Beijing's provocative actions. Yet they spotlight worrisome trends in US domestic politics and foreign policies, which raise important questions about the reliability of the US security guarantee, and the "all the way with the USA" strategic posture adopted by both of Australia's major political parties. Questioning the extent to which Australian policymakers can confidently rely upon shared values with the United States, they warn of a decline in US democracy, the ongoing influence of Trump's nationalist and isolationist tendencies, and criticise Australia's overly militarised relationship with the United States.

Despite considerable differences across the three chapters, the authors agree that Australian policymakers should pursue greater cooperation with China on areas of common interest, including climate change, global health and regional security issues. While acknowledging the considerable challenges posed by China's rise and its worrisome domestic and foreign policy trends, all three chapters offer ample evidence of the dangers of relying exclusively upon military solutions to meet Australia's security challenges. Ultimately, all three contributions point towards the potential for creative and calm diplomacy to help restore a more stable and productive relationship with China – one that is clearly in Australia's long-term national interests.

# 2
# What a difference a decade can make

*Geoff Raby*

Before the 2022 federal election, the Australia–China relationship had plumbed its lowest depth since diplomatic relations were established a half-century ago. In 2017, Australia's official position towards China began to change. Domestically, media and public discussion focused on an increasing threat from China to Australian domestic politics and security. A succession of events – including the Sam Dastyari affair, high-profile banning of Huawei and ZTE from Australia's future 5G network, anti-foreign interference legislation clearly aimed at China, cyber attacks purportedly executed by Beijing, and influence activities on campuses – culminated in April 2020 with the Australian government calling, unilaterally, for an investigation into the origins of COVID-19.

Internationally, with the Hague Dispute Settlement Court's comprehensive rejection of China's claims in the South China Sea, Australia became China's most vociferous critic over its actions in the area. During the Trump presidency, the United States came to define China as a strategic competitor, a position with which Australia closely identified. Australia also began actively promoting security architecture in the region, notably the Quadrilateral Security Dialogue (the Quad) and the AUKUS pact – with its commitment to purchase nuclear-powered submarines, intended for operations in North Asia – to push back against China's bad behaviour.

These discrete events are connected by deep structural changes in the international system. Australia found itself having to respond to the greatest global power shift in history, from the United States to East Asia. The rise of China has ended the US liberal unipolar order. Without a compass, Australia has hewed more closely to the United States amidst the uncertainty of the newly emerging multipolar order. This has been at profound cost to its relations with China.

An Australian prime minister has not been to China since 2016, when Malcolm Turnbull visited for Asia-Pacific Economic Co-operation (APEC), a multilateral meeting. Premier Li Keqiang visited Australia in early 2017 for a bilateral meeting. The drawbridge has since been raised and we have stared at each other across a moat that, until the election of the Labor government in May 2022, had been inexorably widening.

This is the longest gap between high-level visits for decades. When Bob Hawke embraced China's vision of reform and engagement in the international system and understood what it could mean for Australia, both sides had endeavoured to maintain annual high-level exchanges.

Ever since diplomatic relations were established in 1973, regular official high-level contact had been sustained. Never before had Australia been denied access to the highest levels of the Chinese political system as it has been for the past five years. It is in this sense that relations are at their "lowest ebb", notwithstanding the fact that bilateral trade flows are at record levels. Elements of the conservative populist media rejoiced in this sorry state of affairs.[1] The contrast to the 40th anniversary could hardly be greater.

## The path into the abyss

Over the past 50 years of diplomatic relations, Australia and China have been through difficult times, but none so emphatic as today. On the Australian side, officials rightly say that China has increasingly engaged in bad behaviour, notably in the South China Sea, in cyber attacks, in attempting political interference in domestic politics, and

---

1    Raby 2019.

monitoring and influencing student behaviour on our campuses.[2] There are other grievances: theft of technology, unfair and non-reciprocal investment rules, and breaches of World Trade Organization ( WTO) subsidy commitments to mention a few more.

Many of these were not new. Fifteen years ago, for instance, China resumed assertive, muscular and, on occasions, aggressive tactics in the South China Sea. Certainly, China pushed harder than ever before and, in 2016, had a ruling against it by the International Dispute Settlement Court, which it flouted. China has long been accused of state-sponsored intellectual property theft, of providing its state-owned enterprises with unfair advantages, especially subsidies, and restricting and distorting inward foreign investment.

Beijing has all too often adopted bullying behaviour in its foreign relations, be it trying to interrupt the lucrative tourist trade with Taiwan to express displeasure over the outcome of a presidential election, curtailing travel and trade with South Korea over the deployment of terminal high-altitude area defence (THAAD) missiles, seizing Philippine fishing vessels in the Paracel Reef, or – much further back – discouraging Japanese auto sales over the Senkaku/Diaoyu Islands dispute.

As China has risen, it has needed to adopt a more confident and mature foreign policy commensurate with its weight and standing in the world. The Chinese government's hyper-sensitivity to criticism is out of place with a country that exercises great influence owing to its economic strength and deep structural changes in the international system.

With its ever-increasing presence and influence in world affairs, Beijing has failed to behave like a leader, rather than a victim. Instead, as President Xi Jinping tightened his authoritarian control of Chinese politics and promoted a personality cult as part of the process, Chinese diplomats have increasingly met international challenges with "wolf-warrior" diplomacy.[3]

From Beijing's perspective, the discrete elements that have led to the current situation are readily identified. Friction rose substantially over Australia's strident criticism of China over the South China Sea.

---

2    Bergin 2016.
3    Zhu 2020.

Many countries also criticised China's behaviour, but Prime Minister Turnbull and Foreign Minister Julie Bishop were ahead of others in the frequency and stridency of their criticism of China. In her Fullerton Lecture in Singapore in 2017, Bishop went so far as to imply that China was not fit for regional leadership because it was not a "democracy".[4]

This was an extraordinary statement for a foreign minister to make. It also introduced a sharp ideological edge into Australia's China policies. At the time, it was not recognised that this was the first public affirmation that Australia was to follow the United States, and even lead, in redefining relations with China in terms of strategic competition rather than co-operation.[5]

Domestically within Australia, the China Threat syndrome gained momentum with some sensational television reports of spies and agents of influence. That there was fire where there was smoke in the form the Dastyari Affair encouraged something of a political feeding frenzy.[6]

Amid this, and with anti-China fear being whipped up by the shock jocks, Prime Minister Turnbull made his disastrous statement, in reasonable Mandarin, during the federal election campaign that the Australian people had stood up to China by introducing anti- foreign interference laws.

Such laws were perfectly reasonable and long overdue. China could have no objection to them and did not. But when Turnbull channelled Mao Zedong's statement supposedly made at the founding of the People's Republic of China (PRC), which referred to standing up to over 100 years of foreign occupation, depredations, oppression and war, this was seen in Beijing as being gratuitously offensive. Which it was.[7]

With the increasing challenge of China to the United States's dominant global position, Australia began to align itself more closely with the United States and strategic competition intensified. It was justified primarily in ideological terms. And Australia signed up.[8]

---

4    Bishop 2017.
5    The marked shift in Australia's stance towards China and closer alignment with US rhetoric is carefully traced in Collison 2017.
6    Passant 2017.
7    Curran 2022, 224–5.
8    Raby 2020.

## From pragmatism to ideology

For the first 45 years of bilateral relations with China, Australia at both the official and community levels largely adopted a pragmatic stance. Ideology was virtually absent: we each recognised that we had differences based on values and systems of political and social organisation. This enabled both sides to concentrate on interests.

From the time the United States began to treat China as a strategic competitor until China applied economic measures against Australia to express its anger over Prime Minister Morrison's unilateral call for an inquiry into the origins of COVID-19, Australian governments sought publicly to maintain the position of China as a strategic partner, while moving decisively to treat China as a strategic competitor.

Late in Turnbull's term as prime minister and at the start of Morrison's, both gave similar, reassuring speeches about the convergence of interests in the relationship. In this, the mutual economic benefits were stressed while noting that differences that existed should be handled constructively.[9]

In view of the huge economic dependency Australia has on China and the fact we have no border issues or any historical grievances on either side, how could it be otherwise? In fact, policy had already changed to treating China as a strategic competitor.

As James Curran argues, Turnbull's shift on China policy was influenced both by the external challenges of dealing with the newly elected Trump administration and domestic internal Liberal Party politics.[10]

The flip side of Australia's enduring commitment to the US alliance is that Australian officials are perpetually in a state of anxiety over the United States' level of commitment to the alliance and its resolve to defend Australia in times of crisis. The Trump administration both questioned the value of alliances generally and engagement in East Asia specifically, a nightmare for Canberra's strategic analysts.

Turnbull felt he needed to demonstrate Australia's fidelity. Immediately following Cabinet's National Security Committee meeting

---

9    Curran 2022.
10   Curran 2022.

that decided to ban both Huawei and ZTE from the fifth-generation (5G) broadband network, Turnbull tells us in his memoir that he rang Trump to boast that Australia had introduced the world's first formal ban on these companies. As Turnbull records, Trump was "both impressed and a little surprised that we'd taken this position".[11]

Scott Morrison, as Minister for Home Affairs, announced to the parliament that Huawei would be blocked from participating in any aspect of Australia's 5G network. It was a blanket ban like no other from any other government up to that time. Under enormous pressure from the United States, the British still did not implement such a ban until 2020, and then with a five-year phase-in. Canada only announced its ban in 2022. Many European countries still entertain Huawei on their networks, albeit with strict operating protocols to protect sensitive areas.[12]

Similarly, and under pressure from the United States, Australia has not signed up to any of the Belt and Road Memoranda of Understanding. Some 152 countries, including 18 from Europe, have signed relevant memoranda to participate in the Belt and Road Initiative (BRI). Several international bodies, including UN agencies, also now participate. In 2021, legislation clarifying the Commonwealth foreign relations powers was introduced principally to force the state of Victoria to abrogate unilaterally the BRI Memorandum of Understanding it had signed previously.

Joining the BRI is costless in terms of taking on any new obligations or surrendering any aspect of Australia's sovereignty. At most, Victoria's signing the non-binding memorandum added legitimacy to the BRI, which it had achieved well before Victoria signed up. Australia was quick to follow the United States in viewing the BRI more in ideological terms than commercial. The United States regards the BRI as an instrument for challenging the US-led order and establishing a Sino-centric order, and so does Australia. From Beijing's perspective, Australia's actions, rather more than its words, revealed a fundamental shift in how Canberra would from then on view the relationship.[13]

---

11  Turnbull 2020, 434–5.
12  Raby 2020.

By the time Morrison replaced Turnbull, the shift in China policy was completely entrenched within the government and bureaucracy. The relationship was already in the deep freeze with no high-level official contact occurring either in Australia or China, and not even on the margins of major multilateral meetings. The relationship was now entering its tit-for-tat stage.

## Rock bottom

Rock bottom was reached in April 2020. This occurred when the Australian Prime Minister unilaterally called for an international inquiry into the origins of COVID-19. The implication was clear: China was to blame. Morrison's intervention came in the early months of the pandemic, when President Donald Trump was accusing China of unleashing what he variously called the China or Wuhan virus.[14]

Against the backdrop of an already frozen relationship, a furious Chinese leadership imposed economic sanctions on Australia. Imports of Australian wine, lobster, barley, cotton, timber and coal were hit with measures the Australian government quickly labelled as economic coercion ("sanctions" are when we apply economic measures against other countries; "coercion" is when others apply them to us).[15]

Worried about the possible political blow-back from affected sectors and workers, the Morrison government effectively developed a narrative that it was standing up for Australian "values". Australia was not going to be bullied by China. It was China that had changed and not Australia. By implication, it was up to China to fix the relationship. Australia had nothing on its side to do.[16]

This was enthusiastically echoed by conservative political commentators, who castigated members of the business community for personal special pleading if they dared to suggest that Australia's

---

13   Raby 2020.
14   Kelly 2020.
15   Roggeveen, Kassam and Scott 2020.
16   Greene 2021.

economic interests in the relationship were important. As Michael Wesley observed:

> There has been a systematic delegitimization of the economic interests and mutually beneficial relationships that have undergirded the relationship. Anyone in business speaking in defence of pragmatic relations is accused of craven self-interest, while many university partnerships are held up as evidence of a naive surrender to Chinese influence and intellectual property theft.[17]

The notion that there may be ways to balance the defence of our values while pursuing Australia's economic interests was ridiculed. The new mantra was diversification and decoupling critical supply chains from China.[18]

Following Beijing's application of economic measures against Australia and an unprecedented ramping up of insulting accusations from China's wolf-warrior diplomats now off the leash, Canberra decided on a raft of measures to retaliate against China. It was time for Australia to resolve the contradictions in its China policy, be clear about the threat and retaliate.

Some of the measures taken were high profile, such as otherwise inexplicable decisions to block Chinese foreign investment into Australia. Perhaps the most egregious was the Treasurer's decision in 2020 to block the sale of a Japanese-owned Australian dairy firm to a Chinese firm. Others were less obvious such as denial or delaying visas for certain officials or academics, or harassment of Chinese state-owned media organisations operating in Australia.[19]

Over this period, the Defence Minister, in particular, increasingly set about talking up the China military threat in the region. Bizarrely, Australia seemed to become obsessed about an imminent military invasion by China of Taiwan, despite the unlikelihood of that occurring in any relevant policy-planning time horizon. He continued to do this

---

17  Wesley 2020.
18  Wilson 2021.
19  Kehoe et al. 2021; Maiden 2021; Reuters 2020; Tillet 2020.

into the Australian election, despite silence from our regional neighbours and even the United States over this apparent imminent threat.[20]

In the latter part of the Morrison government, Australia hardened its position on China still further. At the public level at least, China's ongoing trade measures against Australia and ever-sharper wolf-worrier diplomacy clearly rankled. China's Foreign Ministry statements were needlessly and heedlessly provocative. In December 2020, China's accusations over Australian alleged war crimes in Afghanistan deeply angered the Prime Minister and senior members of the Australian government.[21]

Earlier the deputy head of the Chinese embassy in Canberra, Wang Xining had been permitted by the authorities in Beijing to give a somewhat conciliatory speech at the National Press Club in August 2020. While its nuances were both wittingly and unwittingly missed by Canberra's political commentators, he himself undid the effort by subsequently handing a television journalist a list of 14 points on which China was upset by Australia.

It was convenient for the Prime Minister to cast these as a diplomatic *demarche* (a formal demand) when what they were, in diplomatic terms, was an *aide memoir* (a note to remind of, or list matters under discussion or that have been discussed). Governments do not issue demarches by handing lists to journalists. This, however, played to the narrative of China's bullying. It was treated as the smoking-gun evidence, as if any were needed. The Prime Minister gleefully passed this list around, seeking support for Australia's position on China, at the Group of Seven (G7) meeting in Cornwall, which he attended as a guest, along with the representatives of four other countries in June 2021.[22]

With this, the Prime Minister moved from defending Australia's values from Chinese bullying to becoming an international advocate of the West hardening its resolve to resist China's rise and push back on its bad behaviour.

---

20   Thompson 2022.
21   Needham 2020.
22   Shoebridge 2021.

This marked a profound shift in the behaviour of Australian prime ministers, from seeking to build coalitions to constructively consider regional and global challenges of interest to Australia to one of advocating confrontation and containment of a neighbouring state and our largest trading partner.

Despite the Australian media's spin on the Cornwall meeting, the G7 as a group was cautious and nuanced in responding to the Australian prime minister. The G7 statement was silent on Australia, though it did have a reference, among many other issues, to being opposed to economic coercion. This motherhood re-statement of an obvious and shared principle was hailed by the Australian media as a great diplomatic achievement. Morrison was emboldened in his view of himself as the leader of the China Threat coalition of states and doubled down on his anti-China rhetoric.[23] Commenting on the Cornwall Consensus in the *Financial Times*, Jillian Tett described it as merely "an advisory memo" and cautioned readers "not to laugh".[24]

Australia also became the leading advocate of a range of groupings, such as the Quad and AUKUS, intended to constrain and challenge China. While there is nothing inherently wrong in supporting a network of different alliances that can raise the cost to China of its bad behaviour, it is unwise to position a middle power like Australia, for whom China is still the major economic relationship, as a leading global enthusiast for such arrangements. As President Truman might have said, Australia talks loudly and carries a toothpick.

Alone among the liberal Western democracies, Australia has managed over the past five years to have isolated itself in the management of its relations with China. Australia has become an outlier, with no official contact. While most countries have their disputes with China at various levels of intensity, all, with the recent exception of Lithuania, have managed to maintain normal diplomatic relations.[25]

---

23  Cornwall Consensus 9 June 2021; Open Societies Statement 2021; Raby 2021.
24  Tett, *Financial Times*, 11 June 2021.
25  Agence France-Presse, 21 November 2021. The dispute was ostensibly over nomenclature to describe the representative office of Taiwan in Vilnius. Bilateral tensions over human rights and other issues had been building for

More importantly, Australia stands alone in the East Asian region (and even in the much-vaunted Indo-Pacific) in having had all high-level political contact suspended. In 2021, the recently-arrived Japanese ambassador, no doubt with encouragement from the leading China Threat proponents in Canberra's intelligence and security establishment, intervened in domestic politics to assert, wrongly, that Japan was in the same position as Australia with its relations with China.

To the contrary, Japan, which has deep historical issues with China and live border disputes, could be something of a model for Australia in how to maintain constructive, working official relations while managing complex and potentially incendiary differences. With no historical or territorial disputes with China, the state of Australia's relations with China, compared with that of Japan and many others in the region, highlights the failure of Australian diplomacy under successive Coalition governments.[26]

Australia must live with China and deal with it as it is, not as we would wish it to be. The collapse of Australia–China relations is a story in two parts. It is how China has (but also has not) changed as it has risen to become a leading global power, capable of shaping the world order in its interests (unlike Australia) and how a failure of Australian diplomacy brought the relationship to its present nadir by not recognising that the changed world order necessitated different diplomatic responses and positioning than simply doubling down on the US alliance.

## The new order

Since the 40th anniversary of diplomatic relations between Australian and China, the international order has changed profoundly. This is attributable not only to China's economic rise and US domestic political divisions over the United States' responsibility for maintaining world

---

some time before this. Beijing viewed this as a direct provocation on top of senior-level officials' visits to Taipei.

26   Hurst 2021.

order but because China has been willing and able to build new coalitions and international arrangements in collaboration with many other countries to re-fashion the US-led post-World War II order.

These developments were inevitable, not just because of China's economic ascendency, but due to the overall shift in the weight of world economic activity from the Atlantic to East Asia and the Indian Ocean.

Australia's response to these changes in the international order has been largely one of denial – hoping to keep our vital commercial interests with China growing, while aligning more closely with the United States ideologically, politically and especially militarily.[27]

Whether arch realist John Mearsheimer was correct or not when he said the post-Cold War liberal global order was *bound* to fail, it is now a relic of another geopolitical age.[28] In response, when contemplating a rising China, Australia has moved ever closer to the United States. As Alan Gyngell argued in his aptly titled book, *Fear of abandonment*, Australia always had the security, and indeed luxury, of a world order that has been led by a dominant power with whom we shared values, political systems and general outlook. This had led to lazy foreign policy, so that, with the rise of China, Australia sought greater comfort in its relationship with the United States. It became an obsession among Australian foreign policy advisers that everything had to be done to keep the United States engaged fully in Asia.[29]

With China's becoming a power capable of challenging the United States on many fronts, while remaining a one-party, authoritarian state, Washington became gripped by a type of "buyers' regret", which has put it in direct conflict with China. The dominant view that emerged in Washington in the middle years of the last decade was that the United States had engaged China for the past 40 years on the implicit promise that, as its economy grew, markets expanded and it became more deeply integrated in the international system, its domestic politics would become more liberal and pluralistic. In other words, China would become more like us.

---

27  Raby 2020.
28  Mearsheimer 2019.
29  Gyngell 2017.

Former CIA intelligence analyst and now academic Michael Pillsbury argued in an influential book among hawkish policy advisers that all along China had set out to dupe the West (read the United States). According to Pillsbury, China had embarked on a secret "100-year marathon" to replace the United States as the single dominant world power. He argued that China's communist leadership pursued a strategy of warfare first set out by Sun Tzu two-and-a-half thousand years ago in the *Art of War*.[30]

Pillsbury argued that China had adopted Sun Tzu's tactics of co-opting and beguiling an enemy, rather than entering direct conflict. Former President Trump once said of Pillsbury that he was the most knowledgeable person in the United States on China.[31]

For those in Australia who have been engaged with China during most of the past 40 years of its reform and open-door policies, buyers' regret is far from their minds. In Australia, few supported engagement with China on the ideologically premised assumption that somehow China's political system would evolve into a more competitive pluralist one.

While it was hoped that China would become less repressive and that, over time, respect for human rights would grow, none really imagined that with economic growth, rising prosperity and entry into the WTO, China would become democratic in the way that Taiwan and South Korea had – but, note, that Singapore had not.

Australia and many other Western countries supported engagement with China based on well-defined self-interest. In addition to the obvious potentially enormous economic benefits for a country like Australia, with such pronounced complementarities, Australia's security could only benefit from a stable, increasingly prosperous China. After all, a fundamental pillar of national security is economic strength.

The Morrison-led Coalition government drew Australia into the US ideological conflict with China. For a long time it sought to conceal this with reference to co-operation and mutual interests, but by the time

---

30   Pillsbury 2015.
31   Schreckinger and Lippman 2018.

of its end the facade was dropped, and ministers openly spoke of China as a potential enemy.[32]

In 2013, Hugh White in his prescient book *China Choice* set the commentators at each other's throats over how the United States should respond to the rise of China. He argued that the United States will someday need to choose between confronting China and trying to contain it or find a way to accommodate China's rise, which will mean sharing global and particularly regional leadership, and eventually living with the fact that China will become the regional hegemon in East Asia. The choice that the United States would make would have serious and long-lasting consequences for Australia.[33]

Sensibly, White, as a realist, argued that China's rise could not and would not be contained and so the preferable course for the United States would be to adopt a strategy of accommodating China in advance of conflict. White had suggested diplomacy was a preferred strategy to war. He was traduced by conservative commentators in Australia who shamefully accused him of appeasement or worse.[34]

In many ways White had set the tone for the subsequent debate and policy development in Australia. Conservative commentators in bodies such as the Australian Strategic Policy Institute (ASPI), which is funded by the Australian Department of Defence and the US military-industrial complex, would never countenance China's becoming a regional hegemon.


## Weaponised foreign policy

Australia's foreign policy has been "weaponised", with the security, intelligence and defence establishment taking charge of foreign policy towards China and geopolitical policy more generally.

This has framed Australia's response to the end of the old order and seen our security entirely aligned with the United States. While it is natural, and perhaps even inevitable, that the dominant power would

---

32   Barton 2022.
33   White 2012.
34   Sheridan 2012.

seek to resist the ascendant power, it is neither usual nor sensible for a small power to take sides. It is more common for diplomacy to seek advantage from such competition.

Instead, China has come to be seen as seeking to extend its reach and influence in every sphere to the detriment of Australia's security, values and institutions. As a result, Canberra's thinking about China policy became much more confrontational than it was or needs to be.

That the relationship is so poor is seen by some as a badge of honour. Little support exists for doing anything substantive to improve the relationship. The prevalent official view is that this is just how things are going to remain and there is no need to do anything to change the current situation.[35]

The China Threat is said to be everywhere. The domestic dimension is used to feed the narrative that China must be pushed back in foreign policy; bad behaviour by China internationally is used to support the need for greater vigilance domestically.[36]

A proper diplomatic response would begin with the reality that China is here to stay and that it will continue to be of vital economic and geopolitical importance for Australia. Contrary to the prevailing orthodoxy, it would recognise that our interests are best served by a co-operative rather than a confrontational relationship with China. It would understand that our dependence on the US alliance is a high-risk strategy. It assumes, ultimately, that the United States will always have the interests, the will and the capacity to confront China militarily and will be able to prevail. These assumptions are in serious dispute.[37]

Australia's diplomatic response would also acknowledge the reality that Australia needs China more than China needs Australia. It is something that Canberra does not like to hear said but, from a realistic foreign policy perspective, the relationship is asymmetrical. Smaller regional neighbours in the Association of Southeast Asian Nations (ASEAN) and New Zealand have understood this and so have sought not to gratuitously confront China when in fact they can do nothing on their own to affect China's behaviour.

---

35  Maude 2020.
36  Perlez 2018.
37  White 2022.

This is not to say Australia should be supine in its dealing with China or that it should step back from asserting its values and concerns, especially over issues such as borders and human rights. Australia needs also to harden its defences, as it is now well advanced in doing, against both external and internal threats from China.

Rather, it means that Australia needs to be much more skilful in how it handles the relationship, relying further on diplomacy and coalitions with states whose interests are aligned with Australia's, and defining for itself a more independent foreign policy. It must recognise that Australia's and the United States' interests converge on some points and diverge in many other respects. Knowing how to sustain a close alliance relationship with the United States, while giving full expression to Australia's unique and thus different circumstances and interests is the real challenge for Australian diplomacy.

Australia needs first and foremost to return to normal diplomatic relations with China. This should not be at any cost, but equally Australia should recognise that it has agency in this as well, and seek to find creative solutions to lift the relationship while not giving up on core issues. As we are smaller, we need to be more creative and active in this.

## Albanese's China challenge

For the full term of the Morrison government, Labor sought to avoid being wedged by the government for being "soft" on China and therefore not to be trusted with Australia's national security. The Defence Minister, Peter Dutton, went to extreme lengths to talk up a China military threat. To the credit of Anthony Albanese and Penny Wong, they succeeded in their objective. For the three years before the election, not a crack of light could be seen between the government and the opposition on any aspect of national security, most especially China.

The narrative adopted by Labor on Australia–China relations was also that of the government. Labor was supporting the government in standing up for Australia's values and resisting bullying by China. Labor intoned the government's mantra that it was China and China alone that had changed and therefore it was entirely up to China to fix the relationship. It was as if Australia had no agency of its own and so was dependent on the actions of another to take care of its interests.

Wong's sole contribution on China policy during her period as Opposition spokesperson on foreign policy was to criticise the government's rhetoric, as if the problem could be attributable merely to one of language not substance.

By adopting the victim approach and seeing the problem only in terms of language, repositioning of Australia's stance towards China as a constructive partner rather than as a strategic competitor and enemy has not so far been pursued.

The Morrison government glued Australia to the hip of the United States and followed it down the path of strategic competition with China. The US position has not changed under President Biden, although, as in Australia under Labor, the rhetorical packaging has softened. Overall, the messaging is more muted, and this has already been helpful: for example, during the days of heightened United States–China tension when Speaker Pelosi made an official visit to Taiwan.

The discipline among Albanese's ministers and restraint in language is in marked contrast to the Turnbull–Morrison period. It is a helpful first step and will be noted by Beijing.

China has made it clear that it is now seeking to lift the relationship above its present level. China's new ambassador, Xiao Qian, is a highly experienced diplomat and a senior appointment who speaks flawless English. Beijing is signalling that it is time to move forward in the relationship. Xiao made a well-judged presentation to the National Press Club and has followed that with generally well-received appearances on current affairs programs. The message now is that China is prepared to reset relations but is looking for some positive signals from Australia.[38]

Limited high-level engagement also resumed, with two meetings between respective foreign ministers on the margins of multilateral meetings, similarly one between defence ministers, and an exchange of letters between trade ministers. In October, this was then capped by

---

38  Giannini 2022.

a successful bilateral meeting between Albanese and Xi Jinping when they were both attending the Bali 20 Meeting. The pace of interaction has quickened since then. The five-year long freeze in the official bilateral relationship has now ended.[39]

Wong has clearly indicated that she sees diplomacy playing a much greater role in Australia's security. She has the political weight and standing to see the return of a better-resourced and more influential Department of Foreign Affairs and Trade. She has also said Australian foreign policy must reflect Australia's multicultural society and its Indigenous heritage. She is in fact defining an independent foreign policy for Australia – the first time in decades. This is being done not only by what she says and does, but by what she does not say. The Albanese government's silence over Speaker Pelosi's visit would have been deafening in neo-conservative policy circles in Washington.

China policy is and will continue to benefit from this effort to craft a more independent foreign policy. The bilateral relationship can be expected to return to a more normal one, similar to that which most countries have with China. Australia is no longer an outlier in its relations with China. If governments on both sides continue to de-weaponise the relationship, the 60th anniversary of diplomatic relations could well be more hopeful than the 50th has been.

## References

Agence France Presse (2021). China downgrades diplomatic ties with Lithuania over Taiwan row. *Guardian*, 21 November, https://bit.ly/3OiqTi5.

Barton, Greg (2022). Peter Dutton says Australia should prepare for war. So how likely is a military conflict with China? *Conversation*, 19 April. https://bit.ly/41t8Ysv.

Bergin, Anthony (2016). A heavy defeat for Beijing: the South China Sea Tribunal ruling. *Strategist*, 13 July. https://bit.ly/3ptQwm3.

Bishop, Julie (2017). Change and uncertainty in the Indo-Pacific: strategic challenges and opportunities, 28th Fullerton Lecture, Singapore. 13 March. https://bit.ly/3HYVIot.

---

39   Raby 2022.

Collison, Elena (2017). Australia's tilt on China. Australia China Relations Institute, University of Technology Sydney, 4 July. https://bit.ly/3K2r6DC.

Curran, James (2022). *Australia's China odyssey: from euphoria to fear*. Sydney: NewSouth Books.

Giannini, Dominic (2022). Chinese ambassador encourages closer ties with Australia. *InDaily*, 7 September. https://bit.ly/42LCI4J.

Greene, Andrew (2021). Chief diplomat warns China wants Australia to compromise on key national interests to reset relations. *ABC News*, 26 April. https://ab.co/41rHhjx.

Gyngell, Allan (2017). *Fear of abandonment: Australia in the world since 1942*. Melbourne: La Trobe University Press.

Hartcher, Peter (2019). Red flag: waking up to China's challenge. *Quarterly Essay*, 76. Melbourne: Black Inc.

Hurst, Daniel (2021). "We are in the same boat": Japan urges Australia to join forces to address challenge of China. *Guardian*, 21 July. https://bit.ly/3puE45E.

Kehoe, John et al. (2021). Treasurer blacklists China investments. *Australian Financial Review*, 12 January. https://bit.ly/42sljyd.

Kelly, Lidia (2020). Australia demands Coronavirus inquiry, adding to pressure on China. *Reuters*, 19 April. https://reut.rs/3pz9uba.

Maiden, Samantha (2021). Treasurer Josh Frydenberg halts Chinese takeover over national security risk. *news.com.au*, 12 January. https://bit.ly/44KEVzn.

Maude, Richard (2020). Looking ahead: Australia and China after the pandemic. *Asia Society*, 13 May. https://bit.ly/3Bg2fat.

Mearsheimer, John (2014). *The tragedy of great power politics*. Cambridge, MA: Harvard University Press.

Mearsheimer, John (2019). *The great delusion: liberal dreams and international relations*. Cambridge, MA: Harvard University Press.

Needham, Kirsty (2020). Australia demands apology from China after fake image posted on social media, *Reuters*, 30 November. https://reut.rs/42smde0.

Open Societies Statement (2021). [Cornwall Consensus]. https://bit.ly/3MjqDOZ.

Passant, John (2017). Overlooking the real enemy: why Dastyari is small beer. *Independent Australia*, 21 December. https://bit.ly/3BcBO5H.

Perlez, Jan (2018). Pence's China speech seen as portent of "New Cold War". *New York Times*, 5 October. https://nyti.ms/3Bejt82.

Pillsbury, Michael (2015). *The hundred-year marathon: China's secret strategy to replace America as the global superpower*. New York: Henry Holt.

Raby, Geoff (2019). The lowest ebb – the decline and decline of Australia's relationship with China. La Trobe University Annual China Oration, 29 October. https://bit.ly/3LWf3aS.

Raby, Geoff (2020). *China's grand strategy and Australia's future in the new world order*. Melbourne: Melbourne University Press.

Raby, Geoff (2021). Morrison was naked at the G7. *Australian Financial Review*, 21 June. https://bit.ly/42HVLNk.

Raby, Geoff (2022). China relations go back to basics. *Australian Financial Review*, 16 November. https://bit.ly/3O0jG6x.

Reuters (2020). Australia to reject China-backed company's offer to buy dairy firm. *Reuters*, 20 August. https://reut.rs/3nKPYIb.

Roggeveen, Sam, Natasha Kassam and Ben Scott (2020). Wuhan lab claims: is Australia questioning China? Or the US? Both? *Interpreter*, 7 May. https://bit.ly/44R9jI5.

Sheridan, Greg (2012). Asia, done in black and white. *Australian*, 11 August, https://bit.ly/43w0Rwd.

Schreckinger, Ben and Daniel Lippman (2018). The China hawk who captured Trump's "very, very large brain". *Politico*, 2 December. https://politi.co/3BfUH7F.

Shoebridge, Michael (2021). Morrison's G7 trip: "Golden era": of China relations over as united response begins. *Strategist*, 9 June. https://bit.ly/3pxuJdm.

Tett, Jillian (2021). The "Cornwall Consensus" is here, *Financial Times*, 11 June. https://on.ft.com/3LQx0YB.

Thompson, Angus (2022). "The reality of our time": Dutton warns Australians to prepare for war. *Sydney Morning Herald*, 25 April. https://bit.ly/3K134J7.

Tillet, Andrew (2020). China intimidation linked to ASIO raids. *Australian Financial Review*, 9 September. https://bit.ly/3px7aS1.

Turnbull, Malcolm (2020). *A bigger picture*. Melbourne: Hardie Grant.

Wesley, Michael (2020). Trade war: can the China relationship be salvaged? *Saturday Paper*, 19 December. https://bit.ly/41nVmhX.

Wilson, Jeffrey (2021). Australia shows the world what decoupling from China looks like. *Foreign Policy*, 9 November. https://bit.ly/44Nw3J9.

White, Hugh (2012). *The China choice: why we should share power*. Melbourne: Black Inc.

White, Hugh (2022). Sleepwalk to war: Australia's unthinking alliance with America. *Quarterly Essay*, 86. Melbourne: Black Inc.

Zhu, Zhiqun (2020). Interpreting China's "wolf-warrior diplomacy". *Diplomat*, 15 May. https://bit.ly/3pPIhkX.

# 3

# Australia–China security and defence relations at 50: hardening positions on both sides

*Bates Gill*

## Introduction

In the previous volume, *Australia–China Relations at 40*, published more than a decade ago, its contributing authors reflected on the past and likely future trajectory of Australia–China ties, including in the area of strategic and security relations.[1] Four of the authors in particular – Nick Bisley, You Ji, John Lee and James Cotton – considered in separate chapters the security relationship between Australia and the People's Republic of China (PRC or China) and came to quite different conclusions for Australian policy.

Bisley argued for a continued careful balance of Australian economic and security ties with China in order to gain maximum benefit from the relationship. You warned against an emerging tendency he saw in Australian policy circles to treat China as a military threat. Lee emphasised China's vulnerabilities and lack of coercive leverage over Australia and argued that Canberra should therefore not shirk from closer relations with the United States. Cotton underscored the historical undercurrent of unease about China among Australian leaders and

---

1    Reilly and Yuan 2012.

strategists and seemed to question whether Canberra could successfully balance its economic and security interests with respect to China.

With the benefit of ten years' hindsight, we can see that these authors' findings and recommendations were in many ways quite prescient. But in other ways they did not fully appreciate the direction relations would take.

Bisley's balanced approach remained at the centre of Australian China policy (and is still a hoped-for outcome for many), but has come under increasing pressure as both the economic and security relationship with the China has dramatically deteriorated in recent years. Lee, while seeing the continuing importance of US–Australia relations, may have underestimated China's rising influence as a military and economic actor and its implications for Australian security and alliance relations with the United States. You, while correctly foreseeing increased Australian concerns about China as a security threat, did not anticipate the many measures China has since taken to negatively affect Australian security perceptions. In recognising Australia's incessant apprehensions over the decades, perhaps Cotton best understood the challenges Australia–China relations would continue to face.

Most importantly, none of these authors foresaw that the Australia–China security relationship would soon decline to its most acrimonious and distrustful levels since the two countries established formal diplomatic relations 50 years ago. To be fair, it seems no one – including this author – could have foreseen these developments from their vantage points in 2012.

While anything can happen in the next ten years, as the last decade demonstrates, we must do our best to probe a number of important questions. What happened and where do Australia–China security relations go from here? Why have security perceptions between the two countries deteriorated so badly in such a relatively short period of time? What are the implications of these developments for the future and can Australia and China find greater common ground on security and defence issues in the years ahead?

We will address these questions by first considering some of the underlying structural elements that constrain and exacerbate security and defence relations between Australia and China. Second, we will outline some of the specific secondary or "ripple" effects that have flowed from those structural elements and that further erode the bilateral security relationship. Based on those analyses, we will conclude with a look ahead at the prospects for improved security and defence relations between Australia and China in the next five to ten years.

## Structural impediments

At a fundamental level, some of the biggest impediments to a more constructive and less antagonistic security relationship between Canberra and Beijing are structural in nature: that is, they are well-established and long-term factors that have a deep, abiding impact on the perceptions, assumptions and choices of leaders and strategists in both countries. It is not possible in this short essay to delve into these factors in detail and one risks over-generalisation. But at least three key sets of structural factors are worth considering.

### Realist worldviews

First, the overarching world views of the strategic and decision-making elites in the two countries – especially in their security and defence establishments – have rarely sat comfortably alongside one another. Both communities are dominated by "realist" thinking, born of their respective historical experiences and geopolitical circumstances. Realists tend to see the world in stark terms: as competitive and often zero–sum, where nations must do what they can to help themselves to promote and defend their own national interests against others who are seeking to do the same. Realists understand that even in the best of times there are "no permanent friends, only permanent interests" (to paraphrase the famous quote from 19th-century British prime minister Lord Palmerston) and states need to be constantly wary about one another.

For Australia and China, this world view is based on fundamental historical and geopolitical factors that further bolster their mutual wariness and mistrust. Geographically remote and sparsely populated, Australian realism has resulted in an historical reliance on "great and

47

powerful friends" in the words of Australian Prime Minister Robert Menzies – first the United Kingdom, and now the United States – to help the country promote and defend its national interests. In the words of prominent Australian scholars, this reliance on a powerful friend is a "hard-wired" and "non-negotiable" aspect of the country's security and defence strategy and arises from a realist world view that displays a "perennial anxiety" and strategic obsession with Australia's unusual geopolitical and historical circumstances, resulting in a "systemic pessimism" regarding geostrategic power shifts.[2] In this view, a rising and more powerful China, especially to the degree it may threaten Australian national interests, is not a welcome development.

For China, its realist outlook also arises from its geopolitical and historical circumstances. Chinese leaders – both before and since the establishment of the PRC – have long claimed that their rightful status as a powerful and respected country has been wrongfully thwarted by outside powers, including major Western powers and their allies, which are intent on preventing China's rise and return to greatness. In the words of China's paramount leader Xi Jinping, the long-sought "great rejuvenation of the Chinese nation" will be realised by "tenacious struggle" to show that "the time in which the Chinese nation could be bullied and abused was gone forever". He continued:

> We Chinese are a people who uphold justice and are not intimidated by threats of force. As a nation, we have a strong sense of pride and confidence. We have never bullied, oppressed, or subjugated the people of any other country, and we never will. By the same token, we will never allow any foreign force to bully, oppress, or subjugate us. Anyone who would attempt to do so will find themselves on a collision course with a great wall of steel forged by over 1.4 billion Chinese people.[3]

According to the University of London's Steve Tsang, one of the world's leading authorities on PRC politics, the Chinese Communist Party ( CCP) adheres to a "Party-state realism" in its foreign policy, especially

---

2    Beeson and Zeng 2017; Wesley 2009.
3    Xinhua 2021a.

in the Xi Jinping era. This approach, he argues, displays three fundamental characteristics: an instrumentalist approach towards the international system to neutralise criticism of the Party; Party-centric nationalism to secure respect at home and abroad; and a hard-nosed, realist assessment of the Party's power versus its enemies abroad.[4]

Such aggrieved nationalist perceptions are deeply embedded in China's official world views and, for PRC leaders and strategists, justify the country's realist outlook. It is not surprising that Australia, as a Western power closely aligned with the United States, would always be considered a potential adversary intent on impeding China's rise. This is all the more true given Australia's deepening alliance with the United States in recent years (discussed further below).

### Security assessments and responses

A related structural element affecting the Australia–China security and defence relationship has to do with both nations' interpretations of the contemporary global and regional security environment and their respective responses. Importantly, both sides see that environment worsening for their national interests. Even more importantly, each side sees the other as part of that security problem. For example, according to official Australian defence statements, "Australia's region, the Indo–Pacific, is in the midst of the most consequential strategic realignment since World War II". As a result, "[s]trategic competition, primarily between the United States and China, will be the principal driver of strategic dynamics in the Indo–Pacific" and, "[t]hough still remote, the prospect of high intensity military conflict in the Indo–Pacific is less remote than in the past".[5]

Similarly, authoritative PRC assessments of its international and regional security situation express mounting concerns. When Xi Jinping and other Chinese leaders speak of "great changes not seen in a century" on the world stage, they combine a confidence in the opportunities that transformation presents with open acknowledgement of the many challenges those changes pose as well. For example, Xi declared in 2019

---

4    Tsang 2020.
5    Department of Defence 2020.

that "[a] range of risks and challenges threaten the leadership of the Chinese Communist Party and our country's socialist system ... [and] threaten our country's sovereignty, security, and development interests".[6] More recently, his tone took a somewhat darker tone:

> The great rejuvenation of the Chinese nation has reached a critical phase. The risks and challenges we face are clearly increasing. To wish for a peaceful life without struggle is unrealistic. We must fight bravely ... and safeguard the national interests of sovereignty, security and development.[7]

These concerns lead both Australia and China to take steps they believe will improve their security, which contribute to a further cycle of apprehensive action and reaction – a classic "security dilemma", as international relations scholars would say. For Australia, to assuage its "perennial anxiety" and "systemic pessimism" about its changing security environment, a deepening defence relationship with its long-time ally the United States comes as no surprise. Other steps, including Canberra's efforts to bolster the heft and impact of the Quadrilateral Security Dialogue (or "Quad", a loose partnership among Australia, India, Japan and the United States), are also intended to signal resolve and solidarity in response to a rising China.

Perhaps most significant of all, plans for the AUKUS partnership, announced in 2021, if fully realised, will result in one of the most sweeping transformations of Australia's defence posture since the 1950s. These plans include the provision to Australia of a conventionally armed, nuclear-propelled submarine fleet, and co-operation across the three governments on hypersonic weapons, counter-hypersonic defences and on other advanced military technologies.[8]

These measures coincide with Australia's largest expansion in military expenditures since the Vietnam War era, spending that will include the acquisition of long-range strike capabilities such as ship-based Tomahawk cruise missiles, extended range air-to-surface

---

6    Xinhua 2019.
7    Xinhua 2021b.
8    White House 2022.

and anti-ship missiles, land-based precision strike missiles and the capability to manufacture advanced guided missiles on Australian soil by the mid-2020s, as well as enhanced mining capabilities to help secure Australia's maritime approaches. These decisions have clearly been made with China in mind.[9]

For China's part, the past two decades have seen a massive investment in so-called "anti-access/area denial" capabilities. These include land-based ballistic and cruise missiles, a larger and more sophisticated naval force with long-range anti-ship missiles, land- and sea-based airpower, and a more advanced over-the-horizon targeting capability to enable long-range strike systems to attack thousands of kilometres from China's shores. These capabilities aim to deter and, if necessary, defeat potential adversaries such as the United States and its allies who may wish to intervene militarily in these increasingly contested regions. China's expanding military presence in the Indian Ocean and in the straits and waterways to Australia's north, and its plans to establish a close security partnership with Solomon Islands further exacerbate Australian security concerns.[10] Moreover, official statements as well as comments from China's state-owned media have issued admonishments and veiled threats warning Canberra against taking political and military decisions that Beijing deems are contrary to China's national interests.[11]

## Ideological differences

A third area of structural divergence – having to do with ideological differences – is not directly related to the bilateral security and defence relationship, but deeply affects strategic perceptions and trust between the two countries. To a degree not seen since the normalisation of their diplomatic relationship 50 years ago, Australia and China find themselves on opposite sides of a competition over ideas, norms and values, and the relative merits of democratic versus authoritarian systems.

---

9    On these Australian defence plans, see, for example, Department of Defence, n.d.; Macmillan and Greene 2020; Morrison 2021.
10   Lyons and Wickham 2022.
11   *Global Times* 2016, 2021.

This will not be a Cold War-style ideological competition where capitalists on one side and communists on the other struggle to spread their systems. Rather, China's approach to this competition will be more nuanced and, thus far, combines three key elements. First, the Party is increasingly keen to show the superiority of its political and economic system in comparison to liberal democracies in providing the fundamental public goods of stability and prosperity. Second, the Party will insist that its form of Party-State authoritarianism deserves respect and should be accepted and appreciated as a legitimate form of government. Third, the Party and State apparatus are increasingly active in seeking to build up an "international narrative power" (国际话语权) to "tell China's story well and spread China's voice" (讲好中国故事传播好中国声音), offering "Chinese solutions" (中国方案) to reform elements of the international order and proposing that some features of the PRC's economic, social and political model may be appropriate for other countries to consider.

Asserting these ideas is not so much to supplant other systems as to challenge the notion that there is a "universal", one-size-fits-all or "Western" approach for national development and success. Even more importantly for the Party, these ideas send the signal that others outside China should not seek to undermine its rule.

These are uncomfortable and confronting developments for Australian leaders and citizens. Australians appear increasingly concerned that China may seek to dilute or constrain global norms such as market-based economic relations, respect for human rights, the international law of the sea, respect for human rights, peaceful approaches to conflict resolution, an open internet and other aspects of international order on which Australia has relied so heavily to promote its values and secure its interests. If and as the Party succeeds in "making the world safe for autocracy"[12] and builds greater acceptance and admiration for authoritarian systems while deriding democratic ones, it will further exacerbate strategic and security relations between Australia and China.

---

12   Weiss 2019.

## Ripple effects

The structural elements described above have long been part of the Australia–China relationship but, over the decades, have waxed and waned in importance and impact. For much of the period since normalised diplomatic relations in 1972, these structural impediments to the relationship were mitigated somewhat by China's relative weakness in the international system and expectations in Australia that China's polity would evolve towards a more open and just system. Moreover, the highly complementary and lucrative bilateral economic relationship between the two countries also helped to mitigate their structural differences. But in recent years, and especially since the advent of the Xi Jinping era in 2012, these structural factors have intensified to push the security relationship to new lows.

Since 2015–16, the ripple effects of this deteriorating security relationship have become more apparent. Of particular note are the highly sensitive mutual recriminations of domestic political interference. In addition, and not surprisingly, elite and public opinion on each side have increasingly soured towards the other, making it politically difficult to set the security and defence relationship on a more positive course.

### Domestic political interference

Perhaps the biggest single change in the mutual perceptions of Australia and China since 2012 involves concerns over domestic political interference. These concerns have been especially acute and widely publicised in Australia, with a profound effect on the Australia–China strategic, security and defence relationship. But Beijing too has ramped up its accusations of Australian interference in China's domestic affairs – in Xinjiang and Hong Kong, for example – further undermining strategic trust and the possibilities of a more positive bilateral security and defence relationship.

Starting from around 2015 and accelerating quickly thereafter, numerous accusations and public disclosures came to the fore in Australia of Party and PRC government attempts to influence and interfere with political and societal views of China and the Party.

Among the most explosive, these revelations included the Sam Dastyari affair, in which a federal member of parliament accepted personal cash and travel support from Chinese businesses and Party organisations while also expressing his support for certain official PRC policies. At the same time, other revelations emerged that Chinese citizens as well as wealthy Australians with very close political and personal business ties to China had donated millions of dollars – a legal practice at the time – to Australia's major political parties. In addition, concerns arose over the widespread ownership of Chinese-language media in Australia by Chinese state-owned firms and activities of PRC government agents to silence critics and manipulate views of the Chinese diaspora inside Australia.[13] These developments were in addition to other security-related concerns involving PRC investments in critical Australian infrastructure – such as the Port of Darwin, Ausgrid and the national broadband network – as well as ongoing Chinese espionage activities and cyber intrusions by PRC-supported entities.[14]

These and related developments led to the enactment of an extensive suite of domestic security laws and regulations in Australia with the express intent of countering foreign interference. In proposing some of the early legislation, Prime Minister, Malcolm Turnbull, asserted in Chinese that "Australia has stood up" (澳大利亚人站起来了) and otherwise made clear that China was a primary source of concern behind the new laws.[15]

Among other outcomes, the new rules and regulations passed since 2017 restrict foreign donations to political campaigns, require the public registration of lobbyists working on behalf of foreign entities, and effectively ban PRC telecommunications firms from involvement in Australia's fifth-generation (5G) broadband network. The counter-interference laws also oblige certain Australian public

---

13  For details on these and other related activities and allegations, see Sun 2016; Uhlmann and Greene 2016. More extensive discussion of these developments can be found in Gill and Jakobson 2017, especially chapter 4; Hamilton 2018; and Hartcher 2021.

14  Besser, Sturmer and Sveen, 2016; Evans 2021; Hitch and Probyn 2020; Packham 2019.

15  Turnbull 2017.

institutions – including state governments, local councils, universities, and their staffs – to inform the Federal government as to their formal agreements with foreign entities, which the Federal government can in turn terminate if deemed necessary for national security interests. It was under this latter legislation that the Federal government revoked the agreement between the Victoria state government and the PRC's National Development and Reform Commission governing cooperation in relation to China's Belt and Road Initiative.

Two other subsequent developments raised hackles in Australia about PRC influence activities and further soured the bilateral strategic and security relationship. The first was Beijing's fierce reaction to Canberra's call in April 2020 for an international investigation into the origins of the COVID-19 pandemic. Among other actions, the PRC imposed a range of punitive measures, including tariffs and non-tariff barriers, on Australian exports to China such as beef, barley, coal, timber and wine and issued official warnings to discourage Chinese tourists, businesspersons and students from travelling to Australia.

Later in 2020, the PRC embassy in Australia took a second high-profile and highly-unusual step by releasing a list of 14 specific grievances against the Australian government and calling on Canberra to address them if it wished for an improvement in the bilateral relationship. The grievances included: making China the target of foreign interference laws and regulations; banning Huawei, the PRC telecommunications giant, from involvement in the Australian 5G broadband network; funding "anti-China" think tanks; making critical statements about China's policies toward Xinjiang, Taiwan, the South China Sea and Hong Kong; accusing China of cyber attacks against Australia; and calling for an international investigation into the origins of the COVID-19 pandemic.[16] By late-2020, in a poll taken by the Lowy Institute, 82 per cent of Australians polled said they were "personally concerned" with China's influence on Australia's political processes.[17]

As noted in the list of grievances, China too has increasingly raised concerns about Australian attempts to interfere in PRC domestic affairs. In recent years, the Australian government has been far more

---

16    Kearsley, Bagshaw and Galloway 2020.
17    Lowy Institute 2021.

vocal in questioning and condemning PRC policies on issues that Beijing considers "internal matters." These steps by Canberra have included its call, following the Arbitral Tribunal's 2016 decision to reject most Chinese territorial claims in the South China, for Beijing to abide by the ruling. The Australian government has also been especially active in condemning PRC crackdowns in Xinjiang and Hong Kong, in unilateral statements, joint statements with allies and partners, and through multilateral forums such as the United Nations Human Rights Council and in issuing statements supportive of Taiwan. The official Chinese reaction consistently denounces such statements with "grave concern and strong opposition", calling them "blatant interference in China's internal affairs" and urging the Australian government to "discard the outdated Cold War zero–sum mentality and narrow-minded geopolitical perception, view China's development in a correct way, and stop interfering in China's internal affairs ..."[18]

*Souring domestic opinions*

These heightened concerns in both Australia and China over highly sensitive issues of domestic political interference have, not surprisingly, led to deterioration in the perceptions each has of the other.

In Australia, public perceptions of China – as measured in opinion polls – have generally been in decline since 2007 and have dropped precipitously since Xi Jinping came to power in 2012. This is best illustrated by the Lowy Institute's "feelings thermometer", which asks Australians to express their feelings towards other countries in the form of a number between 0 ("very cold") and 100 ("very warm"). When this question was first asked in a Lowy poll in 2007, China was quite favourably perceived, on a par with other countries such as Japan, India and the United States. Since then, Australian views of China have grown progressively "colder", and in 2021 reached their chilliest yet (see Figure 3.1). As Figure 3.2 shows, while the rating of China in 2022 inched up one degree higher than in 2021, the country still ranks lower

---

18   See, for example Consulate General of the People's Republic of China in Sydney 2021; Embassy of the People's Republic of China in the Commonwealth of Australia 2022.

in Australian public perceptions than others such as Japan (74), the United States (65), Taiwan (64), the European Union (62), India (56), Myanmar (46) and Afghanistan (36).

Australian public opinion towards China crossed a critical threshold in 2021 when, for the first time in Lowy polling history, a majority of respondents – 63 per cent to 34 per cent, a margin of nearly two to one – stated that China is more of a security threat than an economic partner. This is a remarkable shift in opinion from only five years prior when 77 per cent of Australians polled felt that China was more an economic partner and only 15 per cent said it was more of a security threat (see Figure 3.3). The concern over China as a security threat is also reflected in the Lowy poll in 2022 in which a record high of 75 per cent of Australian respondents said it either "very likely" or "somewhat likely" that China would become a military threat to Australia in the next 20 years.[19]

This trend is consistent with other data. Whereas in 2016 and 2017, Australians were equally divided on the question of which country – China or the United States – was more important to Australia, by 2020 opinion had shifted decidedly in favour of the United States being the most important partner (55 per cent to 40 per cent favouring China).[20] When asked in 2021 which side is most to blame for tensions in the bilateral relationship, 56 per cent of Australians blamed China and only 4 per cent blamed Australia (38 per cent felt both were equally to blame).[21]

---

19   Lowy Institute 2022a.
20   Lowy Institute 2020.
21   Lowy Institute 2021.

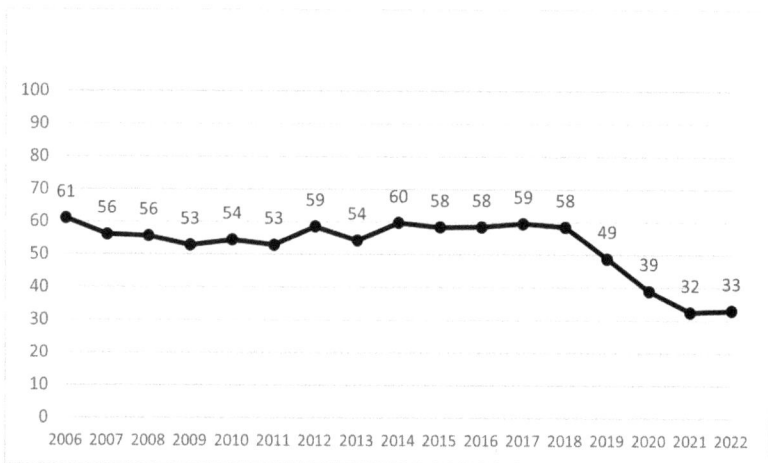

Figure 3.1 Australian feelings of "warmth" towards China, 2007–21 (on a scale of 0 – coldest – to 100 – warmest). Source: Lowy Institute Poll 2022a.

Data on public opinion in China towards Australia is far less extensive. One available poll points to a souring trend in the sentiment among Chinese citizens when asked to express their views about Australia. In a polling conducted in 2020 and again in 2021, Chinese respondents viewing Australia as more of an economic partner than military threat dropped from about 67 to 59 per cent while those who saw Australia as more of a political or ideological threat rose by 5 points to about 34 per cent. This polling also saw declines in Chinese views about Australia as a destination for tourism or to pursue one's studies. Overall, Australia's favourability rating dropped by 10 points between 2020 and 2021, from 65.28 to 55.61.[22]

Interestingly, according to one of the organisers of this polling in China, "the lower a respondent's income and education attainment, the stronger the degree of negativity towards Australia". This suggests that if this particular polling – which mostly concentrated on middle- and high-income respondents in urban areas – had been more nationally

---

22    Chen et al. 2021; Hu 2021.

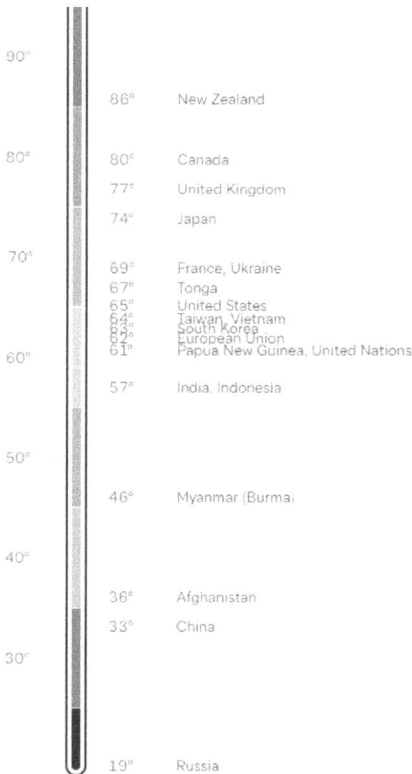

Figure 3.2 Lowy Institute "feelings thermometer" 2022 (on a scale of 0 – coldest – to 100 – warmest). Source: Lowy Institute Poll 2022b.

representative, views towards Australia "would almost certainly be more negative, possibly by a significant margin".[23]

These shifts in attitudes in both Australia and China have an impact on how their respective governments approach the bilateral security relationship. It is more difficult to assess how public opinion affects government decision-making in an authoritarian, one-party

---

23   Hu 2021.

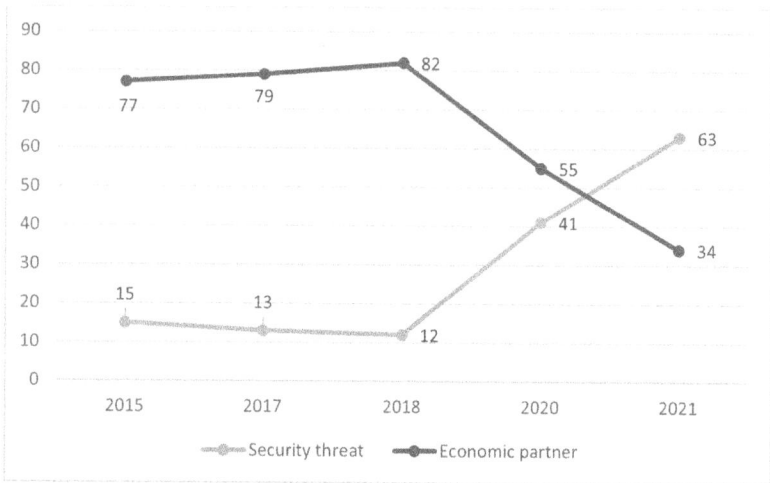

Figure 3.3 China: security threat or economic partner? Percentage of Australian respondents agreeing with one or the other proposition. Source: Lowy Institute Poll 2022c.

system such as China. Nonetheless, even authoritarian leaders need to be conscious of citizens' views, if only to be in a better position to deflect criticism or leverage public sentiment, or both, to align more supportively with the leadership's interests.

It is clearer in democratic systems that politicians will seek to both gauge and shape public opinion for political gain. In Australia, concerns about China as a security threat have entered the political mainstream and have factored more and more prominently in electoral politics. Generally speaking, in both Australia and China, the deterioration in public sentiments towards one another has been both a cause and an effect in the continuing decline in security relations between the two countries.

## Looking ahead

At the 50th anniversary of Australia–China official diplomatic ties, the overall strategic, security and defence relationship between the two countries was at one of its lowest points ever over that period. The flagship "strategic partnership" agreement reached in 2013 between Australian Prime Minister Julia Gillard and Chinese Premier Li Keqiang has been downgraded by Beijing as bilateral tensions have increased. Small, low-level joint training activities between their two militaries – such as the "Panda–Kangaroo" exercise – continued on a sporadic basis through 2019, but have been put on hold for political and pandemic reasons.

Most importantly, the strategic environment in which each side views the other has shifted to introduce greater mistrust, recriminations, and adversarial positioning. As result, the relationship has entered a prolonged period of "bounded engagement": a mix of largely positive economic interactions in parallel with greater uncertainties, deepening mistrust, restricted diplomatic relations, punitive sparring, and heightened security concerns.[24]

Some of these tensions derive from Australia's close political, diplomatic and defence relationship with the United States. Owing to that relationship and its alignment with important Australian values and interests, Canberra can hardly avoid being caught up in the increasingly intense rivalry between China and the United States. Both sides of Australian politics recognise the strategic advantages of the alliance with the United States and will likely seek to deepen ties with Washington – with the 2021 AUKUS agreement being just one major example – in spite of the potential risks entailed in relations with China. This is likely to include an increasing willingness and capacity to confront and counter Chinese threats against US–Australian collective interests.

But in addition, Australian leaders and citizens increasingly recognise that China poses direct threats against Australia, including through greater power projection capabilities, growing security presence in Australia's neighbourhood, cyber attacks, coercive

---

24 Gill 2019.

economic measures, and influence activities. The security agreement reached between China and the Solomon Islands in 2022 stands out as a powerful example of these concerns. These perceptions will not easily change – and in fact will likely become more prevalent in the near to medium term – which will further harden Australian positions towards China.

Given the power asymmetries between China and Australia, the former is far less concerned about threats emanating from the latter. Nonetheless, Beijing has clearly expressed its annoyance with Australian policies that run counter to Chinese interests and has taken actions to counter them. In a classic display of the security dilemma at work, each side takes steps it believes are necessary to defend its interests, but those steps are seen as provocations by the other, and the cycle continues. As this chapter has shown, the elements are in place for this dynamic to remain in place for years to come.

While the Australia–China security and defence relationship is unlikely to improve in the near to medium term, there may be ways to help improve mutual trust, mitigate security tensions and reset defence ties. It was the Australian government, in 2020, that established the National Foundation for Australia–China Relations with the expressed goal to "strengthen understanding and engagement between Australia and China" by supporting businesses, governments, communities and individuals to "provide practical support and expertise, facilitate connections, commission research, and coordinate training and exchange programs".[25] As Ien Ang describes in this volume (see Chapter 10), the foundation had some difficulties in getting started but, in its first two years of operations, it expended just over $8 million in grants to support a range of programs, including joint collaborations between Australians and Chinese people, to conduct research and exchanges on healthcare systems, aged care and emissions technologies, and strengthening people-to-people ties through sports, cultural and youth activities.[26] It is possible such activities will improve bilateral relations, but they are not designed to deal with fundamental strategic differences.

---

25  From National Foundation for Australia–China Relations n.d.a.
26  From National Foundation for Australia–China Relations n.d.b.

It is also possible for the two sides to deepen channels of communication and enlarge a sense of common interests by agreeing to tackle larger strategic and security challenges that both countries must confront. These challenges will include mitigating climate change, preventing the emergence of new pandemics, improving economic prospects and infrastructure in least developed countries, reducing regional instability through preventive diplomacy, resolving conflict and building peace, and slowing the spread of weapons of mass destruction. As China grows stronger, it is increasingly willing and able to take on greater responsibility to meet these and other global challenges. The difficulty for Beijing and Canberra will be to find politically acceptable ways to work together to tackle these and other challenges they face in common. In the absence of deeper government-to-government cooperation in these areas, other collaborations at the sub-national level – for example, between businesses, scientists, entrepreneurs and educators – will help the two sides deal with such commonly shared problems.

With a change in the Australian government following the May 2022 elections, there was some modest hope for a "reset" in relations between Beijing and Canberra. Indeed, some reporting claimed that the Liberal–National coalition lost support in some districts with sizeable ethnic Chinese populations because of its tough rhetoric towards China.[27] The new Labor government promised a different tone in its relations with China, which may help to improve ties. As Wanning Sun points out in this volume (see Chapter 8), the tone among political elites and leading media turned decidedly more negative towards China in recent years. It remains to be seen, but new leaders and restrained rhetoric in Australia may generate a more constructive atmosphere for the bilateral relationship.

After the Labor victory, the two sides re-established ministerial-level communications, with the Australian defence and foreign ministers meeting their counterparts within weeks of assuming office in mid-2022 – a first for the two countries in nearly three years.[28] In another move intended to improve relations, the newly arrived PRC

27   Knott and Sakkal 2022; Rachwani 2022.
28   Barrett 2022; Connors and Smith 2022.

ambassador to Australia, Xiao Qian, delivered a high-profile speech in June 2022 in which he expressed his hope

> [that] Australian colleagues could join us to make concerted efforts by moving towards each other, taking concrete actions, adhering to the principle of mutual respect and mutual benefit, so as to bring our bilateral relationship back on the right track of development at an early date.[29]

(In an indication of continuing difficulties in the Australia–China relationship, the speech was disrupted by anti-PRC protestors.)

While these developments suggest some possibilities for improved relations, both sides acknowledge there remain many obstacles and each side will expect the other to make concessions first. Meanwhile, the fundamental strategic relationship between Australia and China will continue to be fraught with tensions. As discussed by many of the contributors to this volume, the Australia–China relationship has become more "securitised" (that is, more concerned with security than with cooperation), which will make positive progress more difficult between the two. For both sides, hardening realist world views, diverging views on regional security, and widening ideological differences have affected domestic political perceptions in ways that make a change in this trajectory unlikely in the near to medium term. While the past 50 years of Australia–China relations have been characterised by peace and prosperity, the two sides will need to work much harder than in the past to ensure the next 50 years will enjoy the same.

## References

Barrett, Chris (2022). Wong meets Wang as ministers attempt to stabilise China–Australia relations. *Sydney Morning Herald*, 8 July. https://bit.ly/3NeJ08D.

---

29  Xiao 2022.

Beeson, Mark and Jinghan Zeng (2021). Realistic relations? How the evolving bilateral relationship is understood in China and Australia. *Pacific Focus* 32(2): 159–81. https://doi.org/10.1111/pafo.12094.

Besser, Linton, Jake Sturmer and Ben Sveen (2016). Government computer networks breached in cyber attacks as experts warn of espionage threat. *ABC News Four Corners*, August 29. https://bit.ly/3oG38Gm.

Chen, Qing Qing, Zhao Yusha, Xie Jun and Xu Keyue (2021). Chinese less favorable to Australia amid strained ties: GT poll. *Global Times*, 23 June. https://bit.ly/44TzQF0.

Connors, Emma and Michael Smith (2022). Marles, Wei break Australia–China meeting drought. *Australian Financial Review*, 12 June. https://bit.ly/40JCfi2.

Consulate General of the People's Republic of China in Sydney (2021). Chinese FM spokesperson: The US and Australia should stop making waves in the Asia-Pacific region. *Consulate General of the People's Republic of China in Sydney*, 18 September. https://bit.ly/3HZbnUJ.

Department of Defence, Australian Government (2020). 2020 Defence Strategic Update, 1 July. https://bit.ly/3LQeBLw.

Department of Defence, Australian Government n.d. Maritime mining. https://www.defence.gov.au/project/maritime-mining.

Embassy of the People's Republic of China in the Commonwealth of Australia (2022). Embassy spokesperson's remarks on the negative content relation to China of the AUKMIN joint statement. *Embassy of the People's Republic of China in the Commonwealth of Australia*, 21 January. https://bit.ly/42FhIN5.

Evans, Jake (2021). Home Affairs Minister vows to continue to hold China accountable for cyber attacks. *ABC News*, 21 July. https://ab.co/3Y63Udg.

Gill, Bates (2019). Bounded engagement: charting a new era in Australia–China Relations. *Disruptive Asia* 3: 3–6. https://bit.ly/43HLvEK.

Gill, Bates and Linda Jakobson (2017). *China matters: Getting it right for Australia.* Melbourne: Latrobe University Press and Black Inc.

Global Times (2016). "Paper cat" Australia will learn its lesson. Editorial, 30 July. https://bit.ly/3HURu0U.

Global Times (2021). Australia could be caught in Sino-US crossfire. 16 November. https://bit.ly/44MZsD5.

Hamilton, Clive (2018). *Silent invasion: China's influence in Australia.* Melbourne: Hardie Grant.

Hartcher, Peter (2021). *Red zone: China's challenge and Australia's future.* Melbourne: Black Inc.

Hitch, Georgia and Andrew Probyn (2020). China believed to be behind major cyber attack on Australian governments and businesses. *ABC News*, 19 June. https://ab.co/3HZe60p.

Hu, Diane (2021). Public sentiment in China cools toward Australia. *Pursuit*, 1 July. https://bit.ly/42ss5UH.

Kearsley, Jonathan, Eryk Bagshaw and Anthony Galloway (2020). "If you make China the enemy, China will be the enemy": Beijing's fresh threat to Australia. *Sydney Morning Herald*, 18 November. https://bit.ly/3rMtNmg.

Knott, Matthew and Paul Sakkal (2022). Chinese-Australian voters punished Coalition for hostile rhetoric. *Sydney Morning Herald*, 25 May. https://bit.ly/3MeuGfg.

Lowy Institute Poll (2020). Relations with superpowers – US and China. Sydney: Lowy Institute. https://bit.ly/41iIJ7L.

Lowy Institute Poll (2021). Tensions in the Australia–China relationship. Sydney: Lowy Institute. https://bit.ly/44YgOxc.

Lowy Institute Poll (2022a). China as a military threat. Sydney: Lowy Institute. https://bit.ly/3NT4qbF.

Lowy Institute Poll (2022b). Feelings toward other nations. Sydney: Lowy Institute. https://bit.ly/41o0mmH.

Lowy Institute Poll (2022c). China: economic partner or security threat. Sydney: Lowy Institute. https://bit.ly/44Zx8hh.

Lyons, Kate and Dorothy Wickham (2022). The deal that shocked the world: inside the China-Solomons security pact. *Guardian*, 20 April. https://bit.ly/3nO1nqw.

Macmillan, Jade and Andrew Greene (2020). Australia to spend $270b building larger military to prepare for "poorer, more dangerous" world and rise of China. *ABC News*, 30 June. https://ab.co/3nVxkgu.

Morrison, Scott (2021). Australia to pursue nuclear-powered submarines through new trilateral enhanced security partnership. Media statement. *PM Transcripts: Transcripts from the Prime Ministers of Australia*, 16 September. https://bit.ly/3puWh2M.

National Foundation for Australia–China Relations n.d.a. About. https://bit.ly/3VRJwvs.

National Foundation for Australia–China Relations n.d.b. Grant information. https://bit.ly/44JIEgv.

Packham, Colin (2019). Exclusive: Australia concluded China was behind hack on parliament, political parties – sources. *Reuters*, 16 September. https://reut.rs/3plMRqh.

Rachwani, Mostafa (2022). Chinese Australians say Coalition's rhetoric on Beijing could see voters "switch from Liberal to Labor". *Guardian*, 20 May. https://bit.ly/3VPB27Y.

Reilly, James and Jingdong Yuan (eds) (2012). *Australia and China at 40*. Sydney: NewSouth Books.

Sun, Wanning (2016). Chinese-language media in Australia: developments, challenges, and opportunities. Research report. *Australia–China Relations Institute, University of Technology Sydney*, 8 September. https://bit.ly/3DqryYH.

Tsang, Steve (2020). Party-state realism: a framework for understanding China's approach to foreign policy. *Journal of Contemporary China* 29(122): 304–18. https://doi.org/10.1080/10670564.2019.1637562.

Turnbull, Malcolm (2017). Speech introducing the National Security Legislation Amendment (Espionage and Foreign Interference) Bill 2017. *Malcolm Turnbull 29th Prime Minister of Australia 2015–2018*, 7 December. https://bit.ly/3rDYmdT.

Uhlmann, Chris and Andrew Greene (2016). Chinese donors to Australian political parties: who gave how much? *ABC News*, 21 September. https://ab.co/44FU984.

Weiss, Jessica Chen (2019). A world safe for autocracy?: China's rise and the future of global politics. *Foreign Affairs* 98(4): 92–102.

Wesley, Michael (2009). The rich tradition of Australian realism. *Australian Journal of Politics and History*, 55(3): 324–34. https://doi.org/10.1111/j.1467-8497.2009.1520a.x.

White House (2022). AUKUS leaders' level statement. *The White House*, 5 April. https://bit.ly/3OqCewE.

Xiao, Qian (2022). Promote healthy and stable development China–Australia comprehensive strategic partnership in the spirit of mutual respect and mutual benefit. UTS:ACRI Address. *Australia–China Relations Institute, University of Technology Sydney*, 24 June. https://bit.ly/3NXs8DB.

Xinhua (2019). 习近平在中央党校 (国家行政学院) 中青年干部培训班开班式上发表重要讲话 [Xi Jinping delivers an important speech at the opening ceremony of a training session for middle-aged and young cadres at the Central Party School (Chinese Academy of Governance)], 3 September. https://bit.ly/3rM6VDo.

Xinhua (2021a). Full text: speech by Xi Jinping at a ceremony marking the centenary of the CPC. *Xinhua*,1 July. https://bit.ly/3K8oCUf.

Xinhua (2021b). 习近平在中央党校 （国家行政学院） 中青年干部培训班开班式上发表重要讲话 [Xi Jinping delivers an important speech at the opening ceremony of a training session for middle-aged and young cadres at the Central Party School (Chinese Academy of Governance)]. 1 September. https://bit.ly/3Y4I3CW.

# 4
# (Un)reliable partner? Australian security, the American alliance and China in uncertain times

*Brendon O'Connor, Lloyd Cox and Danny Cooper*

When confronted with strategic and security challenges, Australian governments have historically gone to great lengths to strengthen the alliance with the United States.[1] Since World War II, this pattern has been particularly apparent when Liberal Party prime ministers have responded to instability and perceived threats in the Asia–Pacific region. The expansion of communism in Asia in the 1950s and 1960s, the chaos surrounding the independence referendum in East Timor in 1999 and more recently the growing assertiveness of China in Asia and the western Pacific are all developments that prompted Liberal-led Australian governments to strengthen relations with Washington. The conservative Morrison government (2018–2022) amplified Australia's support for and dependence on the United States – not least through the signing of the AUKUS agreement that promised the country nuclear-powered submarines by the 2040s – the effects of which were to worsen already strained relations with China. Yet while the details are of course different, the policy adopted by the most recent Liberal government conforms to a pattern established with Menzies and the creation of the Australia, New Zealand, United States Security Treaty (ANZUS) in 1951.

---

1   See Cox and O'Connor 2012; Bell 1988; and Kelton 2008.

While Labor, in and out of government, has typically been more restrained in its US–Australia alliance advocacy, and has sometimes resisted American policy and preferences (Vietnam and the second Iraq wars being obvious examples), it too has been largely supportive of the US security umbrella, extending right back to Prime Minister John Curtin's necessary embrace of the United States in 1942. Despite periodic recalibrations and changes of tone, such as under the Calwell and Latham leaderships and the Whitlam and Keating prime ministerships, Labor has ensured that support for the alliance has been largely a bipartisan project, especially over recent decades. Prime Minister Hawke's enthusiastic defence of and military support for the US position in the first Gulf War, and the Gillard government's 2011 agreement to have up to 2,500 marines based in Australia's Northern Territory – part of President Obama's original Asia "pivot" – are examples that fit within the general pattern. During the 2022 federal election campaign, Labor leader Anthony Albanese stuck very closely to this script. Nothing that he has said or done since becoming prime minister suggests any significant change with respect to Australia's relationship with the United States or its posture towards the US–China rivalry, which is clearly one of unconditional support for the former over the latter. Despite adopting a more measured tone than that embraced by shrill voices of the Morrison government, the new Prime Minister, and his Foreign and Defence ministers, are all clear that the US–Australia alliance is the bedrock on which Australian security rests.[2] When forced to choose between its largest trading partner and its most important strategic ally, both of Australia's major political parties have clearly made their choice.

---

2   Prime Minister Albanese travelled to the meeting of the Quadrilateral Security Dialogue in Tokyo hours after being sworn in on 23 May 2022. There he reasserted Australia's commitment to both the Quad and the United States, to "make sure we push our shared values in the region at a time when China is clearly seeking to exert more influence". See Stayner 2022. Similarly, in a July 2022 speech to the Center for Strategic and International Studies in Washington DC, Defence Minister Richard Marles called for even closer cooperation between Australia and the United States to counter China's military build-up and to avoid a "catastrophic failure of deterrence in the Indo-Pacific". See Macmillan 2022.

We call this approach to Australia's foreign policy "all the way with the USA" with obvious reference to Harold Holt's 1966 "all the way with LBJ" phrase, which encapsulated the Liberal Party leader's determination to support the US war in Vietnam, regardless of the costs and risks. Just as Australia's involvement in that conflict entailed costs and risks that were insufficiently appreciated or acknowledged at the time, so too does the present Canberra consensus around being all the way with the USA. Most obviously, these risks include the further deterioration of Australia's relationship with China, which involves grave economic, political and military costs for the country. But the risks also include, we will argue, the less commented on over-reliance on a partner whose strategic position in Asia is weaker than often assumed, and whose domestic politics increasingly call into question its medium- to longer-term reliability. Is the United States the reliable guarantor of Australian security that its boosters claim it to be? If it is not, what are the implications for Australia's defence and foreign policy?

In this chapter, we explore these questions within the context of a broader discussion about Australian foreign policy with respect to China and the existing US-led international order. We begin with a consideration of the US-led liberal international order and Australia's support of it and of the United States more specifically. We continue by examining the impact of the US alliance on Australia's relations with China, and the impact of recent Chinese foreign policy on the alliance, which we view as mutually constitutive. We note the challenges that the US-led order faces in Asia, which pose difficult choices for Australia. This is followed with a discussion of America's own febrile domestic politics and the dangers for Australia. These, we suggest, raise important questions about the reliability of the US security guarantee and the "all the way with the USA" strategic posture adopted by both of Australia's major political parties. Finally, we provide a brief sketch of an alternative Australian foreign policy that avoids the pitfalls of over-reliance on one country, albeit one as powerful as the United States.

## Australia and the US-led liberal international order

The American scholar Peter Harris argues that since World War II, American foreign policy has been globally oriented in three regards:

[1] that multilateral security partnerships are essential to defeating and deterring foreign threats to U.S. national security, and that [2] domestic prosperity depends upon the existence of an open world economy … [3] pronounced militarist bias in U.S. government and politics.[3]

In this section, we deploy Harris' frame to focus on how the Turnbull and Morrison governments dealt with Trump's and Biden's support and opposition towards these three pillars of US grand strategy. We suggest that Turnbull and Morrison often tried through their speeches to will into action a "liberal internationalist" America they believed Australia most needed, even when dealing with the patently nationalistic President Trump.

Harris' first pillar of US inter nationalism is a belief in alliances and US security agreements as the basis for global peace, as these alliances tilt the balance of power in the world significantly in America's favour. It is widely believed by the US foreign policy elite that the US-led system of alliances cements in place the status quo of US global hegemony. Australia has fully subscribed to this approach to world affairs and as a result has aimed to form a "special relationship" with the United States.[4] An extension of this view, which some US administrations more than others have been committed to since World War II, is the belief that a US-dominated world is best maintained and served by a commitment to "a rules-based system" or what is similarly called "the liberal international order". For Australian prime ministers Turnbull and Morrison, this language of a US-led "rules-based" or "liberal international" order was a central way of framing America's role in the world and a key element of the claim that the United States (and by extension Australia) should act in a manner that is morally superior

---

3    Harris 2018, 612.
4    Cox and O'Connor 2020.

to how China conducts its foreign affairs.[5] These concepts have been doing a lot of heavy lifting in recent Australian foreign policy rhetoric and have echoes of George W. Bush's over-promotion of his "freedom agenda" to justify the US invasions and occupations of Afghanistan and Iraq. This is not just a mere debating point; the link between the Bush administration's and Morrison's use of the phrase a "world order that favours freedom" can be seen in speeches and strategic documents.

On 9 June 2021, for example, Morrison gave a speech entitled "A world order that favours freedom" in which he argued: "Our challenge is nothing less than to reinforce, renovate and buttress a world order that favours freedom".[6] In 2002, Condoleezza Rice started arguing that US military strength was "special" as it maintained a global "balance of power that favours freedom".[7] The term comes from "The National Security Strategy" of 2002, which is one of the most controversial and militaristic statements of US foreign policy doctrine ever.[8] It was the document that established the claim that the United States had the right to act "pre-emptively" to prevent terrorist attacks (a notion used to justify the invasion of Iraq in 2003). All of this reminds us that phrases like "a world order that favours freedom" are in the end very malleable in the hands of great powers and their allies.

During the Trump administration, seeing the United States as a champion of a "world order that favours freedom," a "rules-based system" or the "liberal international order" was more what Australian leaders hoped of America than the reality. President Trump was clearly no supporter of the idea of a US-led liberal international order. He claimed that maintaining such an order created too many opportunities for other nations to exploit American benevolence. This was one of Trump's many exaggerations, but it was a claim that led to policy action once he was elected. Evidence of this is that, as president, he eschewed the liberal internationalist rhetoric that we are so used to hearing from US presidents; he was unusually comfortable meeting with dictators; and he adopted a more transactional approach to international affairs

---

5    Kelly 2022.
6    Dziedzic 2021.
7    Rice 2002.
8    Rice 2002.

(which extended an attitude to long-standing allies of "what have you done for us recently?"). Faced with this outlook and approach to foreign affairs, Australian leaders were reluctant to publicly criticise Trump, particularly Prime Minister Morrison, and this contributed to a more status quo US-Australian relationship during the Trump presidency compared to more turbulent US relations with Canada, France and Germany. Morrison also promised that, unlike other US partners, Australia could, in his words, "pull our weight" and "do a lot of the heavy lifting."[9] This rhetoric was exactly what Trump wanted to hear from allies. But such promises leave Australia open to being asked by the Americans to do things that are not in Australia's national interest.

In terms of the US commitment to open markets, Trump was a major departure from US post–World War II trade policy. His decision to impose tariffs on a significant range of Chinese exports to the United States created a new trading atmosphere internationally, where the Chinese were also more willing to play the tariff card. This has had negative consequences for Australia given that its economy has historically been heavily oriented to trading internationally. A more mercantilist world where tariffs are commonplace represented a breakdown of the "liberal international order" that had long benefited Australian exporters, and which has been an important element of Australia's long run of prosperity. Turnbull, Foreign Minister Julie Bishop and Morrison all talked up this "liberal international order" as being in Australia's economic interests as well as its security interests. The replacement of Trump's administration with Biden's made Australian rhetoric again align with American liberal internationalist rhetoric. The Biden administration's commitment to long-standing alliances and open markets was on full display when Kurt Campbell, the President's Indo–Pacific co-ordinator, stated in March 2021:

> We have made clear [to China] that the US is not prepared to improve relations in a bilateral and separate context at the same time that a close and dear ally is being subjected to a form of economic coercion.[10]

---

9    Kelly 2022, 134.
10   Hartcher 2021.

Finally, support for US military predominance, which is often reflected in the ubiquity of America's military bases around the world, was one area where the Trump administration presented significant continuity with his predecessors. David Vine, the author of *Base Nation*, contends that America has "800 military bases in more than 70 countries and territories abroad – from giant 'Little Americas' to small radar facilities. Britain, France and Russia, by contrast, have about 30 foreign bases combined."[11] Regarding the global spread of military personnel, Chalmers Johnson quotes a US Department of Defense report that Americans are deployed in "153 countries".[12] Supporting America's global military presence is the area where Australian and American policy is most consistently aligned. Australian governments have reliably – be they Coalition or Labor – wanted greater military interoperability with the American military, greater access to American military technology and intelligence, and a greater US military presence in the Asia–Pacific region. Of course, there have been disputes with the United States over issues like freedom of navigation operations, but there has been significant agreement between Canberra and Washington (arguably more so than with any formal US ally since 1945) because of Australia's "fear of abandonment".[13] This is concerning, as US foreign policy has long over-emphasised military solutions to international challenges. Australia could be seen as encouraging an American pathology that has significantly increased US federal debt this century, and decreased America's standing in the world after each military intervention, from the Korean War onwards. Australia's own emphasis over the last decade of increasing defence and national security budgets, while reducing funding to the Department of Foreign Affairs and Trade, mirrors the American approach under Trump. It points to the general undervaluing of diplomacy and the diplomatic services in both nations. The strength of this military alignment suggests that if America fails to live up to its liberal values at home or abroad in the future, Australia may be willing to largely turn a blind eye and focus on its security relationship with the United States.

---

11   Vine 2015.
12   Johnson 2004, 153–4.
13   Gyngell 2017.

One of the themes of Allan Gyngell's book *Fear of abandonment* is Australia's general willingness to engage in military actions with the United States, in the belief that committing troops provided Australia "insurance" of US support if troubles arose for Australia in the future.[14] Troop commitments to the Vietnam War and 2003 Iraq War are key examples of this approach.[15] This military-first approach to foreign policy and Australia's relationship with the USA is evident in the revival of the Quadrilateral Security Dialogue (the Quad) and the announcement of the AUKUS agreement. The Australian Strategic Policy Institute estimates that the nuclear submarines that are the centrepiece of the AUKUS agreement will cost Australia between $116 and $171 billion.[16] One gets a sense of how significant this financial commitment is when you compare it to Australia's most recent annual budget for its Department of Foreign Affairs and Trade, which was $6.1 billion,[17] and its most recent annual foreign aid budget, which was $4.3 billion.[18]

Due to this Australia–US military alliance first approach, Australian governments have been "flexible" enough to say next to nothing publicly when the United States became protectionist on trade and walked away from months of negotiations on the multilateral free trade agreement known as the Trans-Pacific Partnership, or when President Trump argued against the "liberal world order" the United States had crafted. This is because what the Australian foreign policy and defence department elite is most afraid of is an American ally that is not militarily engaged in the Indo-Pacific. This is revealing and demonstrates in Australia the prioritising of defence policy over diplomacy for a significant period. It is also very revealing regarding how much of a threat to Australian security the Turnbull and Morrison governments perceived China to be.

14  Gyngell 2017.
15  Cox and O'Connor 2012.
16  Tillet 2021. Since the writing of this chapter, it is now estimated at up to $368 billion.
17  Department of Foreign Affairs and Trade 2020.
18  Clare 2021.

We will argue in the final section that the return of Donald Trump or a similar Republican to the US presidency should raise very significant concerns for Australia because of the disdain that leading Republicans now profess to have for the "liberal international order". This liberal international order is possibly more important to Australian security than the American alliance, requiring serious consideration of how such an order can be maintained in the face of a flagging American commitment under future Trump-like figures. After all, Australian policymakers must take seriously the final act of the Trump presidency: the exhortation to violence in a final bid to deny Joe Biden his electoral victory. The key point here is that a country whose leaders show no respect towards liberal and democratic norms at home can hardly be expected to champion them abroad.

Australian policymakers have always felt that Australia's interests are best served by aligning with big and powerful friends, but those friends are expected to stand for something beyond mere militarism and the transactional international leadership characteristic of the Trump era. Australia, like all middle and smaller powers, benefits from liberal rules and norms and understandably fears the consequences of great powers discarding them. Likewise Australia also fears challenges to an order from which they have derived clear benefits. Today, China is often said to be the bearer of precisely such a challenge.

## China and the US–Australia Alliance

It is no coincidence that the deterioration in Australia's relationship with China has coincided with a reassertion of its forthright support for, and strategic dependence on, the United States. This is not to imply that the US–Australia alliance is the only irritant to Australia's relationship with China, or that its deterioration is the key to explaining Canberra's more forthright exaltation of the alliance in recent years. Clearly the world, and particularly the part of the world in which Australia is situated, is far more complex than such a reductive account would allow. That said, it is clear that the dynamics of Australia's relationship with the United States have affected and been affected by Australia's relationship with China. China's recent actions and rhetoric

– its building of islands and military bases in the South China Sea, its efforts to enlarge the Chinese presence in the western Pacific, its tariffs against Australian imports and its shrill denunciations of Australia's alleged subservience to "third parties"[19] – have had the consequence of raising anxiety in Canberra and strengthening the US–Australia alliance. This has in turn hardened Chinese attitudes and actions towards Australia. The two developments are mutually constitutive. The direction of the causal arrows, never easy to disentangle in international politics, runs both ways. Let us begin by considering the Chinese pole of this dialectic.

The spectacular growth of China's economic and military power over the past decade, and China's increased willingness to assertively deploy this increased power to realise its own foreign policy objectives, is at the heart of intensified anxiety in Canberra about Australia's future security. When Xi Jinping became general secretary of the Chinese Communist Party in 2012,[20] China's gross domestic product (GDP) was just over half of that of the United States, at about US$8.53 trillion. By 2020, this had increased to $14.8 trillion, which was over two-thirds the size of the United States' GDP.[21] The Chinese economy is likely to exceed the size of the US economy by 2030, though some would argue that, if purchasing power parity is considered, China already has a larger economy.[22] The sheer size of the Chinese economy is reflected

19  This phrase is clearly a euphemism for the United States. It was most recently used by the Chinese Foreign Minister, Wang Yi, in the meeting with his Australian counterpart Penny Wong, in Bali. In the third of his four conditions for improving bilateral relations with Australia, he suggested "we must adhere to not targeting or being controlled by third parties". See Birtles 2022.
20  In all important respects, this marked Xi Jinping's ascension to the top Chinese leadership, though it would not be until early 2013 that he would become President.
21  Gross domestic product (GDP) at current prices in China and the United States from 2005 to 2020 with forecasts until 2035, see Statista.com, n.d.
22  Naturally there is a degree of uncertainty and contestation around these claims, as it is impossible to predict with certainty rates of growth in various countries. For sources backing the claim that China's economy will exceed the USA by 2030, see Jennings 2022. For sources suggesting that this may be a mirage, see Magnus 2021.

in the fact that it is the largest trading partner of every country in Asia, including Australia. This gives China powerful leverage when dealing with other countries in the region.

Over the past decade, the Chinese leadership has prioritised translating this economic power into military modernisation. While it is important to note that China's military spending is still only about 36.5 per cent of that of the United States, it has roughly doubled in a decade, which implies an average annual growth rate of more than 7 per cent.[23] Among other things, that increased spending has been manifested in new generations of aircraft and missile technology, enhanced cyber-warfare and artificial intelligence capabilities, improved submarine capabilities and the launching of three aircraft carriers that extend China's power projection and capacity for competing with the United States on the high seas.[24] While most defence analysts accept that the US military still has an edge over China, the gap has narrowed considerably since the early 2000s, and will narrow further in the years to come.[25] Moreover, any military conflict between the two countries in the near to medium future will likely occur close to China. This "home-ground advantage", so to speak, would give China tremendous military and logistical advantages in any conventional regional war with the United States, regardless of the latter's naval and technological superiority, which is itself rapidly eroding.

Economic growth and increased military spending do not in themselves represent a threat to Australia's security. It is when they are considered alongside China's deeds and words that threat perceptions are amplified in Canberra and Washington. The list of provocative Chinese actions – seemingly part of a broader policy of projecting power, exerting influence and pushing back against the United States and its partners in Asia and the Pacific – is a long one. China's claiming

---

23   The Stockholm International Peace Research Institute (SIPRI) has regular statistical coverage of national and international military spending and is the source of the data cited here. See Stockholm International Peace Research Institute 2022.
24   Caverley and Dombrowski 2020.
25   Flournoy 2021, 76.

of sovereignty over contested "features" in the South China Sea has been buttressed by the actual building of islands, the establishment of military bases and the seizure of other countries' fishing vessels. China has similarly challenged Japan's control of the Senkaku/Diaoyu Islands in the East China Sea, deploying People's Liberation Army aircraft and naval forces to press its claims.[26] Demonstrations in Hong Kong in 2019 were met with brutal repression, and all political figures in the Hong Kong legislature who opposed Beijing have now been removed. China's economic coercion against Australia and others, and its efforts to establish a greater presence in the western Pacific, dramatised by the announcement of the security deal with the Solomon Islands in April 2022, has been particularly alarming for Australia and its allies. Most importantly, China has loudly reasserted its determination to bring Taiwan under China's control, by 2049 at the latest, with military exercises and numerous violations of Taiwanese airspace symbolising this determination. These developments are clearly part of a broader Chinese foreign policy and set of strategic objectives that concern defence planners in Canberra and Washington. But what are these objectives and what are they not?

For some China hawks – and this seems to be the thinking that was animating the then Defence Minister Peter Dutton's alarmist rhetoric about preparing for war with China – the implicit answer is no less than global Chinese domination.[27] When the assertive actions sketched above are viewed in the context of China's Belt and Road Initiative, its debt diplomacy, its establishment of alternative financial institutions to the International Monetary Fund and World Bank, its overt interference in the affairs of other countries – including Australia[28] – and its energetic efforts to extend its influence in South-east Asia, Africa, the Middle East, Latin America and the Pacific, the conclusion is often drawn that these parts make up a larger whole whose terminus is a world under the heel of authoritarian Chinese control. In this view, modern China is analogous to Nazi Germany or the Soviet Union, and Xi Jinping occupies the position that Hitler and Stalin once did. The

---

26   Hagstrom 2012; Hughes 2016, 111.
27   See Brands 2020; Doshi 2021; Schuman 2021.
28   Hamilton 2018.

political conclusion flows logically from this premise. The democratic West cannot afford to appease or accommodate China's expansionist aims, because appeasement and accommodation will only encourage further aggression and expansion. Instead, the West, under US leadership and with deputising support from allies like Australia, must demonstrate resolve against Chinese aggression, up to and including the use of military force.

This position ignores relevant facts about the world in the 2020s that make it very different from the world of 1938 (when the Munich agreement was signed) or 1947 (when Truman announced the containment doctrine). China is today integrated into the circuits of the global capitalist economy in a way that Nazi Germany or the Soviet Union never were. China's economic prosperity and political stability depend on its continued access to foreign markets and investment, and its continued participation in international forums that help govern the global economy. It derives key benefits from this continued participation, which include employment and improved living standards for millions of Chinese, and a growing middle class that contributes to political stability. A key domestic and foreign policy objective is, therefore, to preserve and grow benefits derived from participation in the global economy, which is the presupposition of China's hard and soft power. Consequently, China's leadership is unlikely to covet a position of global domination because doing so would pose an intolerable risk to its prosperity and power.

This risk is closely related to, and cannot be understood in the absence of, the second relevant difference between today's China and the Nazi Germany and Soviet Union of the past: pre-war Nazi Germany confronted multiple great powers that were *not* nuclear armed; the post-war Soviet Union existed in a bipolar world where its chief adversary was nuclear armed; today, China's power is balanced by multiple powers that possess nuclear weapons. As Hugh White and others have argued, this precludes for China the type of global expansionary ambition that Nazi Germany had and that the Soviet Union allegedly had.[29] As rational actors, the Chinese leadership recognises this even if the China hawks in Washington and Canberra

---

29   White 2022.

do not. The fantasy of global Chinese domination is more about legitimising a particular military and strategic posture – one that seeks to preserve US primacy in Asia – than it is a realistic appraisal of China's ambitions and capacities to realise those ambitions.

To argue that China does not seek global domination is not to deny its regional ambitions or the coercive measures it is prepared to take to realise these ambitions. Nor is it to deny that China at the least seeks to modify the much-vaunted "rules-based international order", which it correctly views as embodying Western values and advantaging Western powers. In regard to its immediate region, China seeks to be the primary power in Asia and to be recognised as such. This entails a challenge to American hegemony in Asia and the western Pacific, which takes material form in the military build-up in the South China Sea, the tense stand-offs around freedom of navigation operations in that contested stretch of water, and Chinese efforts to establish a permanent presence in small Pacific nations. Just as the United States asserts its own primacy in the Caribbean and would not tolerate the intrusion of other great powers, China similarly seeks primacy in Asia and demands recognition of this primacy, which would entail a retreat of the United States from the region (though not necessarily a complete exit). As Hugh White has recently summed up the situation:

> [China] aims to assert its place as the region's primary power, and to undermine America's position, by showing that it is willing to go to war to push America out of East Asia and that America is not willing to go to war to stop it.[30]

And herein lies the nub of the issue for Australian policymakers: ought Australia further sacrifice its relationship with China in order to preserve American primacy in Asia by unconditionally supporting the latter's efforts at preserving primacy?

As recently as October 2019, an Australian prime minister could claim that Australia "does not have to choose between the United States and China".[31] Regardless of whether this was self-deception, duplicity

---

30   White 2022, 36.
31   Morrison 2019.

or a sincerely-held position, the choice made is now clear, if indeed there was any doubt in the first place. Australia's Coalition government unambiguously bet all of its chips on the alliance with the United States, which Morrison described as "our past, our present and our future".[32] Having made that bet, the Coalition then doubled down, as attested to by its announcement of the AUKUS agreement in September 2021, which was received by China as a direct affront to its own security and standing in the world. Morrison would go on to invoke the phrase "red lines" when reacting to the China–Solomon Islands security pact, while his Defence Minister suggested that Australia should prepare for war and that it was "inconceivable" that Australia would not support the United States in a war over Taiwan.[33]

It would be mistaken to think that this is all down to the belligerence of conservative politicians or electoral contingencies driven by domestic political advantage. During the election campaign, the opposition Labor Party was in lock step with the government on national security issues and China, even if it occasionally offered tepid criticisms of the failings of Coalition diplomacy and foreign policy. Since coming into government, Labor leaders have repeatedly voiced their support for the United States, and reacted coolly to Chinese overtures to reset the relationship. When Chinese Premier Li Keqiang sent a letter of congratulations to Anthony Albanese, the latter's first response was to reassert that "Australia's position on national security remained unchanged", while emphasising the importance of the Quad engaging in the Indo-Pacific to counter the activities of China.[34] It is clear, then, that the Labor government is intent on maintaining and strengthening the US–Australia alliance, even if the emphasis and details of its foreign policy shifts relative to the previous, conservative government.

None of this should come as a surprise. Despite the massive economic benefits that Australia has derived from trade with and

---

32　Morrison 2019.
33　Morrison's April 2022 comments on Chinese bases being a "red line" can be found here: Hitch 2022; Dutton's November 2021 comments are reproduced here: Kelly 2021.
34　Graham 2022.

investment in and from China – benefits that continue to accrue even in the midst of sharpened mutual suspicion and recrimination – the longevity, depth and intimacy of its "special relationship" with the United States transcend dry economic calculation. Shared interests and values are buttressed, we have argued elsewhere, by affective attachments that also characterise relations between other members of the "Anglo-sphere".[35] This is manifested in a thousand threads that bind the military, intelligence and political bureaucracies of the two countries, not to mention the shared language and cultural affinities that smooth communication and social intercourse between its peoples. Mark Beeson and Alan Bloomfield have written persuasively of the path dependency of the US–Australia alliance, which is expressed in and reinforced by cultural affinity and high levels of institutionalisation.[36] The willingness of the United States to share its security secrets with Australia within the framework of the Five Eyes intelligence arrangement, and the willingness of Australian governments to support the United States in all of its military adventures since World War II, are but two of the most obvious expressions of this path dependency and the long-standing fraternal relations between the two countries, formalised by the ANZUS Treaty.[37]

Underpinning all this, and lending the alliance a dependable political substratum – despite periodic bouts of Australian public dissatisfaction with US military aggression and particular US presidents – is a generally positive view of the United States and of the alliance within Australia. Lowy Institute public opinion polling extending back to 2005 confirms the high regard in which the United States and the alliance are held, while also identifying widespread distrust of China.[38] Recent developments in world politics have reinforced the reflex towards identifying with, and relying on the assumed security guarantee from, the United States. The global pandemic, the Russian invasion of Ukraine with China's apparent blessing, China's perceived and real aggression towards Australia and

---

35  Cox and O'Connor 2020; Katzenstein 2012; Vucetic 2011.
36  Beeson and Bloomfield 2019.
37  Hayden 2016; Hubbard 2017.
38  Lowy Institute 2022.

others, along with a more generalised sense of uncertainty and instability in global affairs, have all heightened anxieties within Australia's population and political elites about both personal and national security. These febrile conditions have been fertile grounds for stoking Australia's "fear of abandonment", about which Allan Gyngell has so persuasively written.[39] The apparent desire for the protections provided by a "great and powerful friend" are accentuated in the current conjuncture, and few are in doubt that the United States is and should remain that powerful friend.

Yet Australia's dependence on the United States as a security guarantor – and the willingness of Australian politicians to unwaveringly support the United States in its rivalry with China, which is typically viewed as the price of the guarantee – comes with both costs and future risks that have not been sufficiently scrutinised, or even acknowledged, by Coalition or Labor governments. Most obviously, the costs include economic damage that China has shown a willingness to inflict in its recent restrictions on Australian imports of wine, barley, lobsters and coal. But these represent only a small percentage of Australia's overall exports.[40] Despite China's heavy reliance on Australian minerals, the risk is that over time it will escalate its economic retaliation against Australia, as it diversifies the countries of origin from which it draws raw materials to fuel its economic engine. Australia's "all the way with the USA" strategic posture, along with the intemperate language with which it is often articulated, amplifies this risk.

This posture also risks damaging Australia's bilateral relations with other countries. We can already observe this in the fallout over the debacle around the French submarine deal, which has been a significant setback for our relations with a very important Pacific power. But closer to home, the AUKUS deal has raised legitimate concerns in the region that Australia views its security as being better served by being part of a rich white club, rather than by cooperating with local partners, and that this rich white club makes conflict in the region more rather than less

---

39   Gyngell 2017; see also Cox and O'Connor 2012.
40   Wickes, Adams and Brown 2021.

likely.[41] Whether or not this is true is of course a moot point. But the perception here is at least as important as the reality.

The broader risk for Australia, and one about which the previous government and its ideological fellow travellers were virtually silent, a silence that has continued under Labor, is the reliability of the United States itself as a security guarantor. In his recent *Quarterly Essay*, Hugh White makes the case that the American position in Asia – economically, diplomatically and militarily – is not as strong as many imagine, and that it is unlikely that the American electorate will be prepared to pay the price and accept the burdens that military confrontation with China would demand.[42] This makes the US commitment to primacy in Asia more fragile than it appears, and hence its long-term commitment to guaranteeing the security of allies like Australia is no guarantee at all. We do not agree with all of White's uncompromisingly realist assumptions, but he certainly has the merit of highlighting the uncertainties, which many of his critics refuse to even countenance, around the future position of the United States in Asia.

Moreover, the Trump presidency starkly revealed the depths of new and existing strains of isolationism within the United States, while the storming of the Capitol building on 6 January 2021 highlighted the fragility of the democratic constitutional order that we so often take for granted. The nationalist constituency to whom Trump most appealed – and we should remind ourselves that Trump still received 73 million votes in 2020, despite losing – is actively hostile to the idea that the United States should bear the costs of military obligations to allies and that it should be the policeman of the world. We may be only one presidential election away from a return to and a deepening of the isolationism and ambivalence towards allies that marked the previous Trump presidency. Trump is now out of office but Trumpism lives on,

---

41　The Malaysian and Indonesia foreign ministers both expressed their concern when the AUKUS deal was first announced in 2021, suggesting that the agreement might accelerate an arms race in the region and escalate tensions. See Strangio 2021. That same concern was reiterated by Malaysia to the new Labor government in June 2022. See Connors 2022.

42　White 2022, 11–21.

as we discuss in the next section. This raises the stakes tremendously for the type of binary bet that Australia has placed on the United States as Australia's security guarantor.

## "Fight like hell" – the US–Australia alliance in the age of Trump

As we stated at the outset of this chapter, Australia's relationship with the United States is built on the notion of shared values and common culture. At the heart of such values are generally considered to be broad understandings consistent with liberal democratic theory: that legitimate government rests on the consent of the governed; that governments should protect the rights of all citizens regardless of colour or creed; that disputes should be resolved peacefully through compromise and accommodation; and that no single individual is impervious to the rule of law. Cynics may question how well liberal democracies live up to these values in practice, but one cannot doubt the extent to which policymakers in both the United States and Australia identify these values as investing the alliance with a deeper moral significance.

It is for this reason that the events of 6 January 2021 should pose a challenge to the way in which Australian policymakers have historically conceptualised the alliance. After weeks of contesting the legitimacy of the 2020 election, which included multiple failed legal challenges and attempts to influence local election officials to alter the result, President Donald Trump mounted his last stand. Addressing his faithful followers in Washington DC before what should have been the routine counting of Electoral College votes, the president repeated his allegations of a stolen election, telling his followers that they were "under siege" and needed to "fight like hell".[43] Heeding this advice, thousands of loyal Trump supporters ransacked the US Capitol building, ran roughshod over police, endangered the lives of US policymakers – and stained American democracy.

Since this day, there has been no shortage of commentators emphasising the increasingly perilous state of democratic politics in the

---

43    Trump 2021.

United States.[44] The country itself, mainly through the establishment of a January 6 Congressional Committee investigating the events of that day, is still coming to terms with President Trump's attempt to subvert democracy. The chaotic and sinister attempts to overturn the election have been well covered in recent journalistic accounts, most notably Bob Woodward and Robert Costa's *Peril* (2021) and Michael Wolff's *Landslide* (2021).[45] The work of Woodward and Costa is particularly instructive in documenting the extreme lengths to which the president, supported by a cadre of lawyers, went in attempting to overturn the outcome of the 2020 election. Whether it was seizing voting machines "to take control of the vote count", or pressuring the Vice President, Mike Pence, to de-certify the electors pledging themselves to vote for Biden in the Electoral College, there was, to put it mildly, no consideration of democratic values in the last days of the Trump presidency.[46] The eruption of violence was as inevitable as it was tragic, although President Trump shows little remorse with his recent promises to pardon the perpetrators of the violence should he be re-elected in 2024.[47] All of this should give pause to those arguing that "shared values" help strengthen the US–Australia alliance.

The current state of public opinion in America is also suggestive of a darker future. A recent Yahoo News/YouGov poll found that 49 per cent of Americans believe it is "likely" that the United States will "cease to be a democracy in the future".[48] According to a *Washington Post*–University of Maryland poll, approximately "1 in 3 Americans say they believe violence against the government can at times be justified".[49] While the United States has been rocked by questions of racial justice and police brutality against African Americans in recent times, the changes in attitudes are more pronounced on the American right. Believing that President Biden "stole" the election in 2020, coupled with frustrations about pandemic-era restrictions, 40 per cent of

---

44 Gellman 2021; Kagan 2021.
45 Wolff 2021; Woodward and Costa 2021.
46 Woodward and Costa 2021, 193.
47 Palmer 2022.
48 Romano 2022.
49 Kornfield and Alfaro 2022.

Republicans say that violence could be acceptable in comparison to 23 per cent of Democrats.[50] Put simply, 6 January may not have been the unsavoury culmination of Trump-era division. Instead, it may well have been a precursor to a future wave of anti-democratic politics and political violence. Such polls give some credence to George Kennan's observation that "public opinion, or what passes for public opinion, is not invariably a moderating force in the jungle of politics".[51] This obviously does not excuse populist leaders for chipping away at the faith in democratic institutions and fanning the flames of insurrection. But democratic values in America look increasingly fragile when such a large percentage of its citizens is no longer willing to commit itself to the peaceful reconciliation of differences.

Of course, President Trump's influence over the Republican Party has been the subject of much discussion since he left office. These discussions intensified after the Republican Party's modest gains in the 2022 mid-term elections, in which the party failed to retake the Senate but won a slimmer than anticipated majority in the House. A number of candidates endorsed by Trump did not perform overly well, fostering the impression that Trump's influence on the GOP might be starting to wane. But the poll numbers tell a more inconclusive story. According to a Pew Research Center Poll conducted not long after the mid-terms, the number of Republicans saying they feel warmly towards Trump declined from 67 per cent in July 2021 to 60 per cent in October 2022 – hardly a big fall.[52] The biggest decline is among college-educated GOP voters with fewer than half (49 per cent) now providing "positive evaluations" of President Trump – interestingly, 65 per cent without college education remain supportive of the former president. But what this means for the Republican Party, let alone for the future of American foreign policy, is still open to interpretation. After having announced his candidacy for the 2024 presidential election, Trump is not going anywhere, and neither are his most passionate supporters.

---

50   Kornfield and Alfaro 2022.
51   Kennan [1951] 1984, 61.
52   Cerda and Daniller 2022.

Geoffrey Kabaservice, one of the more prominent historians of the Republican Party, supports this claim, arguing that Trump now leads an insurgency that is much different from previous "upwellings of grass-roots anger and enthusiasm".[53] Trump's conservatives, according to Kabaservice, have little interest in the messy, pragmatic compromises involved in governing. He argues:

> conservatism under Trump has reached the point that it is weirdly closer to Trotsky's concept of an endless, all-encompassing, worldwide struggle against established authority than to any political movement, including conservative movements over the past century. The tea party-Trump tribe loosely corresponds to Trotsky's proletarian class, pursuing its own interests against those of every other class in society, without alliance or compromise.[54]

Trump and his conservative supporters in red-leaning states have already made progress simplifying his path back to power, removing and replacing key election officials in states such as Georgia, Michigan and Arizona who refused to buckle under Trump's post-election attempts in 2020 to alter the election outcome. Taking aim at the Republican Party, Barton Gellman argues, "Our two-party system has only one party left that is willing to lose an election. The other is willing to win at the cost of breaking things that a democracy cannot live without."[55] Gellman's point is that without a willingness to abide by a fair election outcome, the United States may face a democratic crisis the likes of which may not have been seen since Lincoln's election in 1860. There is obviously nothing inevitable about this as one could contemplate a future where the Republican Party nominates a candidate more willing to work within the system as opposed to trying to up-end it. But the evidence of the last several years, marked by extremist violence, disputed elections, endless fear-mongering and deep partisan divisions, does not inspire or justify a great deal of optimism.

---

53   Kabaservice 2020.
54   Kabaservice 2020.
55   Gellman 2021.

## Conclusions

What, then, does this mean in a foreign policy sense? Australian policymakers often invoke shared values as the glue that holds the alliance together through thick and thin. But in the age of Trump's conservative nationalism, what exactly is the content of those values? In terms of grand strategy, Trump pursued a form of illiberal hegemony, supporting unquestioned US military strength even as he endlessly criticised democratic NATO allies, coddled dictators from Vladimir Putin to Kim Jong Un, repudiated US support for free trade and withdrew from organisations such as the World Health Organization. Trump fits neatly into what the historian Walter Russell Mead calls the Jacksonian tradition in American foreign policy, the most militaristic tradition that places great primacy on the military being used only to defend core national security interests. For the Jacksonian, Mead argues, "Countries, like families, should take care of their own; if everybody did that, we would all be better off".[56] This aligns nicely with Trump's transactional form of leadership where decisions are made, thinking, as the former President so often put it, of America First.

The questions raised above need to be considered much more deeply, especially by Australian politicians emphasising the importance of shared values. In Australian policy circles, it has often been an article of faith that the United States would act as the reliable custodian of a liberal international order. But, in the age of Trump's conservative nationalism, which allegedly privileges the interests of the American "heartland", how confident can Australia be in America's regional security guarantees? In *Chaos under heaven: Trump, Xi, and the battle for the twenty-first century* (2021), Josh Rogin recounts a candid exchange between President Trump and an unidentified Republican senator. "Taiwan is like two feet [half a metre] from China," Trump is said to have told this senator. "If they invade, there isn't a fucking thing we can do about it." Rogin goes on to emphasise the extraordinary nature of this comment, acknowledging that this would have repudiated a 40-year commitment "to aid Taiwan in its defense".[57] It is

---

56 Mead 2002, 285.
57 Rogin 2021, 44.

also telling in light of the US–Australia alliance. After all, Australian policymakers have often been made aware that if there was any conflict over Taiwan, the United States would expect Australia to promptly align itself with America. In 1999, it was Richard Armitage, who would go on to serve as Deputy Secretary of State in the George W. Bush administration, stating that the United States would "expect Australia's support" in any conflict over Taiwan – indicating that the future of the alliance may depend on it.[58]

It is not simply the unpredictability of US politics that should give Australian policymakers concern. The recent history of conservative governments militarily aligning Australia with the United States has not served Australian interests well. The AUKUS agreement, in our view, is simply the latest iteration of an overly-militarised relationship. Of course, President Biden promises to return the United States to a more conventional liberal internationalist approach, a position much more familiar to Australian policymakers. But in May 2022, while attending a press conference in Japan, President Biden was asked by a journalist whether the United States was militarily obligated to defend Taiwan if China attacked, to which he emphatically stated "Yes".[59] The comment allegedly made some aides uncomfortable as it seemed to repudiate the policy of " strategic ambiguity" at the heart of the US approach to China–Taiwan relations – an approach designed to induce caution on both sides of the Taiwan Strait. But, in more formal pronouncements, the White House has emphasised that official policy has not changed. In the words of a recent readout of President Biden's meeting with President Xi Jinping, the president allegedly told his Chinese counterpart that "our one China policy has not changed, the United States opposes any unilateral changes to the status quo by either side, and the world has an interest in the maintenance of peace and stability in the Taiwan Strait."[60] In our view, this moderate course remains the best approach as it neither signals a flagging commitment to defend Taiwan nor should it needlessly provoke Chinese counter reactions.

---

58   Wesley 2007, 126.
59   Liptak, Judd and Gan 2022.
60   White House 2022.

While we support the administration's formal clarification that its position has not changed regarding Taiwan, Biden's answer should raise questions about the judgement of recent American leaders in times of war and peace. From Somalia and Kosovo in the 1990s to Afghanistan and Iraq in the War on Terror, to Obama's intervention in Libya and Trump's "maximum pressure" campaign on Iran, US interventions rarely go according to plan. This is as true for leaders who are clearly better equipped, both intellectually and temperamentally, than Trump-like figures. After all, it should be recalled that Biden himself as chair of the Senate Foreign Relations Committee voted in favour of the 2003 Iraq War, arguably the most disastrous conflict the United States has waged since Vietnam. American foreign policy, especially on sensitive questions such as Taiwan, can also be complicated by differences in policy preferences between the executive and legislative branches of the US government. Even the passage of the *Taiwan Relations Act* by Congress in 1979 went much further than the Carter administration planned, imposing alleged obligations on the United States to arm Taiwan and come to its defence in any future conflict with China.[61] This remains relevant today when congressional leaders such as Nancy Pelosi opt to visit Taiwan in a bold declaration of ongoing US military support – a visit in August 2022 upon which the Biden administration sent mixed signals, with the President initially claiming that the US military may not think it is a "good idea right now".[62] Of course, Biden eventually defended Pelosi's right to travel to Taiwan, but even outside the intense partisanship of US politics, the system itself can create uncertainty.

The foreign policy missteps of the United States in countries such as Iraq and Afghanistan make it incumbent on Australian governments, whether Liberal or Labor, to pursue a foreign policy that maximises Australia's choices. While it is not our intention here to outline the precise nature of an alternative Australian foreign policy, Australia needs to think creatively about its involvement with regional institutions such as the Association of Southeast Asian Nations (ASEAN) and invest heavily in bilateral relationships with countries

---

61 Mann 2000, 95.
62 Kine 2022.

such as Indonesia. We believe that a number of sensible policy proposals designed to strengthen and deepen economic and cultural ties are advanced in later chapters of this book. These chapters underscore the importance of Australia diversifying its partners and markets, neither relying exclusively on the United States for its security needs nor China for its purchasing of Australian commodities.

Like all nations, Australia must not foreclose the possibility of cooperation with China on issues of deep importance, whether they be climate change, global health or even regional security issues raised by countries such as North Korea. If Australia's voice carries any weight in the United States, then it must surely be used to encourage policymakers in America to identify areas where cooperation with China is possible. Of course, none of this is easy and one cannot neglect the broader regional security dynamics of the region. As always, Australia, as Paul Keating put it, needs to find its security "in Asia, not from Asia". This is the challenge conferred on the current generation of Australian policymakers.

## References

Beeson, Mark and Alan Bloomfield (2019). The Trump effect downunder: US allies, Australian strategic culture, and the politics of path dependence. *Contemporary Security Policy* 40(3): 335–61.

Bell, Coral (1988). *Dependent ally: a study in Australian foreign policy*. Melbourne: Oxford University Press.

Birtles, Bill (2022). China's foreign minister blames Morrison government for poor relations, tells Penny Wong to "treat us as a partner, not a threat". *ABC News*, 10 July. https://ab.co/3I2Zk8V.

Brands, Hal (2020). What does China really want? To dominate the world. *Japan Times*, 22 May. https://bit.ly/3Kqkcbs.

Caverley, Jonathan D. and Peter Dombrowski (2020). Cruising for a bruising: maritime competition in an anti-access age. *Security Studies* 29(4): 671–700.

Cerda, Andy and Andrew Daniller (2022). Before midterms, Trump's image among Republicans had become less positive. *Pew Research Center*, 14 November. https://pewrsr.ch/3O83AWV.

Clare, Angela (2021). 2021–22 foreign aid budget. *Parliament of Australia*. https://bit.ly/3pqAppj.

Connors, Emma (2022). Malaysia adds voice to concerns over AUKUS. *Australian Financial Review*, 28 June. https://bit.ly/3LTpnk3.

Cox, Lloyd and O'Connor, Brendon (2012). Australia, the US, and the Vietnam and Iraq wars: "hound dog, not lapdog". *Australian Journal of Political Science* 47(2): 17–87.

Cox, Lloyd and Brendon O'Connor (2020). That "special something": the U.S.–Australia alliance, special relationships and emotions. *Political Science Quarterly* 135(3): 409–38.

Department of Foreign Affairs and Trade, Australian Government (2020). Budget highlights 2020–21. https://bit.ly/3Ym6z2V.

Doshi, Rush (2021). *The long game: China's grand strategy to displace American order*. New York: Oxford University Press.

Dziedzic, Stephen (2021). Scott Morrison to focus on international trade, climate policy in speech ahead of G7 summit. *ABC News*, 8 June. https://ab.co/42Nw2mA.

Flournoy, Michele A. (2021). America's military risks losing its edge: how to transform the Pentagon for a competitive era. *Foreign Affairs* 100(3).

Gellman, Barton (2021). Trump's next coup has already begun. *Atlantic*, 6 December. https://bit.ly/44WigiL.

Graham, Ben (2022). Anthony Albanese backs US President Joe Biden on Taiwan stance. *news.com.au*, 24 May. https://bit.ly/3nZcywu.

Gyngell, Allan (2017). *Fear of abandonment: Australia in the world since 1942*. Melbourne: La Trobe University Press.

Hagstrom, Linus (2012). "Power shift" in East Asia? A critical reappraisal of narratives on the Diaoyu/Senkaku Islands incident in 2010. *Chinese Journal of International Politics* 5(3): 267–97.

Hamilton, Clive (2018). *Silent invasion: China's influence in Australia*. Melbourne: Hardie Grant.

Harris, Peter (2018). Why Trump won't retrench: the militarist redoubt in American foreign policy. *Political Science Quarterly* 133(3): 611–40.

Hartcher, Peter (2021). "Just not going to happen": US warns China over Australian trade stoush. *Sydney Morning Herald*, 16 March. https://bit.ly/41A0m3m.

Hayden, Michael V. (2016). *Playing to the edge: American intelligence in the age of terror*. New York: Penguin.

Hitch, Georgia (2022). Scott Morrison says Chinese military base in Solomon Islands would be "red line" for Australia, US. *ABC News*, 24 April. https://ab.co/42qQ4DP.

Hubbard, Christopher (2017). *Australian and US military cooperation: fighting common enemies*. London: Taylor & Francis.

Hughes, Christopher W. (2016). Japan's "resentful realism" and balancing China's rise. *Chinese Journal of International Politics* 9(2): 109–50.

Jennings, Ralph (2022). China's economy could overtake US economy by 2030. *VOA News*, 4 January. https://bit.ly/41tBs5k.

Johnson, Chalmers (2004). *The sorrows of empire*. New York: Henry Holt.

Kabaservice, Geoffrey (2020). The forever grievance: conservatives have traded periodic revolts for a permanent revolution. *Washington Post*, 4 December. https://wapo.st/42JAYsB.

Kagan, Robert (2021). Our constitutional crisis is already here. *Washington Post*, 23 September. https://wapo.st/3KLVlz9.

Katzenstein, Peter (2012). *Anglo-America and its discontents*. New York: Routledge.

Kelly, Lidia (2021). "Inconceivable" Australia would not join U.S. to defend Taiwan – Australian defence minister. *Reuters*, 13 November. https://reut.rs/44SaRlm.

Kelly, Paul (2022). *Morrison's mission: how a beginner reshaped Australian foreign policy*. Sydney: Penguin.

Kelton, Maryanne (2008). *More than an ally? Contemporary Australia–US relations*. Aldershot, UK: Ashgate.

Kennan, George ([1951] 1984). *American diplomacy*. Chicago: University of Chicago Press.

Kine, Phelim (2022). How Biden bungled the Pelosi trip: the White House's muddled messaging gave China a big win. *Politico*, 8 March. https://politi.co/3LSr3Kx.

Kornfield, Meryl and Mariana Alfaro (2022). 1 in 3 Americans say violence against government can be justified, citing fears of political schism, pandemic. *Washington Post*, 1 January. https://wapo.st/3I0s1TZ

Liptak, Kevin, Donald Judd, and Nectar Gan (2022). Biden says US would respond "militarily" if China attacked Taiwan, but White House insists there's no policy change. *CNN Politics*, 23 May. https://cnn.it/47cgH26.

Lowy Institute Poll (2022). United States. *Lowy Institute Poll 2022*, 29 June. https://bit.ly/3HZA4QS

Macmillan, Jade (2022). Defence minister urges closer Australia-US ties to avoid "catastrophic failure of deterrence" in Indo–Pacific. *ABC News*, 12 July. https://ab.co/3VQVjtX.

Magnus, George (2021). From economic miracle to mirage – will China's GDP ever overtake the US? *Guardian*, 29 December. https://bit.ly/3NWJuAn.

Mann, James (2000). *About face: a history of America's curious relationship with China, from Nixon to Clinton*. New York: Vintage Books.

Mead, Walter Russell (2002). *Special providence: American foreign policy and how it changed the world*. New York and London: Routledge.

Morrison, Scott (2019). The 2019 Lowy Lecture: Prime Minister Scott Morrison. Lowy Institute, 4 October. https://bit.ly/476JMvV.

Palmer, Ewan (2022). Donald Trump doubles down on pardoning Jan. 6 Capitol rioters, says many not guilty. *Newsweek*, 2 February. https://bit.ly/42iwBVL.

Rice, Condoleezza (2002). A balance of power that favors freedom. Iowa State University: Archives of Women's Political Communication, 1 October. https://bit.ly/3LT6ttt.

Rogin, Josh (2021). *Chaos under heaven: Trump, Xi, and the battle for the twenty-first century*. Boston: Houghton, Mifflin, Harcourt Publishing.

Romano, Andrew (2022). Poll: half of Americans now predict U.S. may "cease to be democracy" someday. *Yahoo News*, 15 June. https://bit.ly/41oauvL.

Schuman, Michael (2021). China wants to rule the world by controlling the rules. *Atlantic*, 9 December. https://bit.ly/3q2UaE9.

Statista n.d. Gross domestic product (GDP) at current prices in China and the United States from 2005 to 2020 with forecasts until 2035. https://bit.ly/3PSc8Ua.

Statista n.d. Gross domestic product (GDP) at current prices in China from 1985 to 2022 with forecasts until 2028. https://bit.ly/3O1qv7z.

Stayner, Tom (2022). Anthony Albanese says Quad will work more closely with Indo–Pacific to counter China's influence. *SBS News*, 24 May. https://bit.ly/3pAeKuP.

Stockholm International Peace Research Institute (2022). World military expenditure passes $2 trillion for first time. SIPRI, 25 April. https://bit.ly/44Nv2kn.

Strangio, Sebastian (2021). Indonesia and Malaysia reiterate concerns about AUKUS pact. *Diplomat*, 19 October. https://bit.ly/3O5DMe3.

Tillet, Andrew (2021). Locally made AUKUS subs almost double the cost: ASPI. *Australian Financial Review*, 1 December. https://bit.ly/3Bf4SJx.

Trump, Donald (2021). Transcript of Trump's speech at rally before US Capitol riot. *AP News*, 14 January. https://bit.ly/42ppwmn.

Vine, David (2015). Where in the world is the U.S. military? *Politico Magazine*, July/August. https://politi.co/44FQCGP.

Vucetic, Srdjan (2011). *The Anglosphere: a genealogy of a racialized identity in international relations*. Redwood City, CA: Stanford University Press.

Wesley, Michael (2007). *The Howard paradox: Australian diplomacy in Asia 1996–2006*. Sydney: ABC Books.

White House (2022). Readout of President Joe Biden's Meeting with President Xi Jinping of the People's Republic of China. The White House, 14 November. https://bit.ly/3OrSwFn.

White, Hugh (2022). Sleepwalk to war: Australia's unthinking alliance with America. *Quarterly Essay*, 86. Melbourne: Black Inc.

Wickes, Ron, Adams, Mike and Brown, Nicholas Brown (2021). Economic coercion by China: the impact on Australia's merchandise exports. Working paper no. 4. Institute for International Trade, the University of Adelaide. https://bit.ly/41vUp7k.

Wolff, Michael (2021). *Landslide: the final days of the Trump presidency*. London: Bridge Street Press.

Woodward, Bob and Robert Costa (2021). *Peril*. London: Simon & Schuster.

# Part Two – Economy

## Introduction to Part Two

Traditionally the bright spot in bilateral relations, since 2017 Australia's trade and investment relations with China have been severely affected by worsening tensions. Fears of over-dependence upon trade with China and anxieties over Chinese investment have led Australia policymakers to pressure businesspeople to diversify their trade ties away from China while discouraging Chinese investors. The three chapters in this section document these worrisome trends, explain the costs of such measures and suggest alternative approaches.

James Laurenceson and Weihuan Zhou begin by arguing that calls for Canberra to take measures to reduce trade within China to mitigate risk are poorly conceived. Drawing on detailed analysis of sector-specific trade data, they demonstrate that, rather than Australia dangerously depending upon China, the trade relationship is best understood as one of mutual dependence. They also insist that Australian firms are far more resilient and flexible than most casual commentary suggests. Grounded in a clear understanding of how businesses assess risks, they demonstrate that Australian firms are already acutely aware that geopolitical fallout might impact their operations and that at a firm, industry and national level there exists a variety of mechanisms to mitigate these risks. Moreover, they point to the often-ignored costs and the considerable difficulty for any government seeking to compel firms to alter their market-driven trading patterns for political reasons. Rather than futile, costly and unnecessary measures driven by political fears, policymakers should consider how they might foster greater diversification of Australia's own export mix while pursuing more effective and less costly risk mitigation measures.

Finally, they point to the potential for Australia to co-operate with China on trade through bilateral and multilateral mechanisms. Reconsidering China's non-market economy status within the World Trade Organization (WTO), for instance, would not only bolster Australia's capacity to deal with bilateral trade disputes, but could also contribute to a general thawing of diplomatic tensions. Australia and China share a concern with the United States' blocking of WTO adjudication mechanisms, as well as a common interest in leveraging WTO initiatives to foster environmentally sustainable development. As founding members of the Regional Comprehensive Economic Partnership, they also share an interest in new multilateral trade agreements. China has also applied to join the Comprehensive and Progressive Trans-Pacific Partnership; as a founding member, Australia has an opportunity to leverage Beijing's interest to encourage further domestic reforms and regional trade cooperation.

In Wei Li and Hans Hendrischke's chapter, our focus is turned to investment, as they draw upon their database of Chinese investment projects in Australia from 2007 to 2021 and extensive interviews with Chinese investors and executives in Australia. They divide the recent history of Chinese direct investment in Australia into the resources boom (2008–12), the integration period (2013–16), and the fallback period (2017–21). The post-2016 remarkable decline and disruption of Chinese investment is due partly to tightening regulatory oversight by the Chinese government, but primarily to Australia's deteriorating political climate for Chinese investment.

Australia's tightening of regulatory restrictions on foreign direct investment (FDI), alongside negative social perceptions and increasing geopolitical tensions as reflected in populist rhetoric have given rise to deepening apprehension among current and potential Chinese investors. Taking a careful look at these drivers, Li and Hendrischke warn that claims of national economic interest can be invoked for a bundle of reasons, including in response to political pressure and in favour of domestic investors. Politicisation of investment amidst surging populism has alienated not just Chinese investors but even many local Chinese Australians, giving Chinese firms the impression that they are less welcome to invest in Australia.

Unfortunately, this heightened politicisation of Chinese investment emerged just as Australian–Chinese business cooperation was diversifying from traditional resources industries into new growth areas where Australian industries have global competitive advantages such as agribusiness, health and services. Australian firms have thus lost opportunities to open up new markets while expanding their access to finance, economies of scale and global value chains. Restoring a healthy investment relationship will require rebuilding social and political trust, presenting a persuasive commercial rationale for desired Chinese investment, reaching a consensus between business and government on investment, and acknowledging the benefits from Australia's and China's growing integration in regional trading blocs. By building on lessons learned over the past decade, Li and Hendrischke conclude, the two sides can establish a more stable foundation for economically sustainable, long-term coexistence.

Glenda Korporaal's chapter augments the two preceding studies by providing firsthand accounts of economic interactions, drawing upon her long experience in reporting on Australia–China economic ties and her extensive interviews with seasoned business executives. She insists that in designing a robust Australian engagement strategy with China, the thoughts and experiences of business leaders deserve to be heard. She echoes Laurenceson and Zhou's finding that business leaders can effectively assess and respond to the risks associated with conducting business with China, citing several examples where Australian businesses have responded to China's recent trade sanctions in a calm and effective fashion.

Her interviews also reveal Australian executives' insightful understanding of key aspects of Chinese political and economic structures and decision-making, particularly at local levels. Australian firms have built upon these insights to identify new and promising market opportunities across the Chinese economy, including in health care, food and agriculture, and legal services. She concludes by urging political leaders to publicly acknowledge that the China trade provides important ballast to the relationship, as well as significant financial benefits for Australia and Australians.

Taken together, these three chapters provide insightful analysis, backed by extensive empirical data and compelling examples, demonstrating how the politicisation of trade and investment ties has entailed considerable costs for Australia. They provide a clarion call for policymakers to push back against an atmosphere of fear and misunderstanding, and to instead offer calm, confident leadership aimed at protecting Australia's economic interests in sustaining viable, secure and mutually beneficial trade and investment relations with China.

# 5
# Australia–China trade: opportunity, risk, mitigation, ballast – progress?

*James Laurenceson and Weihuan Zhou*

## Introduction

From the vantage point of the present, it is easy to forget the exuberance regularly evinced in Australia's discussion of trade with China not all that long ago. Political leaders led the way. In June 2015, at the signing ceremony of the China–Australia Free Trade Agreement (ChAFTA), Prime Minister Tony Abbott addressed the Chinese side that had gathered in Canberra:

> What you have collectively done is history making for both our countries, it will change our countries for the better, it will change our region for the better, it will change our world for the better … We seize this opportunity of more trade and more investment with China … One day we will be able to say to our children and grandchildren, that yes, we were there the day this extraordinary agreement was signed between our two countries.[1]

Despite bilateral political ties beginning to sour in the second half of 2016, at a joint press conference in September 2019 – one where

---

1    Abbott 2015.

US President Donald Trump had declared China to be a "threat to the world" – Prime Minister Scott Morrison remained focused on the economic upside: "We work well with China ... we have a great relationship with China. China's growth has been great for Australia."[2]

A keen appreciation of the benefits that robust trade ties with China delivered extended to the public at large. In the 2018 Lowy Institute poll, 82 per cent of respondents considered China as "more an economic partner than a security threat".[3] Just 12 per cent nominated the opposite. The previous year a poll by the United States Studies Centre asked respondents whether they had a more favourable view of increased trade with the United States or China. The proportion choosing China was 10 percentage points higher than the proportion choosing the United States.[4]

That said, almost immediately after China overtook Japan to become Australia's largest trading partner in 2007, this appreciation of the benefits became tinged with worry about what could go wrong. In 2013, the Lowy Institute commissioned University of Sydney academic Jamie Reilly to provide an assessment of the risk "that the Chinese government will manipulate its trade and investment to undermine Australian autonomy or security".[5] While Reilly concluded the worries were "overblown", they persisted. In a moment of candour in November 2014, Prime Minister Abbott told visiting the German Chancellor, Angela Merkel, that Australia's policies towards China were driven by both "fear and greed".[6] From 2017 there was also an up-tick in media reporting allegations that Beijing was disrupting market access for a variety of Australian exports, including beef, wine and coal, in order to send a political message to Canberra.[7] Even if the evidence supporting such claims subsequently proved equivocal, by the time of the 2019 edition of the Lowy Institute Poll, 74 per cent of respondents agreed with the statement "Australia is too economically dependent on China".[8]

---

2   White House 2019.
3   Lowy Institute Poll 2022.
4   Jackman, Flake et al. 2017.
5   Reilly 2013.
6   Garnaut 2015.
7   Laurenceson, Zhou and Pantle 2020.
8   Kassam 2019.

But it was events in 2020 that dramatically elevated the frame of risk.[9] First, the COVID-19 pandemic emanating from China in January of that year was followed by shortages of some goods in Australia. Some commentators linked these shortages to Australia's exposure to China as a supplier. In March 2020, the executive director of the Australian Strategic Policy Institute (ASPI), Peter Jennings, claimed that "China locks its factories down and within days Australia faces shortages of medical supplies, building components and consumer products of all types".[10] Second, in May that year Beijing launched a campaign of disruption targeting Australian exports.[11] What started with barley and beef subsequently expanded to around a dozen goods by year's end. While the pace of escalation slowed in 2021, none of the earlier moves had been rescinded as of September 2022. In the face of Australian complaints, Beijing responded by claiming the measures were legitimate and permitted by international trade rules. Nor was the economic disruption one-sided: Canberra was blocking Chinese investment with increasing regularity[12] and Chinese goods remained the most prominent target of punitive Australian anti-dumping tariffs, despite expectations in Beijing that the rules embedded in ChAFTA would result in fewer such cases. The negative impact on Australian public opinion of the above events was revealed in a June 2021 poll conducted by the Australia–China Relations Institute and the Lowy Institute. The poll found that, despite China remaining the largest customer for Australian goods and services by far, a majority (53 per cent) of respondents agreed with the statement "Australia's economic relationship with China is more of an economic risk than an economic opportunity".[13] Only one-fifth disagreed. In a dramatic reversal of the 2018 results, the 2021 edition of the Lowy Institute Poll reported that just 34 per cent of Australians regarded China as "more an economic partner than a security threat".[14]

---

9    The background and trigger for the elevation of the frame of risk is discussed in Zhou and Laurenceson 2022.
10   Jennings 2020b.
11   Laurenceson and Pantle 2021.
12   Uren 2020.
13   Collinson and Burke 2021.
14   Lowy Institute Poll 2022.

To date, the Australian government has maintained a bipartisan position that it wishes for robust trade engagement with China to continue, albeit engagement that accounts for risk and does not come at a cost of modifying political choices in the face of coercive pressure. When at the end of 2020 one National Party senator called for Australia to place an export tax on iron ore sales to China in retaliation for Beijing's disruption of other Australian exports, this was immediately rejected by the Minister for Resources and Water.[15] Early on in Beijing's campaign of disruption, Prime Minister Scott Morrison maintained an insistence that commercial interactions with China involve "a judgement Australian businesses can only make ... those are not decisions that governments make for businesses".[16] In September 2021, in a speech otherwise calling for businesses to bolster their resilience through greater market diversification, Treasurer Josh Frydenberg acknowledged that many Australian businesses had "worked hard to access the lucrative Chinese market". This, he said, had "brought great benefits to them and to Australia overall. And they should continue to pursue these opportunities where they can." In March 2022, even after several months of fanning a narrative that China was a strategic and security threat in the lead-up to a federal election, Morrison continued to back this position: "The ongoing engagement between private industry and business with markets like China is very important and I will continue to encourage that, but obviously the political and diplomatic situation is very, very different ..."[17] Nonetheless, the government did send a strong message to businesses regarding the implications of heightened geopolitical risk. In March 2021, Australia's ambassador to China, Graham Fletcher, told a business forum, "You've just got to imagine that, unexpectedly, you may lose your China market for no good reason other than that Beijing has decided to send a message to Canberra".[18] The new Labor government elected in May 2022 has not yet shown any sign of deviating from the above script. Addressing the Australia–China Business Council in September 2022,

---

15  McCulloch 2020.
16  Tillett 2020.
17  Hastie 2022.
18  Dziedzic 2021.

the Assistant Minister for Foreign Affairs, Tim Watts, said that commercial relationships were seen as "complementary" to the government's efforts to stabilise the broader relationship and encouraged those in the audience to "stay engaged in the China market, while accounting for risk".[19]

Yet calls outside government for Canberra to change tack and adopt a more interventionist and prescriptive approach that drives trade ties away from China have not dissipated. In May 2020, ASPI's Jennings asserted that "economic dependence on China is dangerous" and that "steps must be taken to reduce that dependence".[20] There is also the possibility that a future US administration, particularly a Republican one, might head in a more radical "decoupling" direction – and pressure Australia to follow. In August 2021, Matt Pottinger, a former senior Trump administration national security official, wrote on economic engagement with China: "Elected leaders must now take the next step ... Because companies are economic actors, not political ones, it is the government's responsibility to establish guidelines for engaging with adversaries."[21] In some quarters the extent of Australia's trade relationship with China is already seen as an issue for the Australia, New Zealand, United States Security Treaty (ANZUS) alliance. In June 2019, Charles Edel and John Lee of the United States Studies Centre passed on the message: "The United States would like Australia ... to lessen its commercial dependence on China", before themselves going on to advocate for "active diversification".[22] The Biden administration is putting increased store on self-sufficiency and "friend-shoring", the latter of which aims to build supply chains between the United States and security allies like Australia, and that exclude China.[23] There has also been increased discussion of more security-focused arrangements, such as the ANZUS alliance, the Quadrilateral Security Dialogue (Quad) and the Five Eyes intelligence arrangement, being expanded into the economic realm.[24]

---

19  Watts 2022.
20  Jennings 2020a.
21  Pottinger 2021.
22  Edel and Lee 2019.
23  Condon, Kim and Kim 2022.

With this as background, in what follows we argue that calls for Canberra to deploy public policy with the objective of reducing trade with China to mitigate risk are, in general, poorly conceived. To be clear, we do not suggest that trade engagement with China does not present risks. Rather, our contention is that most Australian businesses – the actors that overwhelmingly undertake trade – are already acutely aware that geopolitical fallout might affect their operations and that at a firm, industry and national level there exists a variety of mechanisms to mitigate these risks. Mitigation mechanisms stem from both economic and legal sources and collectively they bolster Australian resilience in the face of coercive measures by Beijing. During a period of prolonged breakdown in senior political-level dialogue, trade engagement delivered not only ongoing direct economic benefits but also ballast to the broader relationship. Further, despite bilateral trade disruption, Australia and China have an alignment of interests in supporting regional and global trade architecture, presenting opportunities ripe for cooperation and to positively shape Australia's external environment.

## China trade risk: economic sources of mitigation

A narrative advanced by some Australian commentators, particularly those coming from a strategic or national security background, is that businesses are naive or indifferent to the risk that this engagement with China involves, at a business or more systemic level or both. This then leads to calls for government intervention to mitigate the risk by reducing trade "dependence".

ASPI's Michael Shoebridge, writing in April 2020, is a typical example.[25] After the initial economic shock caused by the COVID-19 pandemic, Shoebridge warned that Australians should "expect myriad calls to restart our economic relationship with China as it was before". These calls would come "from treasury types in Western governments as well as those with deep self-interest – a lot of wealthy people and leaders sprinkled across our corporate and university landscapes". He

---

24   Laurenceson 2021b.
25   Shoebridge 2020.

exhorted, "we must discount them as we make decisions". This was because "the Chinese state has created unacceptable risks for the rest of us and it will continue to do so unless it changes or until we reduce our dependence on activities within its jurisdiction".

Anecdotes of Australian businesses seemingly making poor decisions with respect to China trade engagement are not hard to find, particularly with the benefit of hindsight. But arguments like that advanced by Shoebridge struggle at a first-principles level. The Australian government's Productivity Commission emphasises that a starting point for effective mitigation is the proposition that risks are best managed by those with direct incentives and capabilities to assess and respond to them, and typically this means businesses, not bureaucrats.[26] The owners of the Australian businesses that engage with China, either as a customer or supplier, do so with their own money on the line. When Beijing effectively blocked Australian barley with tariffs of around 80 per cent in May 2020, it was farmers who faced the fallout: there was no taxpayer-funded bail-out in the offing. Given this, the suggestion that businesses would gloss over risks is a puzzling one. That Australian businesses engaged in trade with China, in fact, take risk seriously was confirmed in a report authored by journalist Glenda Korporaal in December 2021.[27] Korporaal interviewed a dozen business leaders operating at the coalface of trade with China, revealing a sharp appreciation that geopolitical risk was rising. At the same time, oftentimes it still ranked below other challenges in their risk matrix, such as the impact of unexpected shifts in Chinese government regulations. Businesses have also exhibited creative strategies in handling geopolitical risk. When bottled wine from Australia was hit with prohibitive anti-dumping tariffs in late 2020, Treasury Wine Estates pivoted to sourcing product from the United States and France, as well as investing in China's own domestic vineyards.[28] And in any case, the overall level of risk still needed to be compared with the expected returns from engaging with China versus the risk/return equation presented by alternative markets. In August 2021 the chief

---

26   Productivity Commission 2021.
27   Korporaal 2021.
28   Korporaal 2022.

executive officer of trans-Tasman dairy manufacturer, A2, told investors:

> There's no avoiding the fact that the China infant nutrition market is – even though it is challenging at the moment – by far the largest and most interesting opportunity for us. So it is both the biggest risk and the biggest opportunity for us that we must embrace. We have to invest in that to capture that opportunity going forward.[29]

In a November 2021 survey by the Australian Trade and Investment Commission, the Export Council of Australia and the University of Canberra, a higher proportion of businesses looking to diversify to South Korea and Japan, along with other regularly touted alternatives to China such as Taiwan and Vietnam, reported experiencing more barriers in these markets than did business looking to diversify to China.[30]

It is the case that privately-owned businesses do not seek to eliminate risk entirely. Rather, when deciding whether to perform additional risk assessment and mitigation, they compare the expected benefits and costs from doing so. Society might, therefore, insist that a limited number of supply chains are closer to fail-safe than private-sector decision-making delivers and be prepared to incur the costs this necessitates. But this can only serve as justification for highly targeted interventions and is a far cry from the vague calls cited above.

One claim made with particular stridency is that Australian businesses might embrace political lobbying as a tool of risk mitigation, either in the form of demanding taxpayer-funded bail-outs if their China bets go wrong or by putting pressure on Canberra to shift its political positions to ones more agreeable to Beijing. In May 2020, ASPI's Jennings said that business leaders had advocated for a "just shut

---

29   Lynch 2021.
30   Australian Trade and Investment Commission (Austrade), Export Council of Australia and the University of Canberra 2021.

up and take money from China" approach.[31] After leaving office, former prime minister Malcolm Turnbull also complained:

> An Australian prime minister who ends up in conflict with China cannot expect any support or solidarity from the Australian business community. Overwhelmingly, they're totally invested in the economic benefits of the relationship and they'll always blame their own government if problems arise.[32]

Again these assertions struggle once subject to cursory scrutiny. First, in a liberal democracy like Australia, businesses are entitled to press their interests, just as other groups are entitled to push back against such advocacy. Second, while business interests are not the entirety of the nation's interests, they are not in contradiction to it. In June 2020, former director-general of the Australian Security Intelligence Organisation (ASIO) and secretary of Defence Dennis Richardson advised corporate executives that when they are slurred as unpatriotic for emphasising the value of the China trade relationship, "they should punch their accuser right on the nose ... figuratively that is".[33] He then suggested they remind their critics of the employment that their business provides and the tax it pays. Third, the weight of evidence suggests that after Beijing began disrupting trade, rather than amplifying their criticism of Canberra, businesses did the opposite in recognition of the fact that amplification would only invite more frequent pressure in the future.[34] Finally, and perhaps most importantly, even to the extent that some business owners may continue to engage in such lobbying, in the end it is elected officials who get the final say. And the survey evidence since 2020 shows that the public opinion has swung in behind the firm position that Canberra has adopted towards Beijing. The fact that in the 2022 Australian federal election campaign the opposition Labor party was overwhelmingly in agreement with the government's policies towards China makes the

---

31   Packham 2020.
32   Turnbull 2021.
33   Richardson 2020.
34   Power 2020.

point that it saw no electoral advantage in advocating for positions that Beijing might prefer.[35]

The campaign of trade disruption unleashed by Beijing since May 2020 also provides an instructive case study to gauge the scale of systemic risks that Australia's exposure to China as a customer creates. In its breadth and duration, this campaign is unprecedented in the history of modern Chinese economic statecraft. Yet the first outcome to emphasise is that the aggregate value of Australia's goods exports to China in 2020 was steady – and in 2021 jumped by 21 per cent to hit a record high of A$177 billion.[36] Similarly, the value of Australia's imports from China rose by 7 per cent in 2020 and a further 8 per cent in 2021 to hit a record high of $91 billion. That total goods exports and imports reached record levels during a campaign of trade disruption reflects the mitigating factor of China's own self-interest, as well as a fortuitous increase in global commodity prices: between April 2020 and December 2021 the Reserve Bank of Australia's commodities price index jumped by 37 per cent.[37] Exports to China of big-ticket items like iron ore, liquefied natural gas, wool and more have continued to flow unimpeded. This is because China is as reliant on Australia as a supplier as Australia is on China as a customer. It is here that claims Australia is "dependent" on China butt up against the economic reality of there being a mutual dependence. New research shows that the resilience of Australia's exports to China to shocks emanating from the political realm is not only a contemporary phenomenon but stretches back ever since the take-off in the 2000s.[38]

Next, many of the industries hit with disruption were able to effectively mitigate the fallout. An Australia–China Relations Institute study[39] in September 2021 estimated that, for nine of the 12 export goods affected, the value of export losses amounted to less than 10 per cent of total export value. The mitigation mechanism most commonly available for Australian exporters has been access to competitive global

---

35 Collinson 2022.
36 Department of Foreign Affairs and Trade n.d.c.
37 Reserve Bank of Australia n.d.
38 Galley et al. 2022.
39 Laurenceson and Pantle 2021, 1.

markets. Even for goods like cotton, where three-quarters of Australian exports went to China prior to market access being lost, global markets supported local producers redirecting their production to other customers quickly and at low cost. When Beijing blocked goods from Australia, Chinese importers had to source supply from elsewhere. In turn, this created an opening for Australian exporters in those markets that China's new suppliers previously serviced. Another mitigation mechanism available for exporters of affected goods such as lobsters has been "grey markets". This involved local producers first exporting their product to separate customs territories such as Hong Kong before it was then trans-shipped to the Chinese mainland. Some exporters of agricultural and forestry goods also engaged in product transformation to avoid sanctioned categories, such as turning logs into woodchips.[40]

Australia has yet to experience import disruption, albeit some nationalistic Chinese tabloids appear to have enjoyed preying on local fears that it might.[41] China's self-interest again helps to mitigate the risk. Not only would Chinese exporters lose sales to Australia but it would also damage China's reputation as a reliable supplier globally and so provoke a mitigating response. In 2010, Japanese officials perceived that Beijing was threatening to cut off the country's supply of rare earths, albeit the details of the case were contested.[42] Predictably, this triggered a supply chain resilience-building exercise by Tokyo, including investing in the establishment of alternative suppliers.

Nonetheless, the fear of being targeted by Beijing on the import side of the equation loomed sufficiently large such that in May 2021 Treasurer Frydenberg tasked the Productivity Commission with reviewing Australia's supply chain vulnerabilities. The resulting study began by clarifying that, contrary to some commentary, "Australia's supply chains proved generally resilient in response to the COVID-19 pandemic".[43] It then found that nearly a quarter of Australia's import product lines (1,327 out of 5,862) were "highly concentrated" – a situation where the main supplier accounted for over 80 per cent of

---

40   Ferguson, Waldron and Lim 2022.
41   GT staff reporters 2021.
42   Johnston 2013.
43   Productivity Commission 2021.

Australia's imports of that product. Yet, as the above discussion showed in the case of exports, there is also no simple relationship between exposure and risk when it comes to imports. In the event that Beijing disrupts supply, what matters is whether alternative sources are available. To make this point the Productivity Commission's study cited the example of the chemical chlorine:

> Australia sources chlorine primarily from China, but the global market for chlorine is not concentrated and China is not the leading exporter of chlorine. This suggests that Australia could source chlorine from another economy in the event of a disruption to Chinese supply.[44]

After taking alternative sources of supply into account, it was concluded that just 5 per cent (292 of 5,862) of Australia's imported product lines could be considered "vulnerable", with China supplying two-thirds of this number. Even then, fewer than half of all "vulnerable" imports (130 of 292) were found to be used in industries that could be regarded as "essential". Many of these were "unlikely to constitute critical inputs" with examples cited including "women's swimwear from China". In the end, the study highlighted a number of chemicals and personal protective equipment (PPE), such as face shields and isolation gowns, as being examples of goods worthy of further investigation into how supply chain resilience might be enhanced. Such a sober conclusion was in stark contrast to reports by think tanks and statements by politicians seemingly more intent on generating alarmist headlines.[45]

Finally, given that public policy resources are finite, and interventions are not cost-free, any measures aimed at bolstering systemic-level resilience must be chosen with effectiveness rather than political expediency in mind. The mitigation mechanism most frequently privileged in policy circles and public commentary is promoting greater customer and supplier diversification. But it should be recognised that a medium-sized economy like Australia will inevitably develop significant exposures to much larger economies, like

---

44   Productivity Commission 2021.
45   Laurenceson 2021a.

China and the United States. Benchmarked against peer economies, for the most part Australia's overall export exposure to its single largest customer does not, in fact, stand out. What does mark Australia as an outlier is the degree of product concentration found in the export basket.[46] The real diversification challenge for Canberra is not so much convincing other capitals to further prise open their markets to the goods that Australia currently exports but rather in enhancing the domestic economy's ability to competitively supply a broader basket of goods and services internationally.

Further, if policymakers obsess on diversification – of either the market or product variety – then other, potentially more effective or less costly mitigation options, or both, can be missed. For example, despite an iron ore price boom adding billions of dollars to federal government coffers since 2020, there have been no additional injections into the Treasury's Future Fund. An opportunity to self-insure against the income loss that might result from a future shock to exports has been missed. Similarly, measures to encourage supplier diversification must be weighed alongside other supply chain resilience options such as maintaining government stockpiles, mandating or subsidising private stockpiles or subsidising domestic production.[47]

## Trade risk: legal sources of mitigation

Legal sources of risk mitigation carry particular weight in the case of Australia and China because, even in their bilateral disputes, both countries cite World Trade Organization (WTO) rules in justifying their actions, such as WTO provisions around dumping, and sanitary and phytosanitary protocols,[48] while also continuing to demonstrate a willingness to submit to adjudication by its resolution processes. The risk mitigation the WTO affords is far from perfect. The litigation process itself can stretch to years. But its independence can act as a circuit-breaker in what might otherwise become an increasingly

---

46   Laurenceson et al. 2021.
47   Productivity Commission 2021.
48   WTO 2021a.

acrimonious bilateral dispute. And even if a party refuses to comply with a WTO decision, it still conveys reputational consequences that other members will factor into their dealings with that party.

Canberra has now initiated cases at the WTO with respect to Chinese tariffs on Australian barley[49] and wine,[50] while Beijing has done likewise with respect to Australian tariffs applied on Chinese wind towers, deep-drawn stainless-steel sinks and railway wheels.[51] The case brought by Beijing is of particular consequence because it involves a matter of long-standing disagreement: specifically, Australia's treatment of China as a non-market economy in its application of anti-dumping measures to Chinese goods.[52]

It is also significant that in the absence of a functioning Appellate Body at the WTO – owing to the United States blocking the appointment of new judges as the terms of serving judges expired – in May 2020 both Australia and China, along with around 20 other countries, voluntarily committed to an interim appellate review procedure known as the multi-party interim appeal arbitration arrangement (MPIA).[53] The two sides adhered to this procedure in their ongoing disputes concerning China's anti-dumping duties on Australian barley[54] and Australian tariffs on the above bundle of Chinese goods.[55] This contrasts with China's confrontational approach against non-MPIA parties, particularly the United States. In a recent dispute, China appealed "into the void" after the WTO panel found in favour of the imposition of safeguard measures by the United States on certain Chinese crystalline silicon photovoltaic products.[56] China's different litigating strategy can be seen as an attempt to dissuade the United States from continuing to block the appointment of Appellate Body members, an end that Australia supports.[57]

---

49   WTO n.d.a.
50   WTO n.d.b.
51   WTO n.d.c.
52   Zhou 2015.
53   WTO 2020.
54   WTO 2021b.
55   WTO 2022.
56   WTO 2021c.
57   For a recent discussion on how to resolve the Appellate Body crisis, see Gao 2021b.

There is scope for enhanced cooperation in dealing with bilateral disputes under the WTO framework. For example, in 2005 the Australian government promised recognition of China as a market economy as a precondition for free trade agreement negotiations.[58] Later that year, a Senate committee supported the move and made clear what effect the "market economy" designation was expected to have: "Chinese imports will now be judged no differently for anti-dumping purposes to imports from the US and the EU."[59] This is not what eventuated in practice. At the very least, Australia's anti-dumping authorities could extend more meaningful opportunities for the Chinese government and Chinese exporters to demonstrate that market forces play a decisive role economy-wide or in the industries and economic sectors involved and then make a decision on a case-by-case basis upon an objective assessment of the evidence.[60] While this approach would entail more work for Australian authorities, over time this approach could meet China's concerns about Australia's (ab)use of anti-dumping or countervailing measures, or both. With Australia reconfirming China's market economy status, this approach also has potential to contribute to a thawing of bilateral political tensions. The opposite – that is, if Australia maintains its current approach – is likely to promote a situation in which China adopts similar tactics, imposing more frequent and higher anti-dumping duties against Australian goods.[61]

When we widen the aperture away from bilateral disputes, Australia has also been careful to put some distance between itself and the United States on trade matters involving China. For example, after the United States launched its campaign of coercion against China in 2018, in November that year Trade Minister Simon Birmingham stated, "[We've] been very clear in our position all along that we do not approve or support the US actions of increasing tariffs in a unilateral

---

58   Senate Standing Committee on Foreign Affairs, Defence and Trade (2005). *Opportunities and challenges : Australia's relationship with China*, chapter 11.

59   Senate Standing Committees on Foreign Affairs, Defence and Trade 2005.

60   For a discussion of the recent developments of China's anti-dumping practices, see Zhou and Qu 2022.

61   Zhou and Qu 2022.

way on Chinese goods".[62] In the subsequent disputes that China brought against the United States at the WTO, Australia joined as a third party.[63] This is not to say that Australia does not to some extent share US concerns around China's adherence to trade rules and the functioning of the WTO, but its approach to dealing with these issues has been to engage with China and not obstruct the WTO's functioning. When the United States, the European Union and Japan pushed for initiatives that would tighten the rules on Chinese state-owned enterprises and industrial subsidies, Australia also seems to have tried to avoid any official statements that would be seen as supporting the initiatives. In two recent joint statements with Japan and the other Quad countries (the United States and India) respectively, there was no direct reference to China's state-led economic regime and industrial policies. In its statement on China's WTO Trade Policy Review in October 2021, Australia criticised China's non-market practices, state intervention in commercial activities and industrial subsidies. But Australia was careful enough that it did not step further to advocate the development of new rules that singled out China.

Both countries are also proponents for a growing range of WTO initiatives to restructure the nexus between trade, environment and sustainable development, including co-sponsoring an initiative that seeks to tackle plastic pollution in pursuit of environmentally sustainable plastics trade.[64] The WTO's joint initiative on ecommerce,[65] originally initiated by the United States, the European Union and Japan and now led by Australia, Japan and Singapore, has received support from a majority of the membership with China becoming one of the most active participants in the negotiations over time.[66] Moreover, the fact that the ChAFTA is one of the few free trade agreements in which China agreed to a stand-alone chapter on ecommerce also provides a solid foundation for China and Australia to advance ecommerce rules on a bilateral basis and then seek to influence the development of the

---

62  Minister for Trade, Tourism and Investment and Minister for Finance 2018.
63  WTO n.d.d.
64  WTO 2021d.
65  WTO n.d.e.
66  Gao 2021a.

global ecommerce governance at the multilateral level in light of their common position.

Another initiative is trade facilitation. Although the WTO agreement on trade facilitation[67] remains plurilateral at this stage, Australia and China are among the very first group of signatories[68] and both have fully implemented their obligations.[69] This demonstrates their shared vision and commitment to "freer" trade by reducing unnecessary delays, red tape and associated costs at the border. With political will, this shared vision and commitment could extend to re-igniting negotiations to upgrade ChAFTA. This upgrade has long been foreshadowed but negotiations stalled in 2017 along with the deterioration in the political relationship.[70]

Aside from a shared commitment to cleaving to the WTO in bilateral disputes, and to the utility of the WTO more generally, both Australia and China have also demonstrated a shared interest to expanding the rules-based framework beyond it. Both countries were founding members of the Regional Comprehensive Economic Partnership, which entered into force at the beginning of 2022.[71] China has also requested to join the Comprehensive and Progressive Trans-Pacific Partnership (CPTPP) in September 2021,[72] an agreement of which Australia is a founding member. Trade Minister Dan Tehan welcomed the opportunity to engage with China in potential accession talks, albeit reiterating that such talks would depend on assessments of China's compliance with existing trade rules and China's resort to coercion is evidence of non-compliance.[73] China would also be expected to undertake domestic reforms needed to meet the high standards of the CPTPP. On this point, some trade law experts have argued that China's ability to meet these standards is more achievable than is generally understood.[74] Meanwhile, some of Australia's other

---

67  WTO n.d.f.
68  WTO n.d.g.
69  WTO n.d.h.
70  Department of Foreign Affairs and Trade n.d.a.
71  Department of Foreign Affairs and Trade n.d.b.
72  Ministry of Commerce 2021a.
73  Tehan 2021.
74  Gao and Zhou 2021.

strategic partners are less inclined to be supportive of its objectives around trade architecture. India withdrew from the Regional Comprehensive Economic Partnership negotiations prior to the deal's signing, and the Biden administration in the United States continues to show no interest in joining the CPTPP. In November 2021, Commerce Secretary Rina Raimondo put on the public record that the CPTPP "is not something that America would be part of at this time".[75]

Finally, there is an opportunity for Australia and China to work together to head off major challenges to the rules-based order around trade, such as the ever-expanding scope of national security to cover unfettered economic interests and preventing the abuse of security-related measures at the cost of trading partners.[76] The unilateral and retaliatory measures on security grounds embarked upon by the United States in its trade war with China,[77] although affecting other countries too, is the most extreme example. A useful starting point would be for Australia to understand China's evolving approach to national security and the reasons behind it. Recently, China's approaches at international and domestic levels have largely been driven by the actions taken by other key players, particularly the US abuse of economic sanctions on security grounds. At the international level, for instance, China challenged the US trade war measures at the WTO[78] and submitted proposals to reform the relevant WTO mechanisms.[79] In essence, China's position is that security measures should be subject to close scrutiny by the WTO, must not be abused and can be retaliated against if they are applied in bad faith. At the same time, China has also stressed, in its third-party submission in the *Russia – Traffic in Transit* dispute, that the WTO's judicial review of security measures must be conducted with caution so as not to unduly interfere with members' rights to protect national security.[80] Australia's position, as reflected also in its third-party submission in

75   Takita 2021.
76   Cohen 2020; Heath 2020.
77   Bown and Kolb 2022.
78   WTO 2018a; WTO 2018b; WTO 2018c; WTO 2019a.
79   WTO 2019b.
80   WTO 2019c.

the same dispute,[81] is well aligned with China's insistence on ensuring that the judicial review maintains a proper balance between rights and obligations of WTO members. Accordingly, there is room for Australia and China to take collective actions to influence the future development of security-related laws and practices.

At the domestic level, China has rolled out a series of new laws and regulations to establish a comprehensive framework for the protection of national security. This regulatory effort began with the enactment of a new *National Security Law* in 2015.[82] This law treats all harms or threats to China's fundamental economic principles and system, and to the development of major industries and economic sectors as matters of economic security, and creates a non-exhaustive list of security interests subject to further development according to China's own needs. Faced with the US trade war sanctions, China introduced a series of measures in a short period of time, mainly including Measures on the Unreliable Entity List in 2020,[83] the *Export Control Law* also in 2020,[84] *Rules on Counteracting Unjustified Extra-Territorial Application of Foreign Legislation and Other Measures* in 2021,[85] and most recently the *Anti-Foreign Sanctions Law* of 2021.[86] In all these measures, economic security has become an embedded element of national security acquiring growing prominence. Beijing has also instituted a retaliatory mechanism to authorise the use of a broad range of countermeasures against foreign actions that adversely affect China's economic security. While China's regulatory actions were triggered primarily by US sanctions, they have become part of China's overarching strategy to develop sufficient domestic regulatory tools to combat foreign security actions and to pursue its own security and economic interests. Based on this understanding of China's position, Australia's future engagement with China on security-related issues would wisely be built on the principle of non-discrimination to avoid unnecessary frictions. That

---

81  WTO 2019c.
82  President of People's Republic of China 2015.
83  Ministry of Commerce 2020.
84  President of the People's Republic of China 2020.
85  Ministry of Commerce 2021b.
86  President of the People's Republic of China 2021.

is, any actions that Australia takes should target the security risks associated with imports and exports rather than China. Moreover, where there is a need to impose security-related measures on China, there ought to be prior consultations before proposed actions are taken. This would not only show due respect to China's interests but may also lead to a mutually acceptable solution that would avoid countermeasures. Over time, this would also contribute to rebuilding the habits of cooperation so that the two sides can shift their recent focus on political disagreements to one of furthering and expanding mutual economic interests.

## Conclusion

Australia has historically viewed trade ties with China through the frame of opportunity. In recent years, as the bilateral political relationship has broken down, the exposure to China as a customer and supplier has increasingly been seen through the frame of risk. Calls for Canberra to respond by using public policy to drive businesses away from engaging with the Chinese market have grown louder. Beijing's willingness to disrupt Australia's exports since 2020 means that an increased emphasis on risk is not without cause. Yet, as this chapter has explained, for the most part, deploying public policy to reduce trade exposure to China struggles as a coherent strategy in response.

Geopolitical risk is part of a suite of risks that private business owners already regularly monitor and adjust for. Without any government prompting, some will assess that reducing their exposure to China is an optimal risk mitigation response. Others will elect to maintain an existing exposure, confident in the knowledge that, if access to the Chinese market is disrupted, then they have access to alternative mitigation mechanisms. The scope for public policy to improve outcomes, therefore, is mostly limited to the management of risk at a systemic level. As the evidence raised in this chapter has also shown, the scale of systemic risk that trade engagement with China creates is often exaggerated or misdiagnosed, such as when Australia's diversification challenge is depicted overwhelmingly in terms of exposure to the Chinese market rather than in terms of being exposed to a narrow range of products that the Australian economy can competitively supply on global markets.

While some of the earlier euphoria around trade with China was likely overdone, the key lesson learned from the passage of time is that public policy that does not discriminate against businesses and households getting on with the engagement they regard as mutually beneficial, remains consistent with Australia's interests. Beyond the direct economic benefits, robust trade ties provide ballast for the broader bilateral relationship. There is also an alignment of interests in expanding the rules-based framework around trade, including the Regional Comprehensive Economic Partnership, the CPTPP and the WTO, providing an opportunity for Australia and China to cooperate in positively shaping the region they share.

The arrival of a new Australian government in May 2022 and the restart of senior political dialogue the following month has provided further optimism around limiting potential political shocks spilling over to hurt trade. This is not because the structural challenges in the relationship will be resolved – a "reset" in political relations is not in the offing – but a more diplomatic tone from Canberra is readily apparent, as is a commitment to "stabilising" the relationship on the basis of the two countries' Comprehensive Strategic Partnership.

## References

Abbott, Tony (2015). Address to the China–Australia Free Trade Agreement Signing Ceremony Luncheon, Canberra.Transcript. *PM Transcripts: Transcripts from the prime ministers of Australia*. https://bit.ly/3KcqgnS.

Australian Trade and Investment Commission (Austrade), Export Council of Australia and the University of Canberra (2021). *Australia's international business survey 2021: building resilience through diversification*. Report. https://bit.ly/3OoQLZD.

Bown, Chad P. and Melina Kolb (2022). Trump's trade war timeline: an up-to-date guide. Trade and Investment Policy Watch Blog, Peterson Institute for International Economics. https://bit.ly/3O5lLg4.

Cohen, Harlan Grant (2020). Nations and markets. *Journal of International Economic Law* 23(4): 793–815.

Collinson, Elena (2022). The China consensus. Research report. *Australia–China Relations Institute, University of Technology Sydney*, 14 March. https://bit.ly/3Bw69wh.

Collinson, Elena and Paul Burke (2021). UTS ACRI/BIDA Poll 2021: Australian views on the Australia–China relationship. *Australia–China Relations Institute, University of Technology Sydney*, 16 June. https://bit.ly/3Mh6VmM.

Condon, Christopher, Heejin Kim and Sam Kim (2022). Yellen touts "Friend-shoring" as global supply chain fix. *Bloomberg*, 18 July. https://bloom.bg/3I16GKi.

Department of Foreign Affairs and Trade, Australian Government n.d.a. ChAFTA Joint Committee meetings. https://bit.ly/3DstkID.

Department of Foreign Affairs and Trade, Australian Government n.d.b. Regional Comprehensive Economic Partnership. https://bit.ly/3Qc1dox.

Department of Foreign Affairs and Trade, Australian Government n.d.c. Trade statistical pivot tables. https://bit.ly/3DqASvu.

Dziedzic, Stephen (2021). Australia's ambassador to China says Beijing's trade behaviour is "vindictive". *ABC News*, 26 March. https://ab.co/3qbdKho.

Edel, Charles and Lee, John 2019. The future of the US–Australia alliance in an era of great power competition. *United States Studies Centre*, 13 June. https://bit.ly/44ZIv80.

Ferguson, Victor, Scott Waldron and Darren Lim (2022). Market adjustments to import sanctions: lessons from Chinese restrictions on Australian trade 2020–21. *Review of International Political Economy* (July 2022): 1–27.

Gao, Henry (2021a). Across the Great Wall: e-commerce Joint Statement Initiative negotiation and China. In Shin-yeo Peng, Ching-Fu Lin and Thomas Strains (eds), *Artificial Intelligence and International Economic Law: Disruption, Regulation, and Reconfiguration* (295–318). Cambridge, UK: Cambridge University Press.

Gao, Henry (2021b). Finding a rule-based solution to the Appellate Body crisis: looking beyond the multiparty interim appeal arbitration arrangement. *Journal of International Economic Law* 24(3): 534–50.

Gao, Henry and Weihuan Zhou (2021). Opinion: China's entry to CPTPP trade pact is closer than you think. *NIKKEI Asia*, 20 September. https://s.nikkei.com/3BiHpaq.

Garnaut, John (2015). "Fear and greed" drive Australia's China policy, Tony Abbott tells Angela Merkel. *Sydney Morning Herald*, 16 April. https://bit.ly/3O0zRAU.

Galley, Jane, Vishesh Agarwal, James Laurenceson and Tunye Qiu (2022). For better or worse, in sickness and in health: Australia–China political relations and trade. *China Economic Journal* 15(3): 290–309.

GT staff reporters (2021). China produces urea in full swing for fertilizer use, emissions reductions amid global shortage: industry practitioners. *Global Times*, 19 December. https://bit.ly/3Ot1jH6.

Hastie, Hamish (2022). PM urges businesses to diversify amid warning China relationship may not improve for years. *Sydney Morning Herald*, 16 March. https://bit.ly/3KeVQ4h.

Heath, J. Benton (2020). The new national security challenge to the economic order. *Yale Law Journal* 129(4): 1020–98.

Jackman, Simon, Gordon Flake, et al. (2017). *The Asian Research Network: survey on America's role in the Indo-Pacific.* United States Studies Centre at the University of Sydney and Perth USAsia Centre at the University of Western Australia, May 2017. https://bit.ly/42HQWne.

Jennings, Peter (2020a). National security strategy can help build alliances. *Australian*, 2 May. https://bit.ly/3BhB9zS.

Jennings, Peter (2020b). Coronavirus: Why we could be in a world of trouble. *Australian*, 6 March. https://bit.ly/3VR64wo.

Johnston, Alastair Iain (2013). How new and assertive is China's new assertiveness? *International Security* 37(4): 7–48.

Kassam, Natasha (2019). Lowy Institute Poll 2019. *Lowy Institute*, 25 June. https://bit.ly/41mutet.

Korporaal, Glenda (2021). Behind the headlines: why Australian companies are still doing business with China. Research report. *Australia–China Relations Institute, University of Technology Sydney*, 7 December. https://bit.ly/3O07OBl.

Korporaal, Glenda (2022). Penfolds' Chinese made wine hits shelves. *Australian*, 29 September. https://bit.ly/3Bfd6kX.

Laurenceson, James (2021a). Australia's China supply chain "vulnerability" – much ado about nothing? *Policy Forum*, 19 May. https://bit.ly/3Y425xF.

Laurenceson, James (2021b). Will the Five Eyes stare down China's economic coercion. *Interpreter*, 15 April. https://bit.ly/470deU5.

Laurenceson, James and Thomas Pantle (2021). Australia's export exposure to China: assessing the costs of disruption. Working paper. *Australia–China Relations Institute, University of Technology Sydney*, 9 September. https://bit.ly/3MhtM1C.

Laurenceson, James, Thomas Pantle, Phillip Toner and Roy Green (2021). Australia's export mix, industrial base and economic resilience challenge. Research report. *Australia–China Relations Institute, University of Technology Sydney*, 3 November. https://bit.ly/42pAEzK.

Engaging China

Laurenceson, James, Michael Zhou and Thomas Pantle (2020). Interrogating Chinese economic coercion: the Australian experience since 2017. *Security Challenges* 16(4): 3–23.

Lowy Institute Poll (2022). China: economic partner or security threat. *Lowy Institute*. https://bit.ly/3O1asXJ.

Lynch, Jared (2021). A2 stays course on China, despite profit collapse. *Australian*, 26 August. https://bit.ly/41Ho7qh.

McCulloch, Daniel (2020). Minister rules out Chinese iron ore levies. *West Australian*, 14 December. https://bit.ly/3LTdEC0.

Minister for Trade, Tourism and Investment and Minister for Finance (2018). Interview on RN Breakfast with Fran Kelly. Transcript. 6 November. https://bit.ly/3Q9FqxS.

Ministry of Commerce, People's Republic of China (2020). *Bu kekao shiti qingdan guiding* [Provisions on the Unreliable Entities List]. 19 September. https://bit.ly/42psirz.

Ministry of Commerce, People's Republic of China (2021a). China officially applies to join the Comprehensive and Progressive Agreement for Trans-Pacific Partnership (CPTPP). 18 September. https://bit.ly/3rMnD5W.

Ministry of Commerce, People's Republic of China (2021b). *Zuduan waiguo falv yu cuoshi budang yuwai shiyong banfa* [Rules on Counteracting Unjustified Extra-territorial Application of Foreign Legislation and Other Measures]. 9 January. https://bit.ly/3NYWvcM.

Packham, Ben (2020). Economy overrides security: business. *Australian*, 13 May. https://bit.ly/3LSHnLy.

Pottinger, Matt (2021). Beijing's American hustle: how Chinese grand strategy exploits U.S. power. *Foreign Affairs*, 23 August. https://fam.ag/3pywgj4.

Power, John (2020). As China tensions mount, Australia's dovish voices calling for engagement are fading away. *South China Morning Post*, 12 June. https://bit.ly/3OsIDaF.

President of People's Republic of China (2015). *Zhonghua renmin gongheguo guojia anquan fa* [National Security Law of the People's Republic of China]. 1 July. https://bit.ly/41lTvu4.

President of the People's Republic of China (2020). *Zhonghua renmin gongheguo chukou guanzhi fa* [Export Control Law of the People's Republic of China]. 17 October. https://bit.ly/3I0cDHc.

President of the People's Republic of China (2021). *Zhonghua renmin gongheguo fan waiguo zhicai fa* [Anti-Foreign Sanctions Law of the People's Republic of China]. 10 June. https://bit.ly/3W3sIBG.

Productivity Commission (2021). Vulnerable supply chains: Executive summary and findings. Productivity Commission Study report. July. https://bit.ly/3DXOtLf.

Reilly, Jamie (2013). Analysis: China's economic statecraft: turning wealth into power. 27 November. https://bit.ly/3NZPisQ.

Reserve Bank of Australia n.d. Index of commodity prices: 2022. https://bit.ly/3LXsCHi.

Richardson, Dennis (2020). Webinar: Australia–China relations during a time of rising tensions between Washington and Beijing. Conference presentation. *China Matters*, 3 July. https://bit.ly/42sIeJG.

Senate Standing Committee on Foreign Affairs, Defence and Trade (2005). *Opportunities and challenges: Australia's relationship with China* (report). Parliament of Australia, 10 November. https://bit.ly/3nUHr5l.

Shoebridge, Michael (2020). The Chinese state and Australia's economy: "snapping back" must not mean business as usual. *Strategist*, 27 April. https://bit.ly/3rVvjmp.

Takita, Yoichi (2021). U.S. won't join CPTPP but will seek new framework: Raimondo. *NIKKEI Asia*, 16 November. https://s.nikkei.com/3DFv958.

Tehan, Dan (2021). National Press Club Address – economic statecraft in a challenging time. Speech. 22 September. https://bit.ly/3DE4jKD.

Tillett, Andrew (2020). Businesses "must weigh trade risks", *Australian Financial Review*, 27 May.

Turnbull, Malcolm (2021). *A Bigger Picture: With new foreword*. Melbourne: Hardie Grant.

Uren, David (2020). Why China thinks it's been duded on free trade deal. *Australian Financial Review*, 16 June. https://bit.ly/42rAub2.

Watts, Tim (2022). ACBC Networking Gala Dinner. Speech. 13 September. https://bit.ly/3DCbhjt.

White House (2019). Bilateral meeting with the President of the Unites States of America. *PM Transcripts: Transcripts from the prime ministers of Australia*, 20 September. https://bit.ly/42ujKQy.

World Trade Organization n.d.a. DS598: China – anti-dumping and countervailing duty measures on barley from Australia. https://bit.ly/455obBW.

World Trade Organization n.d.b. DS602: China – anti-dumping and countervailing duty measures on wine from Australia. https://bit.ly/42PXgsZ.

World Trade Organization n.d.c. DS603: Australia – anti-dumping and countervailing duty measures on certain products from China. https://bit.ly/3VS28LU.

World Trade Organization n.d.d. DS543: United States – tariff measures on certain goods from China. https://bit.ly/42xXzZO.

World Trade Organization n.d.e. Joint initiative on e-commerce. https://bit.ly/3BhwqhK.

World Trade Organization n.d.f. Trade facilitation. https://bit.ly/42rG79a.

World Trade Organization n.d.g. Ratifications list. https://bit.ly/44QoYH0.

World Trade Organization n.d.h. Progress on implementation commitments by member. https://bit.ly/3LWDxki.

World Trade Organization (2018a). United States – tariff measures on certain goods from China, request for consultations by China, WT/DS543/1. 5 April. https://bit.ly/3YaxMoT.

World Trade Organization (2018b). United States – certain measures on steel and aluminum products, request for consultations by China, WT/DS544/1. 9 April.https://bit.ly/3KcjAWM.

World Trade Organization (2018c). United States – tariff measures on certain goods from China II, request for consultations by China, WT/DS565/1. 27 August. https://bit.ly/44TAD7K.

World Trade Organization (2019a). United States – tariff measures on certain goods from China III, request for consultations by China, WT/DS587/1. 4 September. https://bit.ly/471ew1f.

World Trade Organization (2019b). China's proposal on WTO reform – communication from China, WT/GC/W/773. 13 May. https://bit.ly/3rJR8Fv.

World Trade Organization (2019c). Russia – measures concerning traffic in transit, WT/DS512/R. 26 April. https://bit.ly/3O53Gyt.

World Trade Organization (2020). Statement on a mechanism for developing, documenting and sharing practices and procedures in the conduct of WTO disputes, JOB/DSB/1/Add.12. 30 April. https://bit.ly/477mGVJ.

World Trade Organization (2021a). Committee on Sanitary and Phytosanitary Measures. Notification of emergency measures, 6/SPS/N/CHN/1194. 12 January.

World Trade Organization (2021c). United States – safeguard measure on imports of crystalline silicon photovoltaic products, notification of an appeal by China under Article 16 of the Understanding on Rules and Procedures Governing the Settlement of Disputes, WT/DS562/12. 20 September. https://bit.ly/3DsrmrH.

World Trade Organization (2021d). Launch event: ministerial statements on trade, environment and sustainable development. 15 December. https://bit.ly/3LUWowo.

World Trade Organization (2022). Australia – anti-dumping and countervailing duty measures on certain products from China, agreed procedure for arbitration under Article 25 of the DSU, WT/DS603/4. 20 September. https://bit.ly/3Qc9BEx.

Zhou, Weihuan (2015). Australia's anti-dumping and countervailing law and practice: an analysis of current issues incompatible with free trade with China. *Journal of World Trade* 49(6): 975–1010.

Zhou, Weihuan and Laurenceson, James (2022). Demystifying Australia–China trade tensions. *Journal of World Trade* 56(1): 51–86.

Zhou, Weihuan and Qu, Xiaomeng (2022). Confronting the "non-market economy" treatment: the evolving WTO jurisprudence on anti-dumping and China's recent practices. *Journal of International Dispute Settlement* 13(3): 510–31.

# 6

# Lessons from the rise and fall of Chinese investment in Australia

*Wei Li and Hans Hendrischke*

## Introduction

The rise and fall of Chinese direct investment in Australia over the last two decades has taught lessons to Australian hosts as well as Chinese investors. The lessons are reflected in two debates that have accompanied Chinese outbound direct investment (ODI) in Australia: the economic debate about the commercial benefit of Chinese ODI for Australia and the Chinese investors, and the sociopolitical debate on Australia's dependence on China during the period of geostrategic realignment with the United States. We draw on two unique sources to analyse the fluctuation of Chinese ODI and its shift from resource seeking to market and asset seeking. The first is the KPMG and University of Sydney proprietary database of Chinese investment projects in Australia from 2007 to 2021.[1] The second source is interviews with Chinese investors and executives from major Chinese multinational enterprises in Australia on their corporate motivations and local integration published in our reports.[2] We find Chinese multinational enterprises are motivated by economic opportunities and

---

1   KPMG and University of Sydney China Studies Centre 2007–21.
2   KPMG and University of Sydney China Studies Centre 2007–21.

learn from their localisation and institutional adaptation in Australia. At the same time, Australian governments, businesses, communities and opinion leaders, through trial and error, have learned to integrate Chinese investment into the local economy. We conclude the chapter with an outlook on the sustainability and prospects of Chinese ODI in Australia.

## The rise and fall of Chinese ODI in Australia

Up to 2007, the volume of Chinese investment in Australia was low. The 1987 Channar Joint Venture with Rio Tinto was China's largest overseas foreign investment and the only large-scale mining project between China and Australia. It had started in 1985 when Australian Prime Minister Bob Hawke stood on top of Mount Channar with Chinese Communist Party General Secretary Hu Yaobang, holding hands in recognition that this venture would link China's long-term industrial future to Australian resources.[3] As China embarked on its industrial modernisation by building a steel industry with limited resources of its own, the joint venture, 60 per cent owned by Rio Tinto and 40 per cent by Sinosteel, proved more successful for the Chinese investors than anticipated. Highly profitable for Australian and Chinese investors, the project helped break open the China market for Australian iron ore and other resources exports that lead to the long-term stable growth in bilateral trade with China. In 2009, China became Australia's largest export market and trading partner.

In contrast, Chinese direct investment in Australia has fluctuated markedly between 2007 and 2021, as shown by the KPMG and University of Sydney data (Figure 6.1). The history of Chinese ODI in Australia can be divided into three distinct periods: the resources boom period (2008–12), the integration period (2013–16) and the fallback period (2017–21). The resources boom and integration periods expanded trade and business interaction between the two countries from resources to a wide range of industries. During the fallback period, Chinese ODI shrank back to a few core sectors. According to

---

3    Curran 2022, 59–95.

the Department of Foreign Affairs and Trade, in 2020 China's ODI stock accounted for 4 per cent of total foreign direct investment in Australia.[4] In the following sections, we will discuss the three periods, the main target industries and the key driving forces of China's investment in Australia.

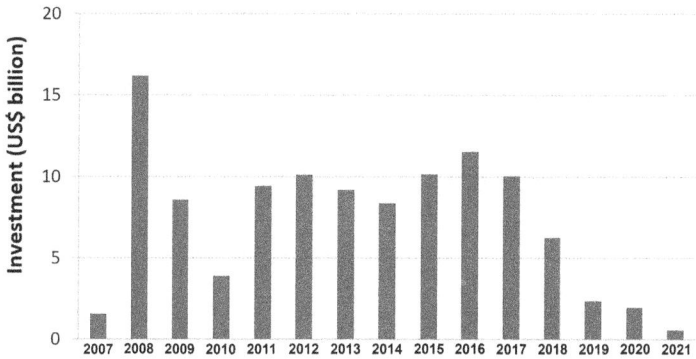

Figure 6.1 Flows of new Chinese ODI into Australia 2007–21 (US$ billion).
Source: KPMG and University of Sydney China Studies Centre database.

## The resources boom period, 2007–12

From 2008, Chinese ODI in Australia increased significantly and attracted public attention and controversy.[5] In 2008, as the result of Chinalco's purchase of a 12 per cent stake in Rio Tinto, Chinese ODI suddenly rose to US$16.2 billion and then fell back to US$8.6 billion and US$3.9 billion in 2009 and 2010 respectively, before stabilising around US$10 billion per annum from 2011. Chinese ODI in Australia was concentrated in iron ore and coalmining industries in the initial years from 2007 to 2009. Mining investment on average accounted for 91 per cent of the total investment. With investment in energy resources gradually catching up, by 2012 a total of US$5.5 billion was

---

4    Department of Foreign Affairs and Trade n.d.
5    Drysdale and Findlay 2009.

invested in mining and US$4.8 billion in energy resources (Table 6.1). Up to 2012, Australia was the globally leading recipient country of Chinese ODI. The average size of the completed deals was significantly larger in Australia than in other countries. Consistent with China's state control over the resources sector, Chinese investment in Australia was dominated by large state-owned enterprises. Notable companies include central enterprises such as CITIC Group and Sinosteel, and provincial-level ones, such as Hunan Valin Steel and Yankuang Group. State ownership of investing companies and the rapid growth of Chinese ODI gave rise to Australian public concern that Chinese investment was government-directed rather than commercially motivated. The reporting from the Australian Department of Foreign Affairs and Trade that China's ODI in 2013 constituted no more than 3.5 per cent of the total stock of foreign direct investment in Australia[6] failed to alleviate concerns about China's economic influence.

Table 6.1 Chinese investment flow into Australia by industry in 2012.

| Industry | Value (US$ billion) | % |
|---|---|---|
| Mining | 5.472 | 48 |
| Energy (gas) | 4.785 | 42 |
| Others | 1.127 | 10 |
| Total | 11.384 | 100 |

Source: KPMG and University of Sydney China Studies Centre 2013. Demystifying Chinese Investment in Australia: Update March 2013, 6.

The boom in Chinese resources investment was driven by China's demand for resources commodities and the Chinese government's expectation to secure long-term supply from Australia. In 2008 China rolled out an infrastructure stimulus plan to mitigate the impact of the

---

6    Department of Foreign Affairs and Trade 2015.

Global Financial Crisis that pushed up demand for mining resources such as iron ore. China, as the world's largest iron ore importer, lacked influence over iron ore supply and prices, as global mining companies consolidated their control.[7] Domestically, the Chinese government encouraged the amalgamation of iron and steel enterprises through alliances, mergers and reorganisations. Externally, the Chinese government incentivised iron and steel enterprises to "go out" and acquire overseas mining assets. For example, China's Ministry of Finance and Ministry of Land and Resources promulgated the "Administrative Measures for Special Funds for Risk Exploration of Foreign Mineral Resources"[8] and stipulated that "for mineral resource exploration projects, special funds will be supported in the form of free subsidies" and "for mineral resource development projects, special funds will be supported in the form of loan discounts". In response to these incentives, Chinese state-owned iron and steel companies increasingly entered the Australian resources sector, mainly through mergers and acquisitions. The resulting increase in mining capacities and output led to the mining boom of 2008 and beyond.

Resources investment temporarily slowed down in 2009, when Rio Tinto rejected Chinalco's US$19.5 billion takeover bid. In a statement, Chinalco President Xiong Weiping said that the firm was "very disappointed" with the failure of its investment plan.[9] In the same year, Australian citizen and former Rio Tinto executive Stern Hu was detained in China in July for bribery and industrial espionage. Chinese mining companies were concerned that Australia was becoming less welcoming towards Chinese ODI. Meanwhile, failed mining investment ventures and project-specific problems made Chinese companies more wary of investing in Australian resources. A shift of investment to energy resources in oil and gas led to a temporary recovery of investment volumes in 2011 and 2012.

---

7    Uren 2012, 65–86.
8    Food and Agriculture Organization of the United Nations 2005.
9    Xinhua 2009.

## The integration period, 2013–16

The integration period began in 2013 when Chinese investment diversified into non-resources sectors including grid infrastructure, and industry and consumer sectors such as agribusiness, commercial real estate, renewable energies and health care. Smaller, local state-owned enterprises and privately owned enterprises in these sectors started to invest in Australia (Figure 6.2). In 2013 investment in resources and energy (gas) dropped to half the percentage of the preceding year, down from 48 per cent and 42 per cent to 24 and 21 per cent, respectively. By 2014, more than half (51 per cent) of Chinese investment was in commercial real estate and 26 per cent in infrastructure. The year 2016 set some significant records including the largest number of deals overall and the largest number of deals by privately owned firms. As seen in Table 6.2, commercial real estate accounted for 36 per cent, followed by infrastructure (28 per cent), health care (9 per cent), agribusiness (8 per cent), and energy (8 per cent), while mining investment only accounted for 5 per cent of the total volume. Privately owned enterprises concluded 78 deals out of a total of 103 deals. Among these companies were large established players in the Chinese markets, such as Fosun and New Hope, smaller real estate companies and a variety of private equity investors.

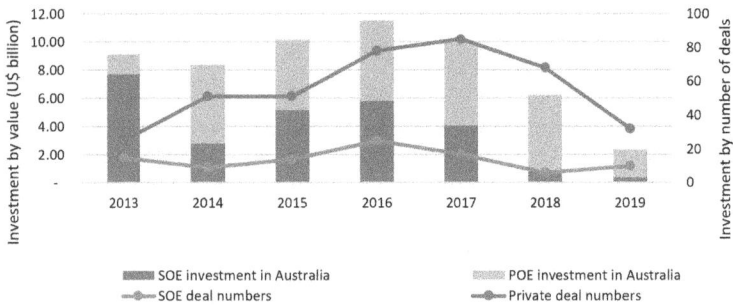

Figure 6.2 Chinese ODI in Australia by ownership, 2013 to 2019 (US$ billion).
Source: KPMG and University of Sydney China Studies Centre database.

Table 6.2 Chinese investment in Australia in 2016 by industry.

| Industry | Value (A$ billion) | % of total Chinese investment |
|---|---|---|
| Commercial real estate | 5.549 | 36 |
| Infrastructure | 4.340 | 28 |
| Healthcare | 1.354 | 9 |
| Agribusiness | 1.202 | 8 |
| Energy (gas and oil) | 1.149 | 8 |
| Mining | 0.839 | 5 |
| Transport | 0.391 | 3 |
| Renewable energy | 0.343 | 2 |
| Others | 0.195 | 1 |
| Total | 15.361 | 100 |

Source: KPMG and University of Sydney 2017, 11.

Despite Treasurer Scott Morrison blocking some very large Chinese investment projects in 2016, such as in the infrastructure company Ausgrid and the agribusiness S. Kidman & Co., Australia was still the second-largest recipient country of accumulated Chinese investment behind the United States. The industrial diversification in Chinese investment that occurred during this integration period marked a significant shift in focus towards Australia's domestic economy and away from Australia's traditional role as a supplier of resources and raw materials. Large and small Chinese multinational enterprises discovered that Australia offered goods and services demanded by

Chinese middle-class consumers in sectors such as health, tourism, education, food, professional services and technology. These were also the new sectors in which the Chinese government's 13th Five-Year Plan (2016–2020) now encouraged investment. Chinese corporations also discovered the usefulness of the Australian market for their globalisation strategies as Australian companies became strategic partners in China's expansion of its global value chains. Our interviews confirm that, in addition to securing long-term supply of resources, Chinese enterprises now integrated their Australian investments into their domestic and global operations by seeking diversified assets and markets, and globalising corporate strategies and capabilities.

Confidence-building measures between the two governments such as the 2014 Comprehensive Strategic Partnership and the conclusion of the China–Australia Free Trade Agreement (ChAFTA) in 2015 opened new modes of cooperation with China. Chinese investment in Australian healthcare companies is a good example of strategic asset-seeking for the Chinese domestic and global markets. Our interviews show that Chinese investment in Australian healthcare services and products served to acquire capabilities that could be used to develop specific market segments in China. Australian healthcare providers were attractive partners for their "packages" of hi-tech services, advanced technology applications, provision of care, health products and their "clean, green and healthy" image. These "packages" could be replicated and projected into the Chinese market once they were customised to fit the specific needs of China's middle- to high-end consumer markets. Chinese enterprises also partnered with Australian healthcare providers in setting up private hospital chains in third- and fourth-tier Chinese cities that lacked advanced health care. In turn, Australian partners were able to upscale up their technologies, and regional and global operations.

Australia's dynamic markets and stable economic growth provided opportunities for Chinese multinational enterprises to operate outside their home market. The compatibility of time zones and the sense that Australia was a preferred destination for Chinese students, tourists and emigrants added to Australia's competitive advantage as an investment destination. Together with the United States and Europe, Australia became a strategic investment destination for Chinese enterprises targeting long-term economic integration in global growth industries.

## The fallback period, 2017–21

The fallback period of the investment relationship began in 2017 amid global uncertainty over the US–China trade war and economic decoupling. It brought an 11 per cent decline of Chinese ODI in Australia in 2017 and a gradual reduction of Chinese investment to the core sectors of new mining, commercial real estate and renewable energy. Infrastructure investment dropped the most, to only two small projects. Commercial real estate investment was characterised by risk minimisation and declining deal sizes. The sector that proved to be most resilient and least affected by the changing regulatory, political and economic landscape was mining. Global demand for coal, lithium and cobalt and other non-ferrous metals led to significant growth in mining investment for the first time in several years. By 2018, amidst global uncertainty and newly-imposed foreign currency controls by the Chinese government, Chinese ODI in all developed economies declined sharply, including a drop of 37.6 per cent for investment in Australia. In 2019, the Chinese investment volume of US$2.4 billion was only one-fifth of the volume of 2016. By 2021, Chinese ODI in Australia was down to US$0.6 billion in volume, with little expectation that large-scale Chinese investment would return in the short to medium term. There were 11 transactions recorded across the three sectors of mining, commercial real estate and renewable energy (Table 6.3).

The economic characteristics of the fallback period of Chinese ODI continued to reflect the changing priorities of China's Five-Year Plans (Figure 6.3). China's expansionist 12th Five-Year Plan (2011–2015) had encouraged Chinese investment into more diversified sectors beyond mining, including energy, agribusiness, hi-tech and financial services. The 13th Five-Year Plan (2016–2020) noticeably reduced sector-focused investment in favour of value chain investment and stressed the importance of "bringing in and going out" in support of enterprises establishing cross-border industrial cooperation, value chains and supply chains in strategic sectors.

Table 6.3 Chinese investment in Australia by industry in 2021.

| Industry | Value (A$ billion) | % of total Chinese investment |
| --- | --- | --- |
| Mining | 0.545 | 70 |
| Commercial real estate | 0.208 | 27 |
| Renewable energy | 0.0250 | 3 |
| Total | 0.778 | 100% |

Source: KPMG and University of Sydney China Studies Centre database.

The remarkable decline of Chinese ODI in Australia was not driven by commercial considerations but mainly by sociopolitical factors in China and in Australia. Since late 2016, the Chinese government tightened regulatory oversight of overseas investments to prevent capital flight and ensure that investments were in line with the company's core business and supported China's development goals.[10] Under the new regulations, Chinese ODI was categorised as either encouraged, restricted, or prohibited.[11] For Australia, the new regulations directly affected investment in commercial real estate (defined as restricted by the Chinese government), as well as indirectly restricting cross-border capital movement. According to our interviews, executives, especially in privately owned enterprises, experienced difficulties moving funds from China to Australia from 2017.

For Australia–China relations, 2017 was a year of significant volatility, marked by Australia's political debate about the role of Chinese investment and a series of new regulations to strengthen national security. Australia became the first Western country to officially ban the Chinese telecommunication giants Huawei and ZTE from participation in building the fifth-generation (5G) broadband

10   Allen & Overy 2017.
11   State Council of the PRC 2017.

| Mining boom period (2008–2012) | Integration boom period (2013–2016) | Fallback period (2017–2021) |
|---|---|---|
| • focus on mining and energy<br>• large deal sizes<br>• central state-owned enterprises<br>• preference for investments in listed companies | • focus on a diversified range of sectors<br>• small- and medium-sized private enterprises and local state-owned enterprises<br>• preference for low entry barriers and growth | • focus on value chains<br>• small- and medium-sized deals<br>• a diverse range of firm sizes, ownerships, experiences, resources and capabilities<br>• preference for quality, scalability and long term |

| 11th Five-Year Plan GO GLOBAL | ▶ | 12th Five-Year Plan DIVERSIFICATION | ▶ | 13th Five-Year Plan VALUE CHAIN |
|---|---|---|---|---|

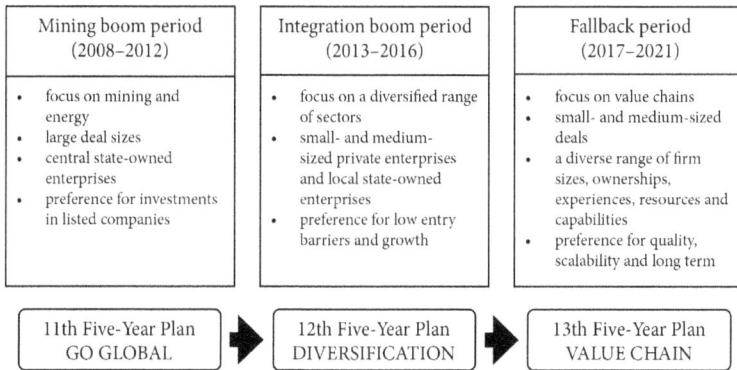

Figure 6.3 Changing characteristics of Chinese ODI in Australia from 2008 to 2021. Source: Authors' data and interviews.

network. The move was widely perceived as Australia's response to rising Sino-American geopolitical tensions. New laws, including a foreign interference law, and the establishment of a university foreign interference taskforce, led to tensions that alienated not just Chinese investors but even many local Chinese Australians.[12]

The resultant mood shift was evident in our interviews, revealing that confidence in the Australian market as a safe investment destination declined between 2014 and 2020. Discussions about Chinese influence and increasing diplomatic tensions had given Chinese companies the impression that they were less welcome to invest in Australia. While some Chinese investors retained optimism about their Australian investments, many investors, especially those in state-owned enterprises, were apprehensive about diplomatic tensions. In 2018, only 35 per cent of interviewees felt welcome to invest in Australia – a notable decline from 52 per cent in 2014. This sentiment was reflected in a further sharp decline in Chinese investment in Australia in both the value and number of transactions in 2019.

---

12    Kassam and Hsu 2021.

The tense relations between Canberra and Beijing since the COVID-19 outbreak continued to affect the investment environment for Chinese ODI in Australia. In March 2020, Australia's Foreign Investment Review Board introduced new regulations to reduce the threshold for mandatory review to zero and extended the review process to six months with no clear sunset maturity time frame.[13] In our interviews, Chinese executives expressed concern about increased commercial costs of investing in Australia due to the higher level of political risks, increased application fees, compliance costs for providing detailed information that was not required before, and unpredictable processing times. Australia's unilateral call for an international inquiry into the origin of the COVID-19 pandemic in April 2020 sparked a furious response from Beijing, followed by trade sanctions on Australian exports worth potentially A$20 billion that hurt local communities but hardly affected the overall trade volume and positive trade balance for Australia.

In sum, unlike Australia's trade with China, the investment relationships between the two countries increasingly came under political pressure imposed by both sides against better economic judgement. Aggravated by the impact of the COVID-19 pandemic, the state of Chinese ODI in Australia in 2022 marks the culmination of deteriorating sociopolitical factors, including Chinese government restrictions on outbound investment, Australia's geostrategic realignment with the United States and populist attitudes against China. A recovery of Chinese ODI in Australia will require a new balance between geopolitical security concerns and market forces aligned with Australia's commercial interests. The basis for such a turnaround lies in the economic complementarity between Australia and China and the lessons in localisation and globalisation that Australian and Chinese businesses have learned from their investment cooperation over the previous decade.

---

13   Hundt 2020.

## Learning from investing in the Australian market

Since the beginning of the integration period of Chinese direct investment in Australia in 2012, a new generation of Chinese investors has entered the Australian market. These investors were not large state-owned resources companies operating under government mandates, but commercially motivated corporate investors. They included central and local state-owned enterprises with increasingly mixed ownership and privately owned corporations ranging from established multinational corporations such as Fosun and Wanda to local manufacturers and family offices.

Most of these companies were private enterprises or of mixed ownership that makes the simplistic division between state-owned and private enterprises more and more difficult. These new investors were less familiar with global markets[14] than the large central government–controlled state-owned enterprises. For their managers and the headquarters in China, Australia became a learning and testing ground before entering larger developed markets in North America and Europe. Operating in the relatively small Australian market enabled them to build brands, reputation, institutional knowledge and managerial experience. While many of these new investors were well established and successful in China, they lacked credentials and successful projects overseas, especially in developed markets. Less-experienced firms found it easier to experiment with entrepreneurial activities in Australia first and then scale up successful Australian operations in other overseas markets. The size of Australia's domestic market, the stable, internationally-oriented regulatory environment, geographic proximity to China and the local multicultural and multilingual population made Australia a "convenient" window for Chinese firms to experiment with new technologies, management know-how and globalisation. Their experiences in corporate governance, expanding value and supply chains, and leveraging their dual presence in local and global markets are lessons that underpin the economic complementarity between the two countries.

---

14   Zu 2021.

## Corporate governance

During the initial mining boom period, Chinese investors emphasised principal–agent relations and direct control over local subsidiaries with limited autonomy and limited links with internal and external partners. During the integration period, the local subsidiaries of Chinese multinational enterprises in Australia gradually gained greater autonomy over investment plans, employment relations and interaction with local firms.

Despite their initial weakness in competing with incumbent local and international firms, Chinese parent firms increasingly delegated strategic control and granted autonomy to local subsidiaries to encourage entrepreneurial initiatives. This approach gave subsidiary managers discretion to take strategic initiatives in response to local circumstances. To maintain strategic control while enabling local initiative, Chinese headquarters appointed qualified managers who enjoyed their trust to manage these local entrepreneurial initiatives. State-owned enterprises such as the Yankuang Group typically appointed senior headquarter executives as local chief executive officers. Private companies such as New Hope frequently looked for trusted managers who had head office work experience. Smaller private investors appointed trusted family members. This arrangement provided ongoing strategic communication and trust between the headquarters in China and their Australian subsidiaries.

As local subsidiaries in Australia grew and became more globalised, a new trend emerged as individual Chinese firms upgraded their main Australian subsidiary to their international head office. This resulted in closer and more substantial interaction between the Australia-based international head office and subsidiaries in other countries including in the United States and the United Kingdom. This flexible governance model enabled the introduction of unified human resources management and corporate social responsibility practices across international subsidiaries as managers of international subsidiaries shared common experience with their counterparts in Australia. These flexible governance mechanisms sustained an entrepreneurial impetus for subsidiaries to pursue opportunities with local partners in new markets and industries.

*Integrating and upscaling value chains*

Since 2017, an increasing number of executives from Chinese firms have emphasised that their companies are not investing for offtake of Australian resources to companies in China but for expanding global value chains and diversifying international supply chains. They referred to products as well as services across all industries that we covered in our interviews, and to the complex integration of supply chains that combine the flow of physical goods and services and deployment of technologies in both directions. Supply chain integration also serves to develop higher quality standards for Chinese firms intending to upgrade and improve their global performance. Chinese investment in Australia is part of Chinese firms' strategic effort to combine national, regional and global value chains to cushion the impact of the trade war and climb up the global value chain of manufacturing. The motivation of value chain integrations is to develop standards and take advantage of various sources of inputs for their production chains and reshape their supply chain so that Chinese firms can achieve industrial upgrading.

One example is lithium mining in Australia. Chinese investment in lithium mining is driven by strong market demand in China and globally, thanks to Australia's status as the major global lithium supplier. At the same time, Chinese firms are building up alternative supplies to their Australian supply with investments in Chile and other locations. Another example is Chinese investment in the agriculture sector. Unlike early investors that focused on offtake, Chinese investors with competitive advantages from their own industry experience, distribution channels and digital capabilities in China are keen to integrate Australian projects into their global value chains. In our study, one company's acquisition of an Australian agribusiness was driven by the Australian company's solid track record of up-to-date technology, industry know-how and strong industry reputation. The Chinese investors had observed the Australian company over several years. After the acquisition, they retained the local Australian management with the plan to integrate the Australian company into their expanding domestic and international markets.

In healthcare investment, we found Chinese companies were primarily investing in Australian healthcare providers to upgrade and diversify their services in the Chinese market. Interviewees emphasised the synergy and strategic match of Australian assets with their Chinese operations as a key requirement for making investment decisions. One Chinese executive mentioned that any asset they acquired needed to have a "China story" that linked it to Chinese domestic demand. They pointed out dynamic coordination and integration with advanced-level Australian operations were required to fully capture first-mover advantages in the Chinese market.

These value chain and scalability requirements have implications for Chinese multinational enterprises' investment strategies. According to our interviews, the new generation of investors takes a long-term approach towards Australian investments. None of them plans to exit the market in the short term. While all of the companies welcome partnerships, they prefer a controlling shareholder position, which gives them the flexibility to combine Australian capabilities with their Chinese domestic and global operations.

### Dual embeddedness

To compete in developed markets like Australia, Chinese investors emphasise the importance of dual embeddedness, especially building local networks in Australia while maintaining and leveraging their networks back in China. Dual embeddedness helps hedge risks through long-term mutual commitment. Flexible funding from headquarters in China or through business networks facilitates business expansion organically and by acquisition. Beyond access to capital, our interviewees argued that China's supportive innovation system and commercialisation of innovations creates technological and cost advantages.

Chinese financial institutions have become thoroughly embedded in Australian markets. They are increasingly strategic partners for Chinese investors but even more for large-scale project finance for Australian firms. Lending by Chinese banks to Australian businesses has grown from almost nothing in 2007 to around A$42 billion in 2020 (Figure 6.4). According to the Reserve Bank of Australia's Assistant Governor Christopher Kent, Chinese banks have become an increasingly important source of financing for many businesses in Australia.[15] Chinese bank finance in Australia is greater than that

Table 6.4 Advantages of access to Australian and Chinese networks

| Australian networks | Chinese networks |
| --- | --- |
| High-quality resource and services | Growth markets |
| Qualified staff | Flexible finance |
| International standards and compliance | International supply chains |
| Branding and marketing | Supportive innovation system and application |
| International innovations | Economy of scale |

Source: KPMG and University of Sydney China Studies Centre interviews.

provided by North American banks and comparable in volume to business credit provided by Japanese and European banks. Dual embeddedness also enables knowledge transfer from Australia to parent companies and other sister subsidiaries. Interviewees from the Chinese banking in Australia sector observed that Australia, as a leader in compliance and anti–money laundering, has helped their headquarters and international subsidiaries gain expertise in areas such as client screening, risk management and cross-border taxation.

---

15    Cranston 2019; Kent 2019.

147

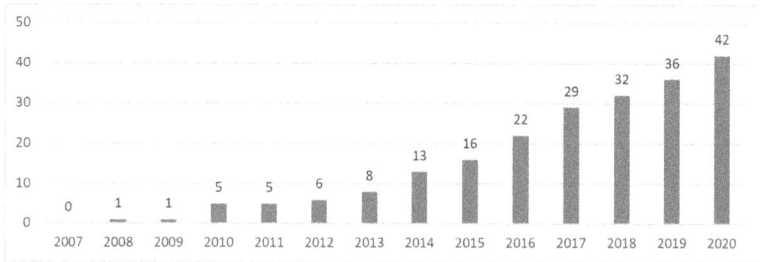

Figure 6.4 Chinese banks in Australia: total gross loans and advances (A$ billion). Source: Australian Prudential Regulation Authority, monthly authorised deposit-taking institution statistics.

Some Chinese firms stand out for building networks in China and extending them into Australia. Chinese wind-turbine manufacturers, for example, entered Australia in the early 2010s when large global firms like Vestas, GE and Siemens dominated the market. These companies cultivated unique network links with energy firms back in China to entice them to enter the Australian market. These energy firms, including major state-owned enterprises like China Energy Conservation and Environmental Protection Group (CECEP) and Guangdong Nuclear Power, invested in wind farms developed by Chinese wind-turbine manufacturers and helped establish a local reputation for them. Chinese wind-turbine companies could not have attained this status by relying purely on upgrading their operational capabilities to the level of their local competitors. The frequent usage of such business networks has positive implications for Chinese investors, such as reduced transaction costs, the large scale of application and price advantages for Australian clients. Networking also creates reputational advantages when competing with established competitors.

In summary, the decline and disruption of Chinese direct investment in Australia occurred when Australian–Chinese business cooperation was diversifying from traditional resources industries into new growth areas where Australian industries have global competitive advantages such as agribusiness, health and services. For Australian businesses, cooperating with Chinese companies and securing their longer-term commitment through investment opened new markets, access to finance, economies of scale, and global value chains. In this process, the institutional and commercial support by Australian regulators, professional services providers, local governments and corporate partners helped Chinese investors integrate and upscale their Australian operations into Australian, Chinese and global markets.

## Lessons for Australia: social and political challenges

Australia has attracted foreign investment for over two centuries, as reflected in its persistent current account deficit. The Organisation for Economic Co-operation and Development (OECD) publishes an annual FDI restrictiveness index[16] with values between 0 and 1 from 0 for fully open to 1 for fully closed. Australia's 2019 FDI restriction index value of 0.153 indicates openness below the OECD average value of 0.094 with a restrictiveness that lies between the United Kingdom with 0.14 and China with 0.34. From a Chinese perspective,[17] the increasing reference to national security holds back investment and creates negative social attitudes and hostile populist rhetoric that reinforce geopolitical tensions. We distinguish five sources of apprehension about foreign investment that concern Chinese investors: clarity about national economic interest; lack of social licence; perceived economic impact; national security; and populism. Some of these concerns have historical roots but have only become virulent during the fallback period. The return to economic normality and long-term sustainable commercial relations will require the combined efforts of Australian and Chinese stakeholders.

### National economic interest

Australia's regulatory institutions apply formal laws, regulations and rules to foreign investors to influence FDI activities and protect domestic industries and national interest. This should not be confused with protectionist intent. The Foreign Investment Review Board's "national

---

16   OECD FDI restrictiveness index.
17   Zha 2013.

interest test" lists formal economic reasons for the Treasurer to withhold approval of foreign investments in addition to national security criteria and effect on government policies (see below). For example, the Treasurer used national interest as a reason to reject the initial applications by Chinese investors for S. Kidman & Co agricultural investment and only approved the deal after conversion to a joint venture structure with majority Australian ownership. Similar concerns existed with other large deals such as Cubbie Station and John Holland, which Treasury resolved in favour of stronger Australian control and focus on international markets. The lesson here is that national economic interest can be invoked for a variety of reasons, including in response to political pressure and in favour of domestic investors.

Australia has traditionally maintained an open policy towards foreign investment but has guided foreign investors to operate commercially and limit foreign state interference.[18] In response to the second phase of Chinese investment since 2012, the approach of the Australian federal government has changed significantly from reluctant acceptance during the mining investment phase to facilitation and proactive regulation, particularly in response to non-resource investment. The Foreign Investment Review Board used conditionality to discourage foreign state involvement and prevent non-market transactions (Figure 6.5). State-owned enterprises in particular can be subject to various degrees of restrictive policies that impose limitations on full or majority ownership, stipulate the use of arm's-length transactions, require mandatory local management teams and regulate other operational matters.[19] The Board's commitment to use approval conditions to deal with national interest concerns features regularly in its annual reports, which document that a growing proportion of applications are approved subject to governance and commercial conditions.[20]

---

18  Gaetjens 2018.
19  Bath 2017.
20  Li and Hendrischke 2019.

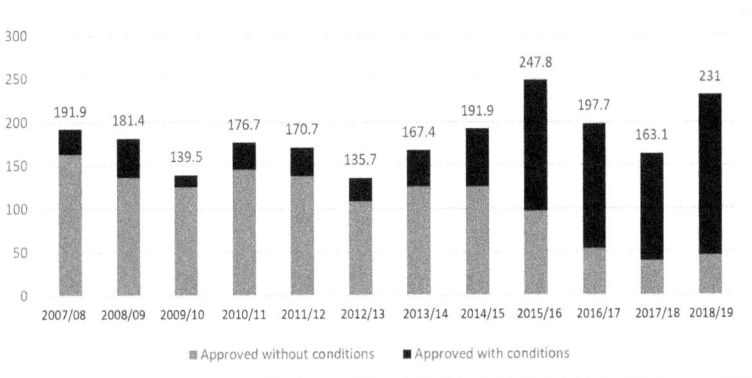

Figure 6.5 Conditionally-approved investment (A$ billion). Source: Foreign Investment Review Board Annual Reports.

This flexible system of foreign investment approvals fulfils its purpose of protecting national economic interest by ensuring localisation of governance, ownership and sales, and mitigating public concerns over Chinese direct investments. For example, the Foreign Investment Review Board restricts vertical integration of supply chains in resources industries by Chinese state-owned enterprises and other multinational companies. Decisions in relation to Chinese acquisitions such as the acquisition of Felix Resources Ltd by Yanzhou Coal Mining Company Limited in 2009 included provisions to ensure that the core management of the company was Australian, a number of board members resided in Australia, offtake from natural resource assets were marketed and sold at "arm's-length terms with reference to international benchmarks", and Chinese ownership was less than 70 per cent.[21] In each of these cases, a balance had to be struck between national economic interest and the interests of foreign investors and their Australian corporate partners, including reducing compliance costs and processing times. Transparent and market-conforming application of national economic interest considerations integrates

---

21    Bath 2017.

foreign investors into the domestic economy and helps them acquire "social licence to operate".

## Social licence to operate

Social licence to operate is a concern in response to the foreignness of Chinese investors who lack familiarity with local institutions, such as local government procedures, legal procedures, compliance requirements and local community concerns. The rise of mergers and acquisitions and joint ventures by Chinese firms to enter developed economies is an ubiquitous feature of the globalised economy and has been documented by a range of consulting firm reports and practitioner-oriented articles.[22] Yet public poll data shows that in developed countries where China has invested heavily, perceptions towards China and Chinese investment are generally negative.[23] The Australian public seems to be concerned about poorly conceived and executed approaches to investment in Australia by Chinese companies. Although cases are limited in number, their examples echo loudly in the press and are used to oppose new investment propositions being put forward.[24]

Several factors can explain this: the institutional and cultural contexts from which Chinese investors have emerged;[25] the active role of the home government;[26] Chinese firms' preference for mergers and acquisitions instead of greenfield investment;[27] their investment being less concentrated in traditional investment sectors, such as manufacturing and resources, and more in consumer-oriented services and information and communications technology;[28] and their unique ownership- or firm-specific advantages and disadvantages.[29]

22  Li and Hendrischke 2020; Rosen and Hanemann 2013; Seaman, Huotari and Otero-Iglesias 2017.
23  CSIS 2016; Lowy 2020.
24  Locke 2017.
25  Marano, Tashman and Kostova 2017.
26  Luo, Xue and Han 2010.
27  For example, Zhang and Ebbers 2010.
28  Ramasamy, Yeung and Lafouret 2012.
29  Cuervo-Gazurra and Genc 2008.

These liabilities of foreignness can be resolved through consultation with host communities and efforts on the part of the foreign investors to integrate in local environments and cooperate with local partners and stakeholders. Like other foreign-invested firms, Chinese companies are expected to act in a way deemed appropriate in their host economy. Such normative pressure determines how foreign-invested firms adopt the shared norms, values, beliefs and culture of a host country.[30] Meeting these concerns requires better public information by Australian governments, corporations, professional service providers and research institutions to create awareness of the "social licence" required by investors: for example, greater openness in employing local staff, better community integration and better communication with the domestic corporate sector.

*Perceived economic impact*

Perceived economic impact of Chinese investment arises when people or groups of people feel their economic interests are threatened. One example was the public perception that Chinese residential real estate purchases were to blame for the housing affordability crisis in Australia's major metropolitan centres. Another example was the threat raised by trade unions that ChAFTA could lead to an influx of low-paid Chinese labour and threaten Australian wage levels and working conditions.

Alleviating these concerns requires detailed and differentiated public information and involvement of the respective interest groups, for example, by providing public information on the limited overall scope of Chinese purchases of residential real estate purchases or farmland, or by defining skill levels and labour conditions for economically responsible labour imports. The register of foreign ownership of agricultural land and foreign ownership of residential real estate are examples of how these concerns can be dealt with.

---

30    DiMaggio and Powell 1983; Francis, Zheng and Mukherji 2009.

## National security

Chinese companies and their operations in Australia are caught up with escalating international and domestic political tensions. In 2020, major reforms to Australia's foreign investment review framework added critical infrastructure and data security legislation, and a raft of new legislation on national security. These reforms have aligned Australian regulations with new screening measures put in place in the United States, the United Kingdom, Canada, New Zealand, Japan, and continental European countries. For example, a mandatory Foreign Investment Review Board approval requirement arises for each action taken by a foreign person that constitutes a "notifiable national security action".[31] With the new investment laws, Australia has introduced international co-ordination where Chinese investment in Australia has fallen in line with core security partners, such as the United States, the United Kingdom, the European Union and Japan.

The political story of Chinese investment has transitioned from commercially driven investment co-operation to cooperation constrained by security concerns. Examples of controversial decisions are the Port of Darwin and Ausgrid projects, which were initially treated as commercial projects and for different reasons later became politicised as matters of national security concern. These examples have shown that national security concerns can arise from domestic or international geostrategic interventions and are not necessarily predictable in their outcomes.

## Populism

Populist objections against foreign investment arise from any of the previous points when investment decisions are taken up in the media and become emotionally charged. The risk with populism is that governments might be forced into action against specific investments to assuage public fears, potentially against better economic judgement. For example, foreign ownership of Australian farmland has provoked populist reactions in the past, which then have the potential to thwart

---

31    Foreign Investment Review Board n.d.b.

commercially desirable deals. Concerns about individual projects or foreign investment in general, particularly from China, become politicised in political discourse and public media. Politicisation opens the door for populist sentiment to enter the debate.

Public perception of Chinese companies investing in Australia continues to worsen. Many Chinese multinational enterprises suffer from liabilities of origin – capability- and legitimacy-based disadvantages associated with the country of origin.[32] This is evidenced in results from public polls. For example, the Lowy Institute Poll in 2019 showed two-thirds (68 per cent) of Australian adults believe the Australian government is "allowing too much Chinese investment in Australia".[33]

Populism must be taken seriously as a form of public resistance and requires a political response based on detailed reasoning and public information. Ad hoc foreign investment restrictions in response to populist public concerns are not a long-term solution. We find that opposition against foreign investment projects is generally quite specific and arises from legitimate economic and political concerns relating to specific industries. Populist concerns are exceptional in that they tend to generalise with little regard for underlying commercial realities.

In short, for Australia to normalise commercial investment relations with China there will need to be a rebuilding of social licence, public and political trust between Australia and China, and a relaxation of geostrategic tensions. Assuming that bilateral issues that are open to diplomatic solutions can be resolved, including the trade sanctions that China has imposed on Australian exports, there will still be a need to tackle the social and political challenges by presenting the commercial rationale for desired Chinese investment, ensuring a consensus between business and government, and mobilising political acceptance for Australia's and China's integration in our region. A commercial rationale for Chinese direct investment into Australia will have to acknowledge Australia's and China's growing integration in regional trading blocs. The experience that Australian businesses and

---

32    Marano, Tashman and Kostova 2017.
33    Lowy 2019.

governments have gained from nearly two decades of integrating Chinese investors, and the lessons that Chinese regulators and corporations have learned from operating in Australia's business and regulatory environment can provide the foundations for an economically sustainable long-term coexistence.


## Moving forward

Chinese investors in 2022 face a very different investment climate compared to 10 years ago. History may provide lessons for the present and guidance for the future. The need to maintain a dynamic balance between political and commercial interests is not new to Australia. Before Australia and China established diplomatic relations 50 years ago, Australia's wheat industry controversially depended on China and expanded its acreage in the 1960s in response to Chinese demand. The arguments in the debate between Australia and the United States about Australian wheat exports to China – a trade in which both countries were involved – have resurfaced at various times, and still sound familiar more than 50 years since they were published.

> the public appears to have developed several distinct attitudes on the subject of these wheat sales. One group openly condemns the sales. Another unreservedly approves of them. And there are those who do not give two hoots about the matter. However, the majority of informed opinion seems to be thinking roughly along these lines: economically, the expansion of the Chinese market is a natural blessing; but these exports constitute a serious danger for our foreign policy.[34]

> The Australian economy has been geared for many years now to receiving those handy trade surpluses from China, but should they unexpectedly dry up our balance of payments position could become quite embarrassing.[35]

---

34  Wilczynski 1965, 44.
35  Wilczynski 1965, 51.

History shows that Australian wheat exports were possible because they were deftly handled by the Australian Wheat Board and tolerated by the United States, whose own wheat exports to China competed at times with Canadian and Australian exports.

Analysing the potential benefits and challenges of Chinese ODI in Australia is important for post-COVID-19 economic recovery. Reducing economic dependence on China needs to be complemented by identifying and promoting cooperation in areas where Chinese ODI in resources, agriculture, manufacturing and services opens markets and opportunities for Australian businesses in Chinese, regional and global markets. The experience of Chinese investment in Australia provides lessons for the future. Chinese entrepreneurs will have to continue their efforts to integrate and adapt to the Australian business environment as part of their globalisation. Australian governments, corporations and public media can use the lessons from the rise and fall in Chinese investment to create a conducive and safe environment for investment from emerging economies, including China.

## References

Allen & Overy (2017). China's new restrictions on outbound investments and remittance. *JDSupra*. https://bit.ly/3KqEh1b.

Australian Prudential Regulation Authority n.d. Monthly Authorised Deposit-taking Institution Statistics. https://bit.ly/3rL5oxx.

Bath, Vivienne (2017). Australia and the Asia-Pacific. In Fabio Morosini and Michelle Ratton Sanchez Badin (eds), *Reconceptualizing international investment law from the global south* (1–46). Cambridge: Cambridge University Press. DOI:10.1017/9781316996812.003.

Cranston, Matthew (2019). Chinese banks lend more to Australia than the US. *Australian Financial Review*, 12 June. https://bit.ly/42Iiw3E.

CSIS (2016). International views of China. Centre for Strategic and International Studies. https://bit.ly/3pw9FUs.

Cuervo-Cazurra, Alvaro and Mehmet Genc (2008). Transforming disadvantages into advantages: developing-country MNEs in the least developed countries. *Journal of International Business Studies* 39(6): 957–79. DOI:10.1057/palgrave.jibs8400390.

Curran, James (2022). *Australia's China odyssey: from euphoria to fear*. Sydney: NewSouth Books.

Department of Foreign Affairs and Trade, Australian Government n.d. China country brief. https://bit.ly/3BmEnBX.

Department of Foreign Affairs and Trade (2015). Australia's position in global and bilateral foreign direct investment. https://bit.ly/3O9BGdc.

DiMaggio, Paul J. and Walter W. Powell (1983). The iron cage revisited: institutional isomorphism and collective rationality in organizational fields. *American Sociological Review* 48(2): 147–60. DOI:10.2307/2095101.

Drysdale, Peter and Christopher Findlay (2009). Chinese foreign direct investment in Australia: policy issues for the resource sector. *China Economic Journal* 2(2): 133–58. DOI:10.1080/17538960903083467.

Food and Agriculture Organization of the United Nations (2005). China: Interim measures for the administration of special funds for risk exploration of foreign mineral resources. https://bit.ly/41yxQyS.

Foreign Investment Review Board n.d.a Reports and publications. https://bit.ly/3OihTZg.

Foreign Investment Review Board n.d.b Key concepts. https://bit.ly/3rLxlW6.

Francis, John, CongCong Zheng and Ananda Mukherji (2009). An institutional perspective on foreign direct investment. *Management International Review* 49(5): 565–83. DOI:10.1007/s11575-009-0011-x.

Gaetjens, Philip (2018). Security before investment: Treasury boss. *SBS News* 8 October. https://bit.ly/44Tmt7x.

Hundt, David (2020). The changing role of the FIRB and the politics of foreign investment in Australia. *Australian Journal of Political Science* 55(3): 328–43.

Kassam, Natasha (2019). Lowy Institute Poll 2019: Understanding Australian Attitudes to the World. https://bit.ly/41mutet.

Kassam, Natasha (2020). Lowy Institute Poll 2020: Understanding Australian Attitudes to the World. https://bit.ly/3Mhp3fl.

Kassam, Natasha and Jennifer Hsu (2021). Being Chinese in Australia: public opinion in Chinese communities. Lowy Institute. https://bit.ly/41yjSgm.

Kent, Christopher (2019). Remarks at the Australian Renminbi Forum Melbourne. Speech, 12 June. *Reserve Bank of Australia*. https://bit.ly/3OwKv24.

KPMG and University of Sydney various years 2012–23. Demystifying Chinese Investment in Australia. https://bit.ly/3pwKeCh.

KPMG and University of Sydney China Studies Centre (2013). Demystifying Chinese Investment in Australia: Update March 2013. https://bit.ly/3pyWjqD.

KPMG and University of Sydney (2017). Demystifying Chinese Investment in Australia: May 2017. https://bit.ly/3LUKjXP.

Li, Wei and Hans Hendrischke (2019). Chinese outbound investment in Australia: from state control to entrepreneurship. *China Quarterly* 243: 701–36. DOI:10.1017/S0305741019001243.

Li, Wei and Hans Hendrischke (2020). Local integration and co-evolution of internationalizing Chinese firms. *Thunderbird International Business Review* 62(4): 425–39. DOI:10.1002/tie.22137.

Locke, Sarina (2017). Chinese investors in agribusiness told to win a social licence or risk rejection by rural communities. *ABC Rural*. https://ab.co/3pps1q2.

Luo, Yadong, Qiuzhi Xue and Binjie Han (2010). How emerging market governments promote outward FDI: experience from China. *Journal of World Business* 45(1): 6–79. DOI:10.1016/j.jwb.2009.04.003.

Marano, Valentina, Peter Tashman and Tatiana Kostova (2017). Escaping the iron cage: liabilities of origin and CSR reporting of emerging market multinational enterprises. *Journal of International Business Studies* 48(3): 386–408. DOI:10.1057/jibs.2016.17.

OECD various years. FDI Regulatory Restrictiveness Index. https://data.oecd.org/fdi/fdi-restrictiveness.htm.

Ramasamy, Bala, Matthew Yeung and Sylvie Laforet (2012). China's outward foreign direct investment: location choice and firm ownership. *Journal of World Business* 47(1): 17–25. DOI:10.1016/j.jwb.2010.10.016.

Rosen, Daniel H. and Thilo Hanemann (2013). *Outward FDI from China: dimensions, drivers, implications.* Peterson Institute for International Economics, Washington D.C.

Seaman, John, Mikko Huotari and Miguel Otero-Iglesias (2017). Chinese investment in Europe. A country-level approach. Report. *Mercator Institute for China Studies*, December. https://bit.ly/43KnLjm.

State Council of the People's Republic of China (2017). State Council issues guideline on overseas investment. https://bit.ly/3rDt8Uc.

Uren, David (2021). *The kingdom and the quarry: China, Australia, fear and greed.* Melbourne: Black Inc.

Xinhua (2009). Rio Tinto scraps marriage with Chinalco. *China Daily* 9 June. https://bit.ly/3OaHSTE.

Wilczynski, Jozeph (1965). The economics and politics of wheat exports to China. *Australian Quarterly* 37(2): 44–55. DOI:10.2307/20634045.

Zhang, Jianhong and Haico Ebbers (2010). Why half of China's overseas acquisitions could not be completed. *Journal of Current Chinese Affairs*, 39(2): 101–31. https://bit.ly/3I2rOQa.

Zha, Daojiong (2013). Chinese FDI in Australia: drivers and perceptions. Lowy Institute-Rio Tinto China lecture. https://bit.ly/42sinBT.

Zu, Haoyue (2021). China's outward foreign direct investment in Australia. *Journal of Australian Political Economy* 88: 5–30.

# 7
# Australia–China ties: why business is a cornerstone

*Glenda Korporaal*

With Australia–China political ties coming back from their low point, the years of tension have highlighted the fact that business – or more specifically trade – is and will continue to be a cornerstone of the relationship. By the end of 2022 there were encouraging signs that the political tensions, which had reached a low point under the Morrison government, were easing with meetings between the leaders of both countries and senior officials of the Albanese government. Both sides managed to celebrate 50 years of political ties with a visit to Beijing by the Foreign Minister, Penny Wong – the first by a foreign minister since 2018. But throughout the darkest days of the relationship breakdown, including tariff and non-tariff barriers affecting some $20 billion of Australian exports, it was clear that business ties remained strong, with China continuing to be Australia's largest trading partner for more than a decade.

Business leaders were among the first Australians to return to China when it opened up its doors in early 2023, attending events including the China Development Forum in Beijing and the Boao Forum for Asia on Hainan Island.

At his speech to the National Press Club in Canberra in August 2022, China's ambassador, Xiao Qian, spelled out the strength of the ties. China has been Australia's largest trading partner since 2009. The volume of two-way trade has soared from less than US$100 million in

1972, when political ties between Beijing and Canberra were opened, to more than US$200 billion in 2021. China accounted for more than 34 per cent of Australia's total imports and exports in the year.[1]

While most countries have a trade deficit with China, Australia enjoys a trade surplus – in 2021 of US$60 billion. Looking through that lens, it is a trade relationship that financially benefits Australia more than China. China is the largest destination for Australia's exports, accounting for 39 per cent of total exports in 2021 and is also Australia's largest source of imports – with goods from China making up 28 per cent of all Australian imports. By 2018 – before COVID-19 travel restrictions hit – China had emerged as Australia's largest source of international tourists, sending more than a million travellers a year, who spent more than A$10 billion a year. Despite the impact of COVID-19, in 2021 Chinese students remained the largest source of international students in Australia, with more than 172,000 Chinese students at Australian educational institutions, making up 30 per cent of total international students, well above the 99,244 students from the next ranking country, India.[2]

Behind these massive figures are millions of transactions – large and small – and individual personal interactions, from business leaders to ordinary people, which have continued despite the heightened major political tensions between the two countries in recent years. With two very different political systems, with China becoming increasingly assertive about its role in regional and international affairs, and with attitudes in the United States shifting from seeing China's economic growth as a positive for the world to a competitive challenge, political differences and tensions between China and Australia, in various forms, still seem set to be part of our landscape for the foreseeable future.

Given this environment, it is more important than ever that alternative voices of cooperation and the experiences of Australian business leaders in working with China are also heard. Trade provides the opportunity for buyers and sellers to get together for deals that are in the best interest of both parties. It does best when there are

---

1   Xiao Qian 2022.
2   Department of Education 2023.

advantages for both sides in the transaction, which can be facilitated with the best possible people-to-people relationships. In the case of Australia, both these things have shown they can work if given the opportunity. Amidst the heightened political tensions of recent years, individual voices of friendship, cooperation and trade have been subdued – and yet they provide so much opportunity for goodwill and benefit on both sides.

A combination of the fundamental complementarity between the two economies – both sides have goods and services that the other one wants – and long-standing and strong personal ties have helped and will continue to provide necessary ballast in the relationship. The trade ties have been turbocharged by the increasing proportion of Chinese-born immigrants, many of whom came to Australia as students, and others with Chinese ancestry and language, who have been ready, willing and able to facilitate trade with China and the Asian region using their own connections. These deepening links are a natural part of Australia's interaction with the Asian region, including China, and yield significant benefits for the country.

For positive business, economic and person-to-person ties to remain, it is critical that doors on both sides remain open. For Australian companies, which operate in a small market of only 25 million people, the chance to access a part of a 1.4 billion market of increasingly affluent customers is a significant attraction for keeping a watchful eye on the opportunities of the China market.

The rise of ecommerce platforms such as Alibaba have provided another potential marketplace, one unaffected by travel restrictions or the need for face-to-face ties between buyers and sellers. Conversely, China's huge population makes mass manufacturing far more economical than in Australia, which has shut down substantial parts of its manufacturing of cars and trucks, clothing and steel. For importers of products ranging from building materials and agricultural chemicals to cars, computers, mobile phones, clothing, furniture, solar panels and computer parts, it makes far more sense to import them from China than make them locally.

The burgeoning trade between the two countries – before the impact of politics and COVID-19 – has proven just how significant the business opportunities can be on both sides. While some politicians have sought to dictate to the business community about doing business with China, lecturing them about the need to diversify away from depending too much on the China market, business has shown itself capable of making its own decisions on global trade.

The impact of political tensions and supply chain issues as a result of COVID-19 shutdowns have provided a wake-up call for business not to have too many eggs in the China market – despite the vast potential of the trade. Business people on both sides are adaptable and know they must constantly be sensitive to shifts in political, trade and regulatory issues if they are to be in the export game. Australian businesspeople in international trade are experienced in handling rapidly changing issues across a range of countries, including China.

While much attention has been given to China's imposition of tariffs on Australian wine and barley, Australian producers have long had to deal with sudden announcements that affect their trade – from Britain's entry into the European Union in the 1970s to tariffs on steel from the Trump administration in the United States (overturned as a result of political lobbying) or limits on chickpea imports in India.

But political tensions – some of which have been stoked for domestic political reasons and others as a result of changing policies in both Australia and China – have caused business leaders to be increasingly careful about their public statements, despite the significant wealth their companies generate for Australia and Australians.

One of the most significant business leaders has been Fortescue Metals Group founder, Perth businessman Andrew Forrest, who has built up one of Australia's largest iron ore exporters to China – a business that has generated billions of dollars in revenue for both state and federal governments over many years, and significant benefits for his shareholders and his thousands of employees. Despite these contributions, his efforts to leverage his China connections to bring in much-needed COVID-19 testing equipment into Victoria at the height of the COVID pandemic crisis in 2020 were criticised when he asked the Chinese consul in Melbourne to say a few words at a press conference to announce the deal. Yet two years later, Australians were vociferously complaining that they couldn't get enough personal COVID testing kits – most of them coming from China. Wary of such public criticism, Forrest and others involved in the China trade and business, including fellow Perth businessman Kerry Stokes, have kept a low profile in their comments on China over the years, despite having long-standing ties with the country.

Australia can choose to have an engagement with China in areas of mutual interest. If it chooses not to, others will continue to do business with China and Australia loses out in having connections with the big player of the region. China has a large, rich and complex population four times the size of the United States and offers many potential areas of co-operation for Australia. Maintaining trade ties is a way of promoting peaceful cooperation and understanding at many levels, something that has significant security implications.

While Australia spends billions of dollars on defence and has wasted billions on chopping and changing its multibillion-dollar submarine policy, investments in diplomacy and trade promotion and connections have the potential to create goodwill across a broad range of sectors and significantly reduce the chances of military conflict for a fraction of the cost of defence spending.

French liberal economist Frédéric Bastiat is credited with the quote: "When goods don't cross borders, soldiers will." While the geographical reality is different – Australia is a long way from China and China's military focus is its near region, particularly in the South China Sea – the underlying sentiment is real. Significant friendly trade relations offer an invaluable opportunity to promote mutual understanding and reduce potential military tensions.

Australia's economic success lies in a robust engagement with Asia, still one of the fastest-growing regions in the world. Doing so requires the sophistication to deal with governments of varying political structures – many of which don't have their origins in British colonialism – and finding points of common ground and mutual benefit. In designing a path forward for Australia's engagement with China, the thoughts and experiences of business leaders deserve to be heard.

## Australia–China trade ties: a brief history

While this book marks 50 years of Australia–China diplomatic relations, the trade ties between Australia and China far pre-date the current era. The gold rushes of the 1850s saw many Chinese come to Australia and go back to China, having made varying levels of fortunes. One of the most famous examples of this is the Wing On department store group in Hong Kong and China, founded by people who made their money in the Australian gold rushes.

The story of Australia's first trade commissioner to China, former British missionary Edward Selby Little, offers another example. After his 1921 appointment by Prime Minister Billy Hughes, Little travelled across Australia, enthusiastically talking to businesspeople and farmers with ideas for products to sell to the Middle Kingdom. Returning to China, he travelled around the country, energetically seeking out potential trade opportunities and sending letters back to Australia outlining possible business deals including imports of Australian railway sleepers and timber, meat, fruit, flour, wheat and cotton. Little recognised that the sheer size of the Chinese market, with some 450 million people at the time, provided new opportunities for a country like Australia with its small market, then only 5.4 million people.[3] Unfortunately, politics brought Little's promising role to a premature demise. He was dismissed in 1923, the victim of political intrigue. It was not until the 1930s that another Australian trade commissioner to China was appointed. One can only imagine what might have happened if the energetic Little had been able to connect Australian sellers with hundreds of millions of Chinese buyers at the time.

The opening up of political relations between Beijing and Canberra in 1972 saw a re-igniting of the trade potential between Australia with its small market and China with a population at the time of 850 million people. In the 1970s, the annual two-way trade of around A$100 million was based on the sale of Australian agricultural products – mainly wheat and wool – and the exports of Australian metals including gold, silver and copper. For their part, Australians were importing China-made clothing and footwear and other finished

---

3    Molloy 2011.

goods. In the 1980s, the efforts by former Prime Minister Bob Hawke, leveraging his connections within China, opened the lucrative new trade of Australian iron ore exports to China.

By 2009, having enjoyed double-digit growth for years, China became the world's second largest economy and overtook Japan as Australia's top trading partner. After years of negotiations, in 2014 Australia signed a free trade agreement with China to considerable fanfare. The China–Australia Free Trade Agreement (ChAFTA) formally came into effect in December 2015, providing another major catalyst for improving trade ties between the two countries.

The growing personal enthusiasm of ordinary Chinese people for both Australian university education and tourism provided another boost to bilateral trade. At its height, just before the COVID-19 outbreak in 2020, there were some 164,000 students from China studying in Australia, with 130,000 of these at Australian universities. The income generated from Chinese students in Australia was estimated to have grown from A$4.9 billion in 2014 to more than A$12 billion in 2020. The number of Chinese tourists visiting Australia was skyrocketing, more than quadrupling from 355,200 in 2009 to more than 1.5 million in 2019, contributing more than A$12.4 billion to the Australian economy.

While these figures led to debate about whether Australian universities were too dependent on the income from Chinese students, they highlighted the fact that Chinese people liked to come to Australia. The influx of visitors and students from China also sparked enthusiasm for Australian goods – including wine, dairy, beef and healthcare products – which they took back home back to China, further boosting Australian exports. Sales of Australian healthcare products, vitamins and infant formula also boomed, as many Chinese Australians promoted iconic Australian goods on China's ecommerce platforms such as those run by Alibaba. Enthusiasm in China for ecommerce also opened up important new channels of business, with the growing Chinese diaspora in Australia also using their connections to sell some of their favourite products back home.

With the free trade agreement clearing the way, China became Australia's largest trading partner. The booming trade ties were built on a solid footing of the natural complementarity between the two economies: Australia's small market and China's huge economy and rapidly growing middle class; China's desire for Australia's clean and green food and agricultural products, and minerals that fuelled its infrastructure growth; and Australians' desire for the finished goods from China which were both well priced and of increasing quality.

## The business community

Having reported on Australia–China business ties over many years, today I find myself struck by the widening gap between the angry rhetoric on both sides, so often in the headlines, and my conversations with sophisticated and experienced businesspeople in Australia engaged in trade with China. At times, it feels as if this is a parallel universe, in which Australian businesspeople retain positive ties with their Chinese counterparts even as political tensions continue to mount.

My discussions with a wide range of Australian businesspeople over many years have introduced me to many leaders of considerable experience in doing business with China. They have their eyes wide open about both the opportunities and the challenges of doing business with China. Yet too often, politicians have adopted an almost patronising tone towards business, presuming to tell them what is in their own best interests. For instance, in a speech to the Australian National University Crawford Leadership Forum in September 2021, Australian Treasurer Josh Frydenberg stated:

Many have worked hard to access the lucrative Chinese market. This has brought great benefits to them and to Australia overall. And they should continue to pursue these opportunities where they can. But, going forward, businesses need to be aware the world has changed. They should always be looking to diversify their markets and not only rely on any one country. Essentially adopting a "China plus" strategy.[4]

---

4  Frydenberg 2021.

In fact, Australian businesspeople are quite capable of assessing and responding to the risks, and the considerable opportunities, of doing business with China. A few brief case studies help highlight this crucial point.[5]

## Treasury Wine Estates

Treasury Wine Estates (TWE), an ASX-listed wine company, was the largest exporter of wine to China before it was hit with tariffs imposed by Chinese authorities in November 2020. These tariffs all but ended the once-lucrative Australian wine exports to China. Yet having established a strong presence in China, particularly for its famous Penfolds brand, the company remained confident and determined to be part of the Chinese market.

Chief executive Tim Ford, who spent many years travelling to China before taking over the top job in July 2020, remains committed to doing business in China because of the significant potential demand for wine in the country. He sees being part of the China market as a key part of the company's future as a global wine maker. Despite political tensions and COVID-19 travel restrictions, TWE has retained the global headquarters of its Penfolds business in Shanghai.

With tariffs on Australian wine making exports unprofitable, TWE responded by developing its Penfolds wine in the Napa Valley of the United States and in France, using these as a base to export into China. It also sourced wine from other countries like South Africa and South America to sell its brands into China. In 2022, after several years of research and development, it announced plans to launch as locally-grown Penfolds in the China market. The company's move to develop a Chinese-made version of Penfolds highlights its determination to remain in the market for the long term.

---

5    The interviews cited in this chapter were conducted for and previously published in a report for the Australia–China Relations Institute (ACRI). My appreciation to ACRI for permission to use this material for this chapter. See Korporaal 2021.

As these flexible responses show, TWE did not need politicians to tell it how to adapt to changing market restrictions while still focusing on the long-term potential of the China market for its product.

In an interview with this author – for a report for the Australia–China Relations Institute at the University of Technology Sydney released in December 2021 – Ford explained his reaction to the imposition of tariffs:

> It was important for us to understand whether this was an Australian country-of-origin issue or a Treasury Wine Estates/ Penfolds issue. But we have found the demand for Penfolds continues to be strong. This is very much an Australian issue, as opposed to a TWE issue.

Evidence of this, Ford adds, can be seen in the fact that Chinese authorities continue to work closely with the company to help stamp out the issue of counterfeit and copycat products that have beset the popular Penfolds brand as a result of its success:

> We have always spent a lot of time and money in China protecting our brand IP [intellectual property]. We continued this when the anti-dumping investigation was underway, and the tariffs kicked in. The program is as strong as ever in enforcing our zero-tolerance approach to infringement.

The company was rewarded with a positive judgement in China's highest court in 2022, which ended six years of legal issues in Australia and China.

Penfolds managing director, Tom King, who is based in Shanghai, believes that the judgement "highlighted China's unwavering commitment to protecting intellectual property rights. We welcome the judgement by the Supreme People's Court of China and thank the Chinese authorities for their continued support in protecting the rights of luxury brand operators." He adds:

> Penfolds has a long and proud heritage in China that's been protected and nurtured since the first bottle of wine was exported

from South Australia to Shanghai in 1893. Our long-term commitment to China, together with international legal protections to prevent infringement of our trademarks, gives our consumers the confidence to continue to enjoy award-winning quality wine from the Penfolds collection.

Like many people in global businesses, TWE chief executive Ford sees his job as constantly watching changing political, regulatory and social trends. "The geopolitical environment is something we monitor really closely," Ford said in his interview for the ACRI report:

It's an important external factor which can impact your business. It's not just China, it's in all the markets we are in. We are in many different markets. You have to balance what the most likely outcomes are and you have to make sure you have your plans in place if sometimes these outcomes do incur some pain.

## King & Wood Mallesons

Global law firm King & Wood Mallesons was formed in 2011 from a merger between Australia's oldest law firm, Mallesons Stephen Jacques, and Chinese law firm King & Wood.

The merger created a unique partnership between the two firms. King & Wood Mallesons now has 28 offices and over 5,000 staff around the world, including more than 400 partners in China and more than 170 partners in Australia.

In an interview for the ACRI report, Sue Kench, the Hong Kong–based global chief executive of King & Wood Mallesons explained that the merger allowed the Australian firm significant growth opportunities in Asia that would never have been available to it had it retained an Australian-base focus:

Australia is a much smaller legal market. It is saturated. If you are a law firm in Australia, you have to ask yourself – can I get growth in Australia or can I get growth offshore? There are too many lawyers in Australia. Do you sit in Australia and fight for an existing share of a reasonably flat, or at times declining market, or do you go offshore and get some growth? That was the decision for us. These are global legal markets. You have to participate and be connected.

"The growth in our business in China has been exponential as China itself has grown as an economy and moved more people into the middle- and higher-income levels," Kench explains. "The firm is now one of the top law firms in China and Asia with a deep expertise about doing business in China."

Australia, Kench adds, needs to realise that, despite US–China tensions, there is still significant business taking place between the United States and China, including US investment into China. "There is incredible connectivity both ways – from China into the US and US into China." These ongoing business ties, she says, also allowed for "support networks and conversation networks when diplomacy is not at its best. Australia lacks that and that's where business can help."

> There is quite strong engagement between China and Australia at a business level. There is a lot in common between the Chinese people and Australians. I would like to see the relationship improve. There are opportunities from a business perspective but also opportunities from an engagement perspective as well. It is naive to think that others will give up that opportunity. The US is not giving up that opportunity.

Kench suggests that Australia should focus on areas of mutual interest with China, pointing to health care as one area of opportunity, with possibilities ranging from helping to reduce child mortality to products and services that improve the health of ordinary Chinese people, to caring for an ageing population.

### Cochlear

One Australian healthcare company that has been doing well in China is Cochlear. The company has been selling its bionic ear implants in China for the past 25 years and moved to set up a factory in the western city of Chengdu in Sichuan province in 2017. More than 50,000 people in China, most of them children, now have Cochlear implants. In an interview, chief executive Dig Howitt told Professor Tim Harcourt of the University of Technology Sydney of his company's strong commitment to the China market:

> Our trading relationship with China is very significant. Hopefully that will continue. It is in the economic interests of both countries to have a strong trading relationship. Clearly, things are more challenging now, but what we are seeing on the ground in China is people are continuing to get implants, parents want their children to be able to hear. Business is going well and we are there for the long run.

## Lendlease

Lendlease, an Australia property and construction company, provides a good example of a firm expanding into China's healthcare and services sectors. In this case, Lendlease has built on its expertise in senior living accommodation to considerable advantage, tapping into a market with exciting opportunities.

The company has developed an upmarket retirement living development on the outskirts of Shanghai, a decision made after more than 25 years of operation in China. Its first phase opened in September 2021 with 250 apartments. "Lendlease has more than 30 years' experience in the senior living sector and is one of Australia's largest owners, operators and developers of senior living communities," its head of Asia, Justin Gabbani, told this author in an interview for the ACRI report. "China is an ideal market to export our expertise, with strong government support."

Gabbani explains that the Chinese government's support for the development of retirement villages has been important in Lendlease's confidence in the market's outlook. "The senior living sector receives strong support from the government, with favourable policies towards retirement and community care sector to meet local market demand." He adds that district governments, which have an influential role in China, have also been very welcoming and open to foreign investment in the sector.

Gabbani, who has lived in Asia since 2011, says doing business in the region involves finding unique propositions for the market, such as Lendlease's experience in senior living. Growing local talent is also important in China, he adds. "Our country leadership team in China has strong local talent, headed by industry veteran Ding Hui. Ding is our country Managing Director for China and has credible experience in the Chinese market with 17 years at IKEA before joining Lendlease."

## Costa

Food and agriculture represent yet another area of significant potential business between Australia and China. ASX-listed Costa Fine Food set up a joint venture in China with American berry company, Driscoll's, one of the world's largest marketers of berries, investing more than A$100 million in its China operations. It also exports citrus fruits – oranges and mandarins – grown in Australia to China, with the China-related businesses generating a combined annual turnover of A$1 billion.

Costa's move into producing in China reflected the importance of understanding local landowning laws and negotiating with local officials. In an interview for the ACRI project, Costa's chief executive, Sean Hallahan, said the company had made the decision to move into China because of the increasing health consciousness of the Chinese consumer with customers being prepared to pay for high-quality fruit. "Chinese consumers, more than any other type of consumer in the world, believe that their health is attributable to the food they eat," he said. He explained that Costa's move had required understanding land ownership structures in China:

> Villagers in China don't own the land but can get long-term leases on it. Costa's China project involves finding areas of land which are climactically suitable to grow berries and approaching villagers in the area to put together leases to farm the berries. They get a stream of income from the rental of their land and are also employed to work on the farms. We band those villages together into a village council. Then they provide an amalgamated long lease holding of the farming land that we need.

Costa has sought to have good relations with the local community by supporting local schools and sponsoring several local village children to enable them to further their education. Doing business in China, Hallahan explains, requires having an ear to the ground on what is happening at the local level as well as a national level:

> There's a difference between what's happening in Yunnan versus what may be being talked about in Beijing, for instance. Yunnan is Yunnan and what is happening in Beijing can be quite separate from that. We have been very focused on having great relationships – in Yunnan overall, and then the level of the provincial governments underneath that. We have many relationships built up over many years from the first time we were there. We want to be seen as someone who is valuable to the communities we operate in.

Hallahan notes that while Costa sought to expand into China, the firm never planned for China to be their exclusive focus:

> One thing we have been very conscious of in China from the start is that we didn't go out for China from an export point of view and make it 80 per cent of our business. That's not even about China. We don't think it's smart to be overly dependent on any country anywhere in the world. We have to have appropriate risk settings. So having about 10 per cent of our export revenue in citrus going to China is appropriate at the moment.

He concludes by explaining why he believes it is important for Australia to have good ties with China:

> There can be a lot of hyperbole about what's going on politically, but it is good to have solid business relationships that show that there is a way of doing things that can continue to happen in the background. I don't think anybody wants Australia and China to stay in a state of argument. We would prefer to get along, wouldn't we?

*Blackmores*

Vitamin company Blackmores has been selling into China for many years. Its products have also proved popular with Australian-based Chinese trans-shipment agents, or *daigou*, who have promoted Blackmores' vitamins to their friends and family back home. This direct access into the China market helped Blackmores' shares reach over A$200 per share by December 2015, as investors became excited about the potential of the firm's China market. In response to this growth potential, the company has continually sought to refine its China strategy, including setting up a wholly-owned subsidiary in the country and refocusing its energies on ecommerce platforms like Tmall Global, JD.com and Ali Health.

Blackmores sees the China market as an important part of its strategy to reach a billion consumers by 2025. Chief executive Alastair Symington says the company's exposure to China has allowed it to learn more about global consumer trends, given the size and speed of change of the China market. "Plugging into the China consumer market gives you a much bigger picture of global trends, which has much broader benefits than just exporting to China," he said in an interview for the ACRI report:

> Products being sold into the China market are being vetted by some of the most discerning consumers in the world. You can take those insights and learnings and apply them to other markets in Asia and even into Australia. We have 6 per cent of our population in Australia of Asian descent.

Blackmores is now designing new products aimed at the Chinese consumer rather than just selling products aimed at the Australian consumer. These include products for pregnant women and for children. Eye care is also a product of particular interest to the Chinese consumer. "Eye care is a very big category in China. It's relatively small in Australia. We are developing products to meet the needs of eye health for the Chinese consumer."

Blackmores' research into the Chinese market also includes the establishment of a China Innovation Centre in Shanghai, announced in February 2020, which is studying the needs of the modern Chinese parent.

Having learned from its experience in China, Blackmores is also taking the ecommerce approach to India, providing a less costly way of getting into the market and allowing it to test out which products work with local consumers before making a big investment. In his interview, Symington echoes the views of many others doing business with China:

> We always have to recognise that there are national security issues, but it shouldn't override our ability to trade with our neighbours. China is not going anywhere. It is going to be our biggest trading partner for a long time, and we have to find a way to make the relationship work.

## Bubs

Infant formula company Bubs has emerged as a major seller to China by meeting the concerns that Chinese parents have in securing high-quality baby food. Bubs' Taiwan-born chairman, Dennis Lin, summed up the importance of the China market to his company in an interview for the ACRI report:

> The Chinese market is simply too big to ignore. In China there are more than 12 million babies born every year. If you assume that babies use infant formula for three years, that's an addressable market of more than 36 million.

Bubs has responded to the potential trade issues in China by continuing to look for new markets overseas, particularly in the United States where it has been successful. It has also responded to changes in the Australian market by restructuring its distribution system to use more sophisticated intermediaries who are now emerging as part of the robust *daigou* trade linking Australia to China. These companies are set up with their own platforms to deal with individual *daigou* in the end markets and handle their orders for Bubs' products, whether they are in Australia or in China. "We consolidated the overall *daigou* trade so we knew exactly where our products were going," Lin explains. "The emerging intermediaries are sizeable businesses in their own right. Our key strategic partner spent close to $100 million making sure he had the relevant cross-border bonded warehouses and the underlying software."

Lin said the *daigou* sellers based in Australia and their links to small Chinese buyers continue to remain an important factor in selling Australian goods into China:

> You have to rely on resellers because, at the end of the day, they are still the biggest advocates and promoters of Australian products. The *daigou* trade is our distinct advantage – a trade which has initially come about because of our education system which in normal times attracts large numbers of overseas students. It is one of our biggest advantages, even compared with the US and the UK.

Lin argues that people doing business with China have to accept its form of government:

> You have to respect the form of government in any country you are operating in. China is run by the CCP [Chinese Communist Party] and that is not going to change. Accepting that, our goal is to ensure we can meet our corporate objectives being able to sell branded baby and toddler nutrition products to Chinese consumers within that environment. My goal is to make sure we provide the best-quality food and to make sure we have transparency across the supply chain.

### Macka's Australian Black Angus Beef

Robert Mackenzie is a fifth-generation beef farmer from northern New South Wales. He exemplifies the strong personal ties that buyers and sellers have developed amidst the long-standing trade between Australia and China. Mackenzie began visiting China in 2015, and started exporting his Angus beef to the country the following year. Since then, he made over 14 visits to China, before COVID-19 stopped travel, and has invited Chinese buyers to Australia to see his farms.

Mackenzie's business was hit sharply by Chinese bans on the meat-processing plants that he was using to sell into China. While he has since sought to diversify his exports to other countries, he still wants to resume the firm's thriving business it enjoyed with Chinese buyers before it was hit with trade sanctions.

"We are supplying products through the Middle East and other countries throughout Asia," he said in an interview for the ACRI report:

> Australian beef is very popular on the world stage. We have no problems selling the beef. I have been able to adapt into other markets relatively easily because of the quality of our product, but we value our Chinese relationships and the Chinese market very much. We are loyal to that market, and we want to move more product into that Chinese market. I have spent so much time and energy developing good, solid, strong relationships with amazing people in China – I don't want to lose that connection.

Mackenzie also used his exports to the China market as an incentive to improve his product, upgrading the traceability of his meat by linking up with a company called Aglive and using its blockchain-based labelling system for his beef exports. While the decision to invest in the Aglive technology was driven by his desire to sell into the China market, it was also a pioneering technology that he plans to use for exports to other countries.

Mackenzie describes the Australia–China trading relationship as a "perfect marriage" where both sides benefit and would like the opportunity to be involved in smoothing out trade tensions, particularly in his sector:

> As a family business and an exporter of fine Australian beef, I would like the opportunity to talk to the Chinese government and be able to say, "Hey, I am a supporter of Australia–China relations. Is it possible we discuss how it is affecting us and our clients? We understand there are some political tensions. Every perfect marriage has its ups and down and needs some counselling and some intervention. Is it possible for governments to put their differences aside and work with a company that has shown loyalty to Chinese customers and open up the market again?"

## Elders

Mark Allison, the chief executive of agribusiness company, Elders, has a long experience of dealing with China. He explains that geopolitical risk is something that exporters are always aware of but also know it is not something they can control. In an interview for the ACRI report, he described the political element in Australia's relationship with China as the base of a relationship triangle, with business and personal relationships making up the other two sides.

While the tariffs on Australian wine and barley have received significant attention, he said tariffs and trade disputes with different countries are a regular part of doing business globally. He cites the example of India, which imposed tariffs of 70 per cent on imports of Australian chickpeas in December 2017, in a move to protect Indian farmers, which he said received little media attention at the time. "It [the imposition of tariffs] crucified the investments Australian chickpea farmers were making to supply the growing Indian market. But we found other markets and adapted. In agriculture you tend to be able to do that pretty well."

Allison pointed out that agriculture is a global market that is constantly rebalancing. If one market is cut off, there are always other opportunities elsewhere. But he adds that the sheer size of the market in China means that it will always be attractive for Australian products. "You cannot ignore a market of 1.4 billion people in close proximity to where you live and where you have a competitive advantage."

## Fortescue Metals Group

As Australia's third-largest iron ore company, Fortescue Metals Group's (FMG) success in challenging mining giants Rio Tinto and BHP has relied heavily upon its long-term relationships with China. In an interview for the ACRI report, FMG chief executive Elizabeth Gaines talked of the importance of developing broader ties in China as a key lesson in doing business with the country:

> Recognising the important cultural considerations to doing business with China, Fortescue has built long-standing relationships that extend beyond the supply of iron ore. These

include procurement, financing arrangements, academic, policy and social linkages, as well as the highly successful direct investment in Fortescue by our second-largest shareholder, Hunan Valin Steel Group.

Gaines said the two Chinese non-executive directors on the FMG board "provide a source of valuable insights on issues affecting our engagement with China. All of these relationships have provided us with a deeper understanding of Chinese business and culture, undoubtedly a key success factor for Fortescue."

A key part of its strategy to strengthen relationships in China has been its support for the annual Boao Forum for Asia on Hainan Island off China's southern coast. Established in 2001 with the support of several influential regional leaders, including former Prime Minister Bob Hawke, the forum was set up as an Asian response to the annual gathering in Davos, Switzerland. Fortescue has sponsored the forum, which is addressed each year by senior Chinese leaders and has attracted diplomats and businesspeople around the world for the past 13 years. In 2021 it upgraded its commitment to the conference to the level of strategic partnership. Gaines says the forum "is an important element of our multifaceted approach to engaging with China and provides a unique opportunity to discuss issues relevant to our region, including long-term opportunities for Australia's resources industry."

Gaines explains why it is important for Australia to maintain a strong relationship with China. "The government and business sectors in Western Australia have worked together to build strong relationships with China. We need to encourage further understanding of the breadth and depth of this bilateral trade relationship to support the growth of our national economy." She adds:

It is a relationship that has been built on decades of engagement. West Australian businesses such as Fortescue have led the way in forging strong, long-term relationships with business and government in China, underpinning the success and longevity of this mutually beneficial partnership. It is critical that we continue to support a strong narrative around Australia's relationship with

China which reflects the experience of the resources sector and the Western Australian and Australian economies more broadly.

Gaines says Australia's trading relationship with China is "critical in providing economic stability and supporting jobs" and in securing FMG's future. Fortescue is expanding its focus from its initial reliance on iron ore to "green energy" with Gaines seeing China playing a key role in the strategy. She concludes:

> As Fortescue diversifies into a green renewables and resources company, we believe that building and maintaining strong trade relationships with key partners such as China will remain critically important. Collaboration will be key to achieving global emissions reduction goals, and this includes ongoing engagement with our customers in the crude steel manufacturing industry in China to learn about the challenges they face in decarbonising their operations.

## Conclusion

The preceding case studies show that, despite all the risks and the potential for ongoing political tensions, even with the improved relations under the Albanese government, the Australian business community is convinced that opportunities in the world's second-largest economy remain. My extensive discussions with these individuals show their sense of the continued opportunities of the China market as well as their appreciation for the nuances and challenges of doing business within this vast and complex country. This should not be a surprise. Individuals involved in global business are experienced in dealing with different regimes, and in assessing the challenges, risks and opportunities on a daily basis.

Going forward, political leaders should acknowledge that the China trade provides important ballast to the relationship, as well as significant financial benefits for Australia and Australians. Instead of cheap political point scoring, those seeking constructive ways to improve the Australia–China relationship should listen to the executives who have spent years engaging with Chinese counterparts, forging relationships, building on-the-ground personal connections, gaining a deeper understanding of China, and creating and seizing business opportunities across this rapidly changing, complex economy. Business leaders can offer real-world insights into China and can help sustain a mutually beneficial economic relationship between Australia and China.

Yet, just as the 1972 diplomatic normalisation opened the door to prosperous trading relationships, as the last few years have shown us, politics also has the potential to close the door on valuable business and trading opportunities. To sustain and expand these relationships and economic opportunities, the political doors must remain open. As Australia and China move into the sixth decade of their diplomatic relationship, political leaders should listen more closely to these voices.

## References

Department of Education (2023). International Student Numbers by Country, State and Territory. Australian Government. https://bit.ly/3QbHC7Z.

Frydenberg, Josh (2021). Building resilience and the return of strategic competition. Speech, Global Realities, Domestic Choices, Australian National University, 6 September. https://bit.ly/3Oy5fXp.

Korporaal, Glenda (2021). *Behind the headlines: why Australian companies are still doing business with China*. Sydney: Australia–China Relations Institute, University of Technology Sydney, 7 December. https://bit.ly/3O07OBl.

Molloy, Bob (2011). *Colossus Unsung*. Exlibris.

Qian, Xiao (2022). Strive to Bring China-Australia Comprehensive Strategic Partnership Back on the Right Track. Address by H.E. Xiao Qian, Chinese Ambassador to Australia as the National Press Club of Australia, 9 August. https://bit.ly/3QfBv2t.

.

# Part Three – Media, education and culture

## Introduction to Part Three

Australia's rich and diverse relations with China extend far beyond the political and economic interactions that tend to dominate news headlines. This third section explores three of the most consequential areas of Australia–China ties: coverage of China in Australian media; the politically sensitive realm of higher education; and the current and potential contributions offered by cultural diplomacy. While embarking from different areas of expertise, the authors share a common concern for how an atmosphere of deepening distrust and fear has spread across diverse realms of bilateral interactions.

Wanning Sun's chapter leads off this section by describing how Australian news coverage has tended to produce an image of China as Australia's national enemy. She argues that adversarial and insinuative journalism is on the rise, with marked similarities to Cold War journalism, particularly speculations about covert activities by Chinese nationals. Investigating the media's construction of a specific threat narrative, Sun outlines and provides examples of frequently used news framing strategies, including the recurrent use of negative key words and phrases in news articles, sensational headlines, audio-visual images used to create an eerie or foreboding atmosphere and putting words in the mouths of interviewees or citing them out of context.

Sun is particularly concerned with the deliberate and repeated citing of certain scholars and institutional spokespeople as sources, further pointing out how China watchers are often promoted to the status of China experts by the media, or the "experts" cited are from the fields of defence and intelligence, who in fact know little about China. Sun explores this media narrative through two case studies: the Australian media's coverage of COVID-19 in China, and the Australian television program "Power and influence", screened by the ABC in 2017. The Australian media has overwhelmingly framed COVID-19 in China in terms of disinformation, censorship and authoritarian control and, in 2020, Australia's tabloid media even engaged in the spread of conspiracy theories and racist tropes about Chinese people. Sun's chapter thus shows that the media has actively contributed to the worsening Australia–China relationship, creating a significant hurdle for engaging China.

Anthony Welch's chapter begins by setting the history of higher education relations within the broader context of Chinese immigration to Australia, and then describing how the various institutional frameworks that both Australia and China participate in provide both structures and resources to support research and educational cooperation. While noting the importance of bilateral research collaboration, Welch rightly focuses upon the massive student flows from China to Australia in recent years. He explains that "persistent underfunding" pushed Australian universities to seek overseas student fees, with Chinese students providing the bulk of international student income for most universities.

Even before the onset of COVID-19, the imposition of foreign interference legislation, enhanced scrutiny of university links with China and a deepening atmosphere of fear and mistrust heightened tensions around China and Chinese students on campuses across Australia. Travel limits imposed by both China and Australia during the pandemic sharply limited student enrolments, imposing considerable financial pain on Australian universities. With the arrival of the new Labor government in Australia and easing travel constraints in China, the prospects for at least a return to the pre-pandemic situation seem brighter. Still, Welch concludes, changing the febrile climate of polarisation and decoupling will take time and work. Governments and universities on both sides will need to adopt calm, considered approaches to restore a more stable foundation for educational and research collaboration going forward.

Providing the final chapter for this section, Ien Ang explores how cultural diplomacy can promote communication and build trust between Australia and China in times of rising geopolitical tensions. Focusing on causes for optimism, Ang provides examples of cultural diplomatic work taking place in Australia at various levels: in particular, in local institutions that have mobilised their cultural resources to engage Chinese immigrant communities. She begins by assessing both previous and current large-scale government-funded projects in Australia. Ang acknowledges the important efforts of institutions such as the Australia–China Council to enhance China literacy among Australians by fostering sustained people-to-people cultural cooperation in culture, education and the arts. Turning to its successor, the National Foundation for Australia–China Relations, Ang expresses some concern over its implementation to date. She describes the foundation's recent initiatives in the arts and education as excessively focused on loyalty concerns, aiming to bind Chinese immigrants more to the Australian nation.

Ang also analyses the impact of bilateral tensions upon Chinese diaspora communities in Australia, particularly the increase in anti-Chinese racism. Here she draws from public opinion surveys conducted by the Lowy Institute, which show a decline in Chinese immigrants' feelings of belonging in Australia and a growing gulf between Chinese Australians and the broader Australian population in their opinions on China-related issues. But Ang also points to modest, grassroots and small-scale initiatives that can help improve relations "from the ground up". Examples of local civic initiatives include increased efforts to include Mandarin speakers in public facilities in Sydney's Hurstville, and the showcasing of more Chinese artists in local galleries across Sydney. Ang concludes by stressing the potential for "softening" tensions through creative and sustained efforts of cultural diplomacy and mutually beneficial exchanges between Australia and China.

This section helps remind us that Australia–China relations are far more than simply fear and greed. The two countries share a long and proud history of social interactions, with Chinese immigrants in particular having made countless contributions to Australia's local communities, schools, universities, culture and society. Adopting a more nuanced approach to reporting on China, openly tackling financial and cultural challenges within the higher education sector and reinvesting in cultural diplomacy – as described in the following chapters – can contribute to restoring a more stable foundation for Australia's engagement with China.

# 8
# Cold War journalism, the China threat agenda, and the framing of Australia–China relations

*Wanning Sun*

In his analysis of Western representations of China's rise, Chengxin Pan defines the "China threat" as a "fundamental image that casts China's rise and its international implications primarily in a negative, alarming, and threatening light".[1] Even though Pan is an international relations scholar, he believes that the best place to trace the discursive formation of the China threat discourse is in the media, since this is where public perceptions and normative concerns are "nurtured and put on regular display".[2] Pan's point about the centrality of the media makes sense, since media institutions produce news, which, writes Michael Schudson in *The Power of News*, is a form of cultural narrative that "incorporates assumptions about what matters, what makes sense, what time and place in which we live and what range of considerations we should take seriously".[3]

Given that China has now been widely recognised as Australia's national enemy, several questions naturally arise for me, as an Australia-based media studies scholar. Most importantly: how does the Australian media produce knowledge about a country that is increasingly imagined as our national enemy; to what extent is the

---

1    Pan 2012, 23.
2    Pan 2012, 23.
3    Schudson 1995, 14.

media responsible for the current state of bilateral relations; and to what extent is the media capable of not only influencing public opinion but also shaping the actions and decisions of the government?

This chapter considers these questions by engaging with some key analytic concepts in critical media studies, in particular, Cold War–mindedness, agenda setting and news framing. It concerns itself with a few key issues in journalism such as news sources, the use of experts and the politics of voice. This discussion makes extensive use of two examples: the Australian media's coverage of COVID-19 in China; and an analysis of the 2017 television program "Power and influence".[4] The chapter asks about the role of the media in establishing "the truth" about the China threat: whose truth counts in the media's production of public knowledge about China, and what kind of truth is legitimated in China reporting.

## Cold War journalism 2.0

Over the last decade, the Australian media's reporting on China has become increasingly adversarial. Here, the term "adversarial" is not about being a "watchdog" over the government or being "the fourth estate" with a core mission of "keeping the bastards honest". Instead, it refers to a kind of reporting that takes as given that the foreign country being reported on is a hostile nation, and that therefore the accepted ways of reporting on it are adversarial in a predetermined way. This adversarial perspective not only dictates what kinds of stories readers should hear and read about China, but it also dictates how these stories are told. In the field of journalism studies, this kind of adversarial journalism is often associated with the Cold War era or, in a contemporary context, with reporting on terrorist states and organisations. The implicit assumption is that China is a hostile nation,

---

4   ABC Television 2017; updated 1 January 2021. This program has now been removed from the ABC's website, and, since early 2021, has been replaced with the following advice: "This program is temporarily unavailable for legal reasons". The video can still be viewed, as of mid-August 2022, via Facebook (https://fb.watch/eX-zm0aSf0/).

and, operating with such an assumption, the ritual of reporting, which usually requires an attempt at balance and the provision of evidence, is no longer necessary.

Central to this form of reporting is what media scholars call a "Cold War–mindedness," a concept that offers a way of making sense of enmity between two hostile nations. Writing about the US media's coverage of the militant group Islamic State in the 1990s, US-based media scholar Barbie Zelizer suggests that Cold War–mindedness did not stop in 1989. Instead, it "went underground, surfacing over time as an available interpretative frame for multiple crises in search of meaning".[5] Surveying the literature on Cold World journalism, we can discern a predictable pattern. Generally speaking, Cold War news assumes the "unseen dimensions"[6] of a war, even though it is an invisible or an imaginary one; adopts a particular view of geopolitical reality that relies on accepting certain strategic notions of enemy formation; reinforces certain understandings of who is "us" (the free world) and who is "them" (for example, the authoritarian, the terrorist, the communist nation); and reports the tension and conflict – the "imaginary war" – by portraying the enemy using discursive strategies such as "stereotypy, black-and-white thinking, polarisation, simplification, and demonization".[7] Similarly, scholarship on British propaganda during the Cold War uncovers instances of government manipulation and "occasional strong-arming", but also observes that, in most cases, consensus about how to report on the enemy (for example, the Soviet Union and its communist allies) was a result of a gradual, negotiated revision of the media's commonsense view of the world. John Jenks, for instance, considers this process of building consensus as a process whereby journalists, publishers, producers, politicians and government officials become sometimes predictable and at other times strange bedfellows.[8]

In the current context, this shift to a Cold War journalistic style of reporting on China has resulted in the blurring of the boundary between

---

5    Zelizer 2016, 6064.
6    Zelizer 2016, 6077.
7    Zelizer 2016, 6062.
8    Jenks 2006.

fact and opinion, between evidence and hunch. Perhaps the most spectacular example of this type of journalism is "Power and influence", an "agenda-setting" *Four Corners* television program on Chinese influence screened by the Australian Broadcasting Corporation (ABC) in 2017.[9] The program can be seen as a defining moment in the Australian media's construction of the China threat narrative. A joint *Four Corners* and Fairfax/Nine Entertainment investigation by Fairfax's Nick McKenzie and the ABC's Chris Uhlmann, the program purports to reveal how the Chinese Communist Party (CCP) is infiltrating Australia. The program highlighted the problem of political donations in Australian politics – an issue worthy of an exposé in its own right. But the program also made a range of claims against Chinese-Australian citizens and Chinese nationals that were not convincingly substantiated. In the absence of evidence, the program establishes "the truth" about Chinese influence through generous use of suspicions about possible links, insinuations about possible crimes and speculations about covert activities. For instance, on the political influence of Sheri Yan, described in the program as "a socialite with connections to senior levels of government, here and abroad", McKenzie asks China scholar John Fitzgerald, "Did you think she might be a Chinese intelligence operative of some sort?" Fitzgerald replies, "I understand that Sheri Yan is very closely connected with some of the most powerful and influential families and networks in China. Once you know that, you don't need to know much more." In another example, the Australian National University security scholar Rory Medcalf, in response to McKenzie's question about Chinese-Australian philanthropist Dr Chau Chak Wing, said, "We have to assume that individuals like that have really deep, serious connections to the Chinese Communist Party". While it was the prerogative of the individual interviewees to make statements as they saw fit, it fell to the journalist to press for clarification and substantiation. Yet statements such as these were presented as self-evident, as if they warranted no further investigation or discussion.

Some media stories have gone beyond what I have called "insinuative journalism",[10] and have now ventured into the territory of

---

9    Chubb 2022.
10   Sun and Yu 2019.

guesswork. An example of this comes from ABC Radio's *Background Briefing* program, with a special episode on China's influence in Australia, broadcast in October 2019. Attempting to offer some speculation regarding the culprit behind the November 2018 cyber attack on the Australian National University, the reporter Mario Christodoulou says:

> The VC [vice-chancellor of the university] doesn't know who was behind the attack. And it's important to note that we don't either … The resources required to pull it off suggests a nation state is responsible. And in that narrow field, China is at the top of the list.[11]

This is a speech act aiming at declaring rather than proving.

The 2017 episode of *Four Corners* resulted in two defamation cases against the ABC, and since then, the media have taken to the free use of disclaimers. Journalists have realised that to accuse someone of being a spy or a foreign agent without proof may land them in legal trouble. So, some reporters now add qualifications such as, "This paper is not suggesting …" But they then go on to say things like, "Questions are being asked about Person X's relationship with China …" or "Concerns have been raised …" Apparently, then, insinuation, with or without disclaimers, often works. Stories might be written so as to implicate someone because they're in the same photo as a Chinese diplomat, or because they attended the same conference as a visiting government official from China. "Connected", "linked", "associated" are the operative words in these media stories.

## Sources, experts and voices in agenda-setting

Cold War–mindedness is one thing but to promote and perpetuate such perspectives requires consistent work on the part of the media, especially news and current affairs. While five decades of research on agenda-setting in news and journalism has engendered a voluminous

---

11   Christodoulou 2019.

body of work exemplifying different focuses, approaches and methodologies, the core idea of this research remains the same: news media coverage influences the public's perception of the importance of issues, both by what it includes and by what it excludes. As Bernard Cohen famously said in his book *The press and foreign policy*, the media "may not be successful much of the time in telling people what to think, but it is stunningly successful in telling its readers what to think about".[12] Since McCombs and Shaw's seminal study of the presidential election in the United States first advanced the theory of agenda-setting and the media,[13] recent scholarship has continued to reiterate its core concern: that the elements that are relevant in the media agenda – such as issues, public figures and descriptions of these issues and figures – will also become relevant elements in the public agenda.[14]

The role of the media in setting the agenda for public debate is certainly borne out in the case of the Australian media's coverage of China and its construction of the China threat narrative. In recent years, for a wide variety of reasons, the Australian media across the board have been much more invested in setting a specific agenda in their reporting on China. For an example of a media outlet that adopts such an agenda, we need to look no further than the *Sydney Morning Herald*, which, in one of its promotional billboard slogans in 2019, said the following: "China's growing influence: If Beijing's ambition affects Australia's future, you deserve to know". In exposing Beijing's ambitions, the *Herald* promised to "shine a light on hidden influences," using "hard news to expose soft power".[15] And in order to achieve this, the newspaper proclaimed that "we do whatever it takes to break the stories." In fact, the *Sydney Morning Herald*'s news agenda on China was so consistently critical that former Labor politician Gareth Evans considered them to be "indistinguishable" from the Murdoch-owned News Corp empire.[16]

---

12  Cohen 1963.
13  McCombs and Shaw 1972.
14  McCombs and Valenzuela 2021.
15  *Sydney Morning Herald* n.d.
16  Evans 2020.

One noticeable change as a result of adopting such a media agenda in China reporting has been the growing reliance on certain sources: individuals and institutional spokespeople who, for myriad reasons, see it as beneficial to consistently toe the "China threat" line. This leads to what Peter Manning has called "access journalism",[17] a kind of reporting in which the journalist unwittingly plays the role of mouthpiece for some individual, government agency or other body to which she or he appears to have "exclusive access". According to Manning, access journalism has a number of features. For instance, its sources usually cannot be named; there is often no evidence base (such as a document or money trail); it lacks transparency, in that any evidence cited cannot be independently verified; it usually serves the agenda of the government or some other entity; and it uses phrases in the text that have little clarity or definition (for example, "is linked to").

What we see now is the curious coexistence of "watchdog" and "guard dog"[18] models of journalism. In reporting on purely domestic politics, the watchdog is alive and alert. It takes on the prime minister, the ministers and powerful institutions. But when it comes to investigating the domestic politics of our China policy, this watchdog has been missing in action. Operating on a guard dog model instead, for some years now the media have been on standby through most of the 2010s to report on gratuitous remarks about China from the Coalition government's backbenchers; to quote security and intelligence agencies who issue yet another warning about the China threat; and to give space to security analysts in universities and think tanks whose new reports always seem to raise "fresh concerns" about China.

The business community – particularly in the beef, wine, barley, seafood and other export sectors – also stands to suffer from the deteriorating relationship between Australia and China. Yet, although trade with China is a significant factor in ensuring Australia's prosperity and the nation's standard of living, criticisms of the China threat narratives from the business sector have been mostly muted. Few dare to speak up, not wanting to be accused of putting economic interests above national security. Peter Hartcher, a senior political reporter at

---

17  Manning 2018.
18  Donohue, Tichenor and Olien 1995.

the *Sydney Morning Herald*, has described some spokespeople from the Australian business sector who express concern over the Australian government's China policy as "craven characters" who privilege money over Australia's sovereignty.[19]

Like climate change, understanding China requires specialised knowledge. China is mostly beyond the expertise of the public, so journalists seek the views of China experts. But China experts have different ideological positions and come from different disciplines, and nobody from the China studies community can speak on behalf of all. But, too often, the media doesn't reflect this internal difference. The public gets the impression that the chosen expert is speaking as an uncontested authority. Too often, the same scholar is interviewed repeatedly – not necessarily because they're the most qualified person, but because they're willing to talk, and are likely to deliver the expected line that suits the media's agenda on China reporting.

But who are the experts? The word "expert" is used a lot in China threat stories, but China *scholars* and China *watchers* are quite different species. China watchers tend to be current or former journalists. Many of them may know little about China, but they are often supremely confident and articulate. After a stint of reporting from China, they might claim to have found the "truth about China", or to have divined the real intentions of the Chinese Communist Party or the inner thoughts of Xi Jinping. They present themselves as reasonable, cosmopolitan and knowledgeable, and so members of the public, who know even less about China, see no reason to doubt their words. A worrying tendency in China reporting is that these China watchers are often promoted to the status of experts. One China critic is now described in his own newspaper as the "global expert tracking the rise of China". As one Chinese-Australian writer jokingly observes, "If you hurl a brick randomly, you can be sure to hit at least one or two China experts".

Equally worryingly, these China watchers, as well as run-of-the-mill journalists reporting on the China threat, themselves need to cite experts, but many favour experts from the fields of defence, intelligence and security, who know little about China. It is indeed ironic that, while the media accuses the security and intelligence establishment of infringing

---

19   Hartcher 2020.

on the media's freedom in relation to certain issues in other contexts, when it comes to China the same establishment is the media's best friend, and the latter's reporting largely reproduces a security and intelligence perspective, with little, if any, interrogation of that perspective.

While the majority of people in the Chinese-Australian communities feel unfairly scrutinised and judged by the media, their voices are very seldom included in mainstream China threat media stories. In fact, the only voices from these communities that the media deem to be legitimate are those of dissidents. Many community members feel that, regardless of one's focus, one must say outright that they are critical of China's policy on Xinjiang and Hong Kong. Unless they do that, they are not likely to be seen as credible. To be sure, giving voice to critics of the Chinese government and calling out China on human rights issues is important, especially given that these voices are not allowed in China. But the Australian media seem to forget that, between these dissidents and those who work for the Chinese government, there is a silent majority whose political views come in 50 shades of grey, even within the Mandarin-speaking community. And not everyone wants to be a card-carrying dissident.

The Australian mainstream media typically does not trust Chinese community organisations or their leaders, and suspects some of them of being linked to the United Front. Nor do many of these media trust WeChat, the most popular social media platform among Mandarin-speaking Chinese Australians, as a source of genuine community sentiment, since its Chinese version, Weixin, and to a lesser extent WeChat itself, is subject to censorship from China. Many Chinese Australians feel they have no legitimate platforms on which to speak, let alone talk back. A constant refrain in WeChat discussions among Chinese Australians is that "we have no voice". As for international students from China, the media mostly portrays them as a hot-headed, angry mob, or as possible spies for the Chinese embassy. Neither are China-born China scholars trusted. A couple of years ago, a security researcher in Melbourne wrote that Australian universities should only hire homegrown political scientists working on China, rather than hiring people educated in China.[20]

---

20    Graham 2019.

While the term "fifth column" is mostly directed at Chinese Australians, language bullets such as "Communist Party agents" are often freely fired at any non-Chinese commentators and scholars who hold a complex position, and who dare to argue for critical engagement with China. While the media amplifies the fear of a China threat, it seldom acknowledges the fear of those Chinese Australians who are subjected to witch-hunts. The media tell us that people both here and in China dare not speak up for fear of persecution by the Chinese Communist Party, but they don't mention the fact Chinese Australians are now increasingly practising self-censorship out of fear of being labelled Beijing apologists. Such a politics of fear is familiar to people who lived through either the Cold War or the Cultural Revolution.

It is perhaps beyond the scope of this discussion to outline in detail why the media seems to need to adopt such an agenda in relation to China. Suffice it to say that there is a multifactorial and complex constellation of reasons, including the priorities of the government in power, the ongoing dynamics of Australia's domestic politics, our economic dependence on China, increasing levels of Chinese immigration and investment in Australia in recent decades, as well as the unstoppable trend towards digitalisation in the technological domain. In addition, the agenda is also shaped by the nature of journalism as a profession and the financial challenges facing media organisations – both of which have become more uncertain and precarious due to the arrival of digital platforms and social media. Furthermore, also at play are the personal ambitions of individual media professionals and the challenges they face in seeking to achieve certain KPIs, justify their employment, receive a promotion or even to win a Walkley Award. These factors impose myriad institutional and individual constraints on the production of media content. These constraints include shrinking budgets and fewer resources, the relentless rhythm of the daily news cycle, the pressure of deadlines and the imperative to produce sensational sound bites and visuals. And this is made more challenging by the most glaring existential geopolitical reality currently facing Australia" namely, that, as John Lyons writes, "our biggest customer is also viewed as our biggest threat".[21]

---

21   Lyons 2022.

## Framing China

Apart from asking about how the media sets the agenda for public debate, we can also critically examine how China-related media stories are framed. In critical media studies, analysing the framing of a media story is important if we want to "draw attention to details of just how a communicative text exerts its power".[22] Frames enable journalists to process large amounts of information quickly and routinely: to recognise it as information, to assign it to their cognitive categories, and to package it for efficient relay to their audiences.[23] As Entman puts it:

> to frame is to select some aspects of a perceived reality and make them more salient in a communicating text, in such a way as to promote a particular problem definition, causal interpretation, moral evaluation and/or treatment recommendation for the item described.[24]

In the context of the Australian media's framing of China-related issues, we can see that a journalist's choice of issues, sources and language determines what we see and how we see it, and what continues to be unseen or ignored. In this sense, framing can be achieved by using certain words, phrases, pictures and emphasis, or simply by omission. Through a range of framing devices, the Australian media contributes to public debate about China not only by presenting the aspects of China it thinks we should talk about, but also by shaping how these aspects will be discussed. To push the China threat agenda means consistently framing China-related issues by emphasising certain elements of any given issue above others, thereby defining "the problem", diagnosing its causes, making moral judgements and even suggesting remedies – all according to an institutional agenda of reporting on China. Therefore, to examine and identify the China threat discourse, we need to look for: the presence or absence of certain keywords; stock phrases; stereotyped

---

22 Entman 1993.
23 Gitlin 1980.
24 Entman 1993, 52 (italics in the original).

images; sources of information; and sentences that provide thematically reinforcing clusters of facts or judgements.

The first of these framing strategies is the use of words or phrases that carry certain connotations. The second is the choice of labels to define a figure, an event or a situation. Both devices are amply illustrated in how the Australian media interpreted a particular statement from the Chinese government. When Labor won the 2022 Australian election, and after the first meeting between the new Labor Foreign Minister, Penny Wong, and her Chinese counterpart, the Chinese ministry issued a carefully crafted statement containing four vaguely worded points that could be taken as either advice, or as principles that both sides should adhere to. Seasoned Australian diplomats experienced in dealing with China considered the statement to be positive and conciliatory[25] but it was interpreted by many in the Australian media as problematic and concerning. The key to this interpretation was the choice of the word "demand" to frame the four points raised in the statement. For example, an ABC story asserted: "Mr Wang has made four general *demands* [emphasis added] of the new government"[26] – without any justification for its use of the word "demands". From then on, "demand" became the most frequently used word in the Australian media to describe the four points. The use of this word over other possible options – for example, "proposed principles" or "suggestions" – led the media angle to congeal around more or less one familiar pre-existing theme: China is again lecturing us and is trying to dictate the terms and conditions of the bilateral relationship.

The third framing strategy, and perhaps the most important of all the framing devices I discuss here, is the deliberate choice of sources and experts who are known to espouse certain angles and perspectives in relation to China, and the omission of others. Journalists who resort to exclusive access to certain sources mostly serve the agenda of only one side of any debate. As discussed in the last section, "access journalism" is a favoured strategy for journalists who claim to have an exceptionally close relationship with security establishments, hawkish politicians, and think tanks that advocate decoupling from China.

---

25   Chey 2022.
26   Birtles 2022.

Discussing the transformation of the Chinese influence narrative in Australia into a matter of national security, and drawing on published comments from both the journalist Chris Uhlmann and ASIO's chief Duncan Lewis, Andrew Chubb believes that the national security bureaucracy was working in a "coalition with the media".[27] He points out that prominent journalists such as Uhlmann were "highly receptive to securitising moves from officials. Once convinced of the threat, they became active securitizers, driving threat perceptions downward and outward to mass audiences."[28] We see many instances in which the two parties indeed work in tandem. Sometimes, this can take the form of being tipped off by security and intelligence. For instance, Hamish McDonald mused sarcastically about Melbourne-based reporter Nick McKenzie, who "just happened to be outside [NSW state Labor MP Shaoquett] Moselmane's home at 6.30am along with a crew from Nine's *60 Minutes* as the raid occurred".[29]

The fourth device is the use of sensational and often misleading headlines. In 2017 I wrote an article for the *Australian Financial Review* about the danger of the Australian media's sensational narrative about China's soft power in creating fear and anxiety about various Chinese communities, but the editor's headline read, "China's soft power alive and well in Australia".[30] Some China scholars have been horrified to find that editors have given their articles a misleading or more sensational title.

The fifth device is to put words into the mouth of an interviewee. This can be demonstrated by a barrage of media stories about how the new Labor Prime Minister responded to China's so-called "demands" (see above). In response to a journalist's question about China's "demands", a number of media outlets – both the *Guardian* on the left and the Murdoch press on the right – reported Prime Minister Anthony Albanese as saying: "Australia does not respond to demands".[31] Regardless of whether Albanese believed that the four points actually

---

27  Chubb 2022, 13.
28  Chubb 2022, 12.
29  McDonald 2020.
30  Sun 2017.
31  Shepherd 2022; Ransley 2022.

*were* demands, his response became a new development in the "demand" narrative. He was effectively "verballed" by a journalist.

The sixth strategy, and perhaps the most egregious, is to quote interviewees out of context. A devastating example of this involved Ms Lupin Lu, the president of the Chinese Students and Scholars Association at Canberra University, who was interviewed in the 2017 *Four Corners* program discussed earlier. The transcript of the episode shows the following exchange between the journalist and Lu:

> NICK MCKENZIE: Students organising anti-communist party protests may be reported to the Chinese Embassy.
> LUPIN LU: I guess as the president of Chinese Students Scholars Association and as a Chinese, I would do this for the safety of other members, other students.
> NICK MCKENZIE: You would tell the embassy that some students were organising a human rights protest, for instance?
> LUPIN LU: Yes. I would definitely, just to keep all the students safe and to do it for China as well.[32]

In a defamation suit against the ABC, Ms Lu alleged that the ABC had "lured" her into doing an interview, claiming that her words were edited "out of context ... to give the misleading impression" that she was acting on behalf of the Chinese government to "infiltrate the Australian political process", and arguing that the episode was "recklessly indifferent to the truth".[33] Ms Lu's defamation action was settled by the ABC in a confidential agreement, but the ABC refused to issue a public apology, as she had requested.

The seventh framing strategy – and perhaps the one that is deployed most often – is sometimes referred to as "cherry-picking". Journalists or editors select and amplify facts or evidence that supports a particular view, but leave out inconvenient or contradictory information. Geoff Raby, a former ambassador to China and one of the people who appeared in the 2017 *Four Corners* program, lamented that there was no attempt at balance on the part of the journalists who made

---

32   ABC Television 2017, at 23 minutes from start.
33   Cornwall 2019.

the episode. He was interviewed for 50 minutes for the program, but only two minutes of this went to air, whereas "those who had tales of dark webs being spun in Australia by the Chinese Communist Party" were given plenty of airtime. He suspected that the journalists had begun with their conclusions and "worked back to find those comments that would best fit their preconceived story". This led him to argue that "the views of an informed observer, providing context and a degree of balance, were left on the ABC's cutting-room floor".[34]

Finally, an examination of framing can never ignore the numerous ways in which images work together with the spoken or written word to encourage certain kinds of interpretation. For example, as this episode of *Four Corners* shows, if no hard evidence or testimony can be presented to establish "the truth", suspicion of clandestine activities can be raised by visually and acoustically creating an eerie atmosphere suggesting secrecy, using ominous music, dark silhouettes and a cinematic mise-en-scène more befitting a John le Carré novel set in the Cold War era than a serious documentary.

A few things can be said about this list of framing devices. First, this is not an exhaustive list, and has not included many other devices, such as the position in which the story is placed (for example, whether it is a leading story on the front page or buried on an inside page), what kind of images are used to illustrate the story (for example, is it a cartoon demonising a Chinese official?), the choice of photos (does it suggest the Chinese government's aggressiveness?), and what captions accompany the images. Second, framing devices of all stripes can work either separately or in tandem. Third, in order to understand the power of framing on the production of the discursive message, analysing these devices is only half the job; the other half is to outline what has been omitted or downplayed. Crafted with the aid of these devices, the portrayal of China as the bogeyman has become a stock narrative. Fourth, these devices may sometimes be applied deliberately, but most often they are adopted unthinkingly or unwittingly, without malice. Fifth, successful framing relies on a close alignment of the efforts of media proprietors, executive producers, editors and journalists in setting the media agenda.

---

34    Raby 2017.

*China, COVID-19 and the Australian media: a case study*

How the Australian media covered the COVID-19 crisis unfolding in China in the initial few months provides a valuable prism through which to explore the role of the Australian media in constructing public knowledge about China. In particular, has the media's coverage of China throughout the crisis been a continuation of the China threat discourse or a departure from it? Motivated by this question, I conducted a critical discourse analysis of major news stories, documentaries, opinion and analysis published in Australia's most influential media outlets between 1 January and 31 March 2020.[35] I used three criteria to determine the suitability of items for analysis. They had to be: key media programs that are widely considered to be authoritative and trustworthy; media stories written by journalists who enjoy the highest level of professional recognition in the field of journalism; or media narratives that elicit the strongest responses from China, the Chinese-Australian community and the English-speaking public in Australia. So, rather than conducting a quantitative content analysis to gauge the accuracy of reporting, I sought to identify the key themes, perspectives and angles in these reports to understand the likely role that opinion leaders, high-impact media programs, news stories and journalistic practices played in shaping public opinion of China and its handling of COVID-19.

True to its reputation as the most trustworthy mainstream broadcaster in Australia, the ABC has played a crucial role in keeping the country informed during the pandemic. But, while it has largely reported on COVID-19 as a health crisis, the ABC's news and current affairs coverage of COVID-19 in China has been framed as a political story. The privileging of this political framework is evidenced in several episodes of *Four Corners*, as well as the ABC's panel discussion program, *Q+A*, and its flagship radio current affairs programs, *AM* and *PM*. The *Four Corners* episode on 24 February 2020, for instance, projected the impression of draconian authoritarian measures, and repeatedly returned to the question of the Wuhan local government's tardy response to the initial outbreak. Related to this constant refrain linking the outbreak of

---

35   Sun 2021.

COVID-19 to political control was the fate of whistleblower Dr Li Wenliang, within the narrative framework of censorship.

These programs' claims of Chinese government censorship of Dr Li, their criticisms of local authorities' failure to inform the public and their denunciation of the severe measures taken by the police and Wuhan's local government followed a well-established narrative framework of reporting on China. China's coercive measures aimed at controlling people's movements, portrayed in terms of heavy-handed policing and infringements of individuals' civil liberties and human rights, were all reported in light of China's political system – the implication being that such practices would not be adopted in a liberal democracy. There seemed to be an implicit assumption that there is "bad authoritarianism", which is readily practised by undemocratic states such as China, and there is "necessary authoritarianism", which is reluctantly adopted by liberal democracies in order to contain and suppress the virus for the greater good of the community and society. While Australia's media seemed to assume the difference between these two kinds of authoritarianism in order to justify the equally heavy-handed approach adopted in Australia, there was little attempt to discursively disaggregate the authoritarian measures China invoked to combat COVID-19, and the authoritarian practices for which China is routinely criticised in the Australian media.

My study found that, while the overall coverage was unfavourable across the board, there was a clear "division of labour" between different media sectors.[36] For instance, the more "respectable" end of the commercial press, such as the *Sydney Morning Herald*, focused its reporting on Chinese Australians' two-way efforts in sourcing masks and medical supplies. The *Herald*'s most controversial story about China and COVID-19 was written by Kate McClymont, who, tipped off by a "whistleblower", wrote:

as the coronavirus took hold in Wuhan earlier this year, staff from the Chinese government-backed global property giant Greenland Group were instructed to put their normal work on hold and

---

36   Sun 2021, 35.

source bulk supplies of essential medical items to ship back to China.[37]

Although the news story refrained from sensationalism and was essentially based on stating "the facts", it enraged many Chinese immigrants, who saw this as a perfectly legal "humanitarian effort" consisting of donations from companies and individuals in Australia.

What seems to be at issue here is not so much the story's factual accuracy; rather, it is that a perfectly legal action by a Chinese company and several individuals was deemed newsworthy since it seemed to cohere with the pre-existing China influence narrative framework. The use of the term "whistleblower" carries the connotation that this was misconduct at best, illegal at worst, even though those involved broke no laws. This report was offensive to many within Australia's Chinese communities, because to them, it implied not only that China's behaviour was predatory, but also that the loyalties of the Chinese diaspora were misplaced. For members of the Chinese-Australian community, who pride themselves on being able to love both their motherland and Australia and on being willing to help both whenever they can, to have their loyalty questioned in this way was deeply hurtful.

The politics of face masks continued to play out as the pandemic unfolded. As COVID-19 became a serious concern in Australia in early March 2020, and as supplies of masks and other personal protective equipment (PPE) became plentiful in China, the Chinese community members in Australia wanted to do their bit, this time by importing masks and medical equipment from China. Ironically, although they acted out of a love for both homeland and adopted country in both cases, they soon realised that neither of their "good deeds" was taken at face value by the mainstream English-language media. A week after McClymont's story, the *Herald's* key contributor to the Chinese influence narrative, Nick McKenzie, wrote a "sequel" about the efforts of some members of the Chinese community to source medical supplies for Australia in China, accusing them of peddling the Chinese government's agenda.[38] Both McClymont's and McKenzie's stories

---

37   McClymont 2020.
38   McKenzie 2020.

continued the *Herald*'s China influence narrative by framing Chinese Australians as objects of suspicion whose loyalty to Australia was questionable.

While the ABC framed COVID-19 in China in terms of disinformation, censorship and authoritarian control, and commercial papers such as the *Sydney Morning Herald* sang from much the same song sheet but with a distinct interest in pushing its China influence discourse, Australia's tabloid and shock-jock media dealt in straightforward racism-tinged sensationalism. This strategy, clearly aimed at attracting viewers and growing subscriptions, adopted two main tropes. The first was that of the conspiracy theory: that COVID-19 was a deliberate Chinese Communist Party plot. The second trope involved racist jokes and headlines at the expense of Chinese people, portraying them as Orientals, alien and repugnant people who ate bats. The tabloid press and shock-jock radio consistently fanned anti-Chinese hatred, often seeming to invoke old fears of the "yellow peril" and anxiety about "reds under the beds". The most significant finding of my research on this topic was a conflation of political authoritarianism with normal public health measures – a key feature of the ABC's reporting of China and COVID-19. My analysis suggests that the coverage of China's experience has been a continuation and embodiment of the "China threat" and "Chinese influence" discourses.

To sum up, this analysis suggests that the Australian media's reporting on China's COVID-19 experience during the initial months of the pandemic says more about Australia's own fears and anxieties and the media's political, ideological and cultural positions than about the reality of how the Chinese government managed, and the Chinese people experienced, COVID-19. It also makes it clear that, while Australia's media may give the impression that there is only one story to tell about China and COVID-19, and that there is only one way of telling that story, in reality the frames, perspectives and discursive positions the media adopts are cultural rather than natural, ideologically influenced and profit-driven rather than objective or balanced. The virus may know no boundaries, but virus-related reporting is profoundly bound up with politics, history and the cultural identity of a nation.

This kind of adversarial reporting also embodies a form of "internal othering", a discursive disenfranchisement of Chinese-speaking communities in Australia. While the media tends to focus on human rights violations that are happening in China, the human and citizen's rights of Chinese Australians are downplayed. By imagining them mostly in the role of agents of the Chinese government, or by casting doubt on their political allegiances, the media often reduce them to individuals without any cultural, emotional, or cognitive conflicts and ambivalence. The logic is clear: you are either with us oragainst us.

## Power without responsibility

The China threat discourse is often justified as being in the public interest and the national interest, but the notion of who "the public" is, and questions about what constitutes the national interest, are contested. The media seldom asks politicians and security experts questions about who stands to benefit from the China threat discourse and who stands to suffer from it. For instance, discourses of foreign influence have proved to have had a devastating impact on Australian citizens of Chinese origin, especially those from mainland China. This negative impact manifests itself in at least two ways. First, even though these Chinese Australians are Australian citizens, their bodies carry their foreignness with them. Repeated media stories casting aspersions on them and hinting at links they may have with the Chinese government as potential agents of interference and influence in Australian politics, media and foreign policy have led to people in this community to become objects of distrust, suspicion and sometimes racist violence; their loyalty to Australia has been openly questioned. This is indeed bad news for social cohesion.

Second, and equally worrying, is the possibility that media discourses of China's influence have pushed many ethnic Chinese to identify more forcefully with China and pro-China nationalism. Despite the real negative impact such Cold War journalism may have on Chinese Australians, the economy and social cohesion, there is a real lack of recognition in the media that along with the power of the media comes the responsibility to report in the public interest, adhere to professional codes of conduct, abide by journalistic ethics and the law, listen to the voices of the public and ultimately to demonstrate a professional commitment to being held accountable to the public. Sadly, much too often, such a willingness to take responsibility is missing. For instance, "Where," asks David Brophy, "are the investigations into Australian decision-making on China, or the role of American pressure behind the scenes?"[39] he continues: "Nor has there been any accountability when China-related stories come unstuck", citing the much-hyped spy story about Wang Liqiang as an example.[40]

Of the two defamation suits arising from the 2017 *Four Corners* episode, the ABC and Fairfax lost one case[41] and settled in the other.[42] The litigant in the case I discussed earlier, the Chinese student Lupin Lu, said she was happy with the settlement, but she was bound by a non-disclosure clause.[43] But neither of these legal cases has reduced the negative impact the program had on Chinese Australians, and till today, this episode is widely credited with the introduction of Australia's foreign interference legislation. Neither the ABC nor Fairfax has issued any retractions or corrections, let alone apologies to the allegedly defamed individuals. The episode has cast a long and dark shadow over the Chinese-Australian communities ever since, and the reputational damage to the individuals involved could be irreparable.

## Conclusion

It would be a mistake to assume that the China threat discourse only started when Xi Jinping assumed the role of paramount leader in China. It is worth remembering that Chengxin Pan's book, which analyses the discourse of China as opportunity and threat in the Western imagination, was published in 2012.[44] In the same year, a

---

39   Brophy 2021, 226.
40   Brophy 2021, 226.
41   McKinnell 2021.
42   Cornwall 2019.
43   Cornwall 2019.
44   Pan 2012.

study[45] of all episodes of the ABC's *Foreign Correspondent* and SBS's *Dateline* during the period 2005–2008 suggests that the concept of threat was circulating not only in reports about Chinese politics but also in coverage of China's economic growth. Moreover, both Lachlan Strahan's book[46] about Australia's perceptions of China, and Colin Mackerras's book, *Western images of China*,[47] had already identified *threat* as a trope that circulated in the history of the West's imagination of China. Mackerras discusses the ways in which Westerners, from the earliest times until the late 1980s, had perceived China – both the China of their own time and the China of the past. Examining a wide range of sources, including literature, journalism and the arts, Mackerras outlines how changing power relations have influenced Western ideas about China, its people and its history, canvassing an enormous variety of Western images of China over the centuries. For instance, at certain times China has constituted a model for schools of thought in the West, while at others the country has been viewed as a threat.

As this discussion shows, the Australian media plays a crucially important role in shaping public knowledge and opinion about China. The media has not merely reported on the worsening of the Australia–China relationship; it has actively contributed to it, and is partly responsible for the emergence of a new Cold War perspective in Australian public discourses. The "fears and phobias"[48] of the previous Coalition government and the security and intelligence establishment in relation to China have been one factor, but establishing this threat and creating a "China panic"[49] in the public imagination requires what Curran calls "Cold Warriors"[50] in the media to collaborate actively. Andrew Chubb pinpoints mid-2017, when the ABC's "Power and influence" went to air, as the turning point in the China threat narrative, and explains the timing as follows:

45   Li 2012.
46   Strahan 1996.
47   Mackerras 1989.
48   Curran 2021.
49   Brophy 2021.
50   Curran 2021.

The People's Republic of China's ( PRC) efforts to influence politics abroad had been well documented since the 2000s and cannot explain the timing of their securitization from mid-2017. It was through the formation of a securitizing coalition of intelligence officials, politicians, and journalists that the PRC as a source of existential threats gained policy traction. But as the coalition expanded from security agencies to politicians and the media, the scope of the threat expanded from an initial concern with PRC party-state activity to the securitization of a much wider array of state and non-state activities under the ambiguous label "Chinese influence".[51]

In the absence of systematic and rigorous audience studies, it is nevertheless safe to speculate, judging by the results of numerous surveys, that the exponential increase in the sheer quantity of China threat reporting has led to a more hostile perception of China and the Chinese in Australian public opinion. For instance, the Lowy Institute's annual poll published in 2021 found that 63 per cent of Australians saw China as a threat, up from 41 per cent in the previous year, and 12 per cent in 2018.[52]

Erik Jensen, the founding editor of the *Saturday Paper*, commented on the inability of the media industry to take criticism on board. Journalism, he says, "might be the only industry in the world where being told you were wrong is taken as proof that you're right".[53] Jensen's PEN Lecture mentioned racism and Islamophobia, but did not mention China-phobia, so the question remains: if the media needs to be accountable and reflect on itself and its practices, should this accountability extend to its coverage of China? In other words, does reporting on an "enemy state" excuse the media from accountability? This chapter is premised on the assumption that China coverage should not be exempted from accountability, and the media, because of its power, should behave like a watchdog rather than guard dog in its

51   Chubb 2022.
52   Power 2021.
53   Jensen 2019.

China reporting. Only then can there be the possibility of genuine engagement between the two countries.

In a 2021 Lowy poll, when asked to assess the Australian media's reporting on China, as many as 61 per cent of respondents said it was "fair and balanced", 26 per cent said it was "too negative" and 10 per cent said it was "too positive".[54] These overwhelming statistics could mean one of two things: either that the Australian media's selective reporting on China has had a significant impact on public perceptions of China, and that the public's trust in the media as fair and balanced is thus misplaced; or that the Australian public form their perceptions of China independently of media coverage, and that the majority of the public just happen to think along the same lines as media practitioners. This discussion has provided evidence to suggest that the former is the more likely scenario. Through a discussion of the media's agenda-setting power and its employment of a series of framing strategies, the analysis in this chapter ultimately drives home the fact that the media works by giving the impression that its news stories are natural and logical rather than ideologically predetermined, so readers come to believe that this is the only story worth telling, and that there's only one way of framing it.

If anything, this discussion points to the enduring power of the media as a form of storytelling. Journalists may believe that their work is pivotal in the pursuit of "the truth" and critical in the fight against a nasty regime. But in many cases, instead of the journalist writing the story, the story is waiting to write itself. Every day, journalists face new events, situations and issues, and, while the details may change from day to day, the frameworks for making sense of these events, situations and issues remain mostly the same. For this reason, this analysis has pointed to a somewhat pessimistic view about the media's capacity for positive change. To be sure, the new Labor government ushered in in May 2022 has presented fresh opportunities for the media to "lift its game" but the onus seems to rest on the government to develop an effective strategy for living with the media, so that its "new approach to

---

54   Lowy Institute Poll 2022.

rising China"[55] does not end up being Hijacked, derailed or jeopardised by the Cold War warriors in the media.

## References

Birtles, Bill (2022). China's Foreign Minister blames Morrison government for poor relations, tells Penny Wong to 'treat us as a partner, not a threat' *ABC News*, 11 July. https://ab.co/3I2Zk8V.

Brophy, David (2021). *China panic: Australia's alternative to paranoia and pandering*. Melbourne: La Trobe University Press.

Chey, Jocelyn (2022). When words matter: reviewing the Wong–Wang meeting. *Pearls and Irritations*, 13 July. https://bit.ly/45kgusT.

Christodoulou, Mario (2019). Are Australians aiding China's surveillance state? *ABC: Background Briefing*, 13 October. https://ab.co/3qd89Hs.

Chubb, Andrew (2022). The securitization of "Chinese influence" in Australia, *Journal of Contemporary China*. https://doi.org/10.1080/10670564.2022.2052437.

Cornwall, Deborah (2019). ABC quietly settled Chinese student's defamation case *Australian*, March. https://bit.ly/44Ph9lz.

Cohen, Bernard C. (1963). *The press and foreign policy*. Princeton, NJ: Princeton University Press.

Curran, James (2021). Cold warriors brew China fears and phobias. *Australian Financial Review*, 18 July. https://bit.ly/3VXCFAv.

Donohue, George, Phillip J. Tichenor and Clarice N. Olien (1995). A guard dog perspective on the role of media *Journalism of Communication* 45(2): 115–32. https://bit.ly/42OcNJO.

Entman, Robert M. (1993). Framing: toward clarification of a fractured paradigm. *Journal of Communication* 43(4): 51–5. https://doi.org/10.1111/j.1460-2466.1993.tb01304.x.

Evans, Gareth (2020). Pressing the pause button on Sinophobia. *Pearls and Irritations*, 19 June. https://bit.ly/3Kozqh5.

Gitlin, Todd (1980). *The whole world is watching: mass media in the making and unmaking of the New Left*. Berkeley: University of California Press.

Graham, Ewan (2019). Australia has too few home-grown experts on the Chinese Communist Party. That's a problem. *Conversation*, 13 August. https://bit.ly/3BgWh9c.

---

55   Robertson 2022.

Hartcher, Peter (2020). The money or our sovereignty: China leaves us no choice. *Sydney Morning Herald*, 1 May. https://bit.ly/3Kg0E9G.

Jensen, Erik (2019). PEN Lecture: Fragile minds. *Wheeler Centre*, 17 July. https://bit.ly/3pznrpv.

Jenks, John (2006). *British propaganda and news media in the Cold War*. Edinburgh: Edinburgh University Press.

Li, Xiufang (Leah) (2012). Images of China: a comparative framing analysis of Australian current affairs programming. *Intercultural Communication Studies* 21(1): 173–88. https://bit.ly/3q3cf55.

Lowy Institute Poll (2022). Australian media reporting about China. https://bit.ly/44Mevgb.

Lyons, John (2022). Will Australia support the US in a war between Taiwan and China? Ask the military chiefs, not our political leaders. *ABC News*, 15 August. https://ab.co/44Q7LhF.

Mackerras, Colin (1989). *Western images of China*. Oxford: Oxford University Press.

Manning, Peter (2018). How "access journalism" is threatening investigative journalism. *Conversation*, 21 December. https://bit.ly/3nX2KmP.

McClymont, Kate (2020). Chinese-backed company's mission to source Australian medical supplies. *Sydney Morning Herald*, 26 March. https://bit.ly/3OwLTSk.

McCombs, Maxwell E. and Donald L. Shaw (1972). The agenda-setting function of mass media. *Public Opinion Quarterly* 36(2): 176–87. https://dx.doi.org/10.1086/267990.

McCombs, Maxwell E. and Sebastián Valenzuela (2021). *Setting the agenda. Mass media and public opinion*. Cambridge, UK: Polity Press.

McDonald, Hamish (2020). Media in the Asian century. *Pearls and Irritations*, 3 July. https://bit.ly/44QuhHb.

McKenzie, Nick (2020). Former Chinese military man behind export of tonnes of medical supplies. *The Sydney Morning Herald*, 31 March. https://bit.ly/3QfotlU.

McKenzie, Nick and Chris Uhlmann (2017). Power and influence. *ABC News Four Corners*, season 56, episode 17, 5 June; updated 2 February 2021. https://ab.co/3M0LapY.

McKinnell, Jamie (2021). Businessman Chau Chak Wing awarded $590,000 in defamation case against ABC. *ABC News*, 2 February. https://ab.co/3I3AG7Y.

Pan, Chengxin (2012). *Knowledge, desire and power in global politics: Western representation of China's rise*. Cheltenham, UK: Edward Edgar Publishing.

Power, John (2021). Australians' trust in China has fallen to record lows, according to new survey. *This Week in Asia*, June 23. https://bit.ly/3Q9GaTK.

Raby, Geoff (2017). Where have all the grown-ups gone on China policy? *Australian Financial Review*, 20 June. https://bit.ly/3WbvBkd.

Ransley, Ellen (2022). Australia 'won't respond' to China's demands, says Anthony Albanese. *News.com.au* 11 July. https://bit.ly/44Iggeg.

Robertson, James (2022). Penny Wong promised a new approach to rising China. Did she deliver? *New Daily*, 26 May. https://bit.ly/3BfgLzr.

Schudson, Michael (1995). *The power of news*. Cambridge, MA: Harvard University Press.

Shepherd, Tory (2022). Australia 'doesn't respond to demands', Anthony Albanese tells China. *Guardian* (Australian edn), 11 July. https://bit.ly/44Iggeg.

Strahan, Lachlan (1996). *Australia's China: changing perceptions from the 1930s to the 1990s*. New York: Cambridge University Press.

Sun, Wanning (2017). Chinese soft power is alive and well in Australia. *Australian Financial Review*, 8 June. https://bit.ly/44PSldl.

Sun, Wanning (2021). The virus of fear and anxiety: China, COVID-19, and the Australian media. *Global Media and China* 6(1): 24–39. https://bit.ly/3O1DoPe.

Sun, Wanning and Haiqing Yu (2019). WeChat, the federal election, and the danger of insinuative journalism. *Pearls and Irritations*, 1 February. https://bit.ly/3nRMZxo.

*Sydney Morning Herald* n.d. Advertisement. Accessed 17 August 2022. https://bit.ly/3O40AfQ.

Zelizer, Barbie (2016). Journalism's deep memory: Cold War mindedness and coverage of Islamic State. *International Journal of Communication* 10: 6060–89. https://bit.ly/3O0DE0S.

# 9

# China–Australia higher education relations: promise unfulfilled?

*Anthony Welch*

Notwithstanding the tendentious claim by President Hu Jintao that famed Ming dynasty Admiral Zheng He [1371–c.1434] had visited Australia during his regional voyages of the early 15th century, there is a long history of Chinese engagement with northern Australia, largely based on trade and seafaring.[1] In his speech to the Australian parliament, President Hu argued, somewhat expansively:

> For centuries, the Chinese sailed across vast seas and settled down in what was called "the southern land", or today's Australia. They brought Chinese culture here and lived harmoniously with the local people, contributing their proud share to Australia's economy, society and thriving pluralistic society.[2]

Some have estimated that by 1859, Chinese settlers formed almost 20 per cent of the male population.[3]

But, while relations between China and Australia have a relatively long genealogy, a strategic vision has often been lacking.[4] In addition to

---

1   Wang 2021.
2   Kendall 2007.
3   Sherington 1990.
4   Fitzsimmons 2023.

more than a century of "historical, cultural and racial baggage in terms of its relations with Asia and China in particular",[5] economic relations have dominated, often to the exclusion of other dimensions. Higher education relations between the two countries are of much more recent vintage – and are currently under significant strain.[6]

## Chinese immigration to Australia

Despite the proportion of Chinese settlers in the colonial era, tensions between Australia's development as a series of British colonies and its location as the only English-speaking settlement of any size in the South Pacific sustained a prevailing racism, supported by contemporary social Darwinism, that postulated a hierarchy of races with white British culture securely placed at the apex.[7] Against this background, including White perceptions of competition for gold and jobs, it was no surprise that – as in North America – racist outbursts and riots, and policies of exclusion and expulsion commonly targeted Chinese labourers.[8] Non-Caucasians should, it was commonly felt, be non-permanent, ineligible to intermarry and restricted to relatively menial occupations. As a result, many Chinese returned home, and China-born settlers declined in number from 38,142 in 1861 to 6,404 in 1947.[9] By then, the proportion of the population that were either non-Caucasian or Indigenous was a mere 0.25 per cent (one in 400): "Australia had become one of the whitest countries in the world, outside north-western Europe".[10] There is little evidence of much school attendance by Chinese, or of higher education participation, during this period. Yet, as Megalogenis' analysis of the impact of immigration argues, Australian racism and xenophobia was broad but not deep. Non-discriminatory immigration has been in place since the mid-1960s.[11]

---

5    Curran 2022.
6    Welch 2022a.
7    Jupp 2002, 7; Welch 1996, 29–30; Welch 2018.
8    Jupp 2001; Lew Williams 2018; Luo 2021.
9    Hugo 2005, 20.
10   Jupp 2002, 9.
11   Megalogenis 2015; Welch 2022b.

## Higher education: China and Australia

Unsurprisingly, Australia's first models of universities, dating from the mid-19th century, as well as most academic staff and educational philosophies, came from the United Kingdom.[12] The beginnings of higher learning in China could hardly have been more different, consisting of a millennia-long tradition of higher learning and related institutions, notably the Confucian model that was widely influential in the region.[13] The first modern Chinese universities date from the dying days of the sclerotic Qing dynasty in the late 19th century.[14] Despite these differences, the emphasis on self-cultivation and fundamental moral qualities underpinning Confucian education were not altogether different to those animating Newman's *The Idea of a University*.[15]

One of Australia's first three diplomatic missions separate from the United Kingdom, established in China in 1941, included links to universities in Kunming, Chengdu and Chongqing.[16] Despite the cessation of diplomatic relations by the Liberal Country Party government in 1949, academic relations continued, via figures such as the well-known Sinologist C.P. (Patrick) Fitzgerald, the highly regarded Wang Gungwu from 1968, Kam Louie and M.A.K. (Michael) Halliday. But the Cold War era resulted in China's exclusion from regional academic mobility schemes such as the Colombo Plan, in part established as a bulwark against communism.[17] Few Western students studied in China at the time, and of the 280 foreign students listed at Beida (Peking University) in 1968, none was from Australia.[18] In this period, China studies at Australian universities often flew under the flag of "Area Studies", and the subject was at times thought to be useful for defence and security purposes. But wider concerns about China's place and role in the world, social change, ethnic minorities and the

---

12  Pietsch 2010, 2013; Sherington 2019; Welch 2021c; Welch 2022c.
13  Hartnett 2011.
14  Hayhoe 2017.
15  Marginson 2014.
16  Holenbergh 2005.
17  Oakman 2004; Organisation for Economic Co-operation and Development 2007.
18  Wong 1996; Holenbergh 2005, 56.

Chinese diaspora were also evident. As Australia's first Ambassador to the People's Republic of China posed in a challenging diplomatic cable in 1976: "Was the aim of a substantive political relationship with China just 'too hard?'"[19]

## Bilateral higher education relations

International relations in higher education take many forms, including framework agreements, academic exchanges, staff and student mobility, joint teaching programs and research collaboration. Considerable benefits to both sides can accrue to such exchanges, as acknowledged by the Asia-Pacific Economic Cooperation (APEC) Vladivostok declaration:

> Facilitating the flow of students, researchers and education providers ... provides opportunities for a significant expansion of cross-border education services to the benefit of all economies ... Increasing cross-border student flows will strengthen regional ties, build people-to-people exchanges, and promote economic development through knowledge and skills transfer.[20]

Several events have helped shape bilateral exchanges, including the evolution of framework agreements underpinning staff and student mobility. The end of the Cold War era made it easier for China to participate in regional academic mobility schemes such as the recent New Colombo Plan (2014), and University Mobility in Asia and the Pacific (UMAP) (1991), although (unlike Vietnam) not in the original Colombo Plan (1950). Of the two newer schemes, the New Colombo Plan initially encompassed a mere four destinations, including Hong Kong. Open to all undergraduates aged 18–28, the scheme currently supports around 10,000 students engaged in study programs and internships, in numerous regional higher education systems, including

---

19   Curran 2022.
20   Australian Council for Educational Research 2015; see also Asia-Pacific Economic Cooperation 2012.

both mainland China and Hong Kong. A much smaller number are offered scholarships.[21]

UMAP embraces 23 Asian and Pacific nations and more than 600 institutional members, who are expected to waive tuition fees for UMAP semester exchange students, and to grant credits towards the student's home institution degree for study undertaken while on exchange.[22] But the range of universities on both sides is rather limited. It includes a mere four mainland Chinese higher education institutions to have signed UMAP's Pledge of Agreement (Nottingham Ningbo, Xi'an Jiaotong-Liverpool, Sias and Zhengzhou Business universities), as well as a single Australian university (Curtin). Major research universities on both sides appear conspicuously absent.

By contrast, of the Universitas 21 consortium's 28 member universities across Asia, the two Australian institutions (University of New South Wales and University of Sydney) and three Chinese universities (University of Hong Kong, Fudan and Shanghai Jiao Tong) are all leading research-intensive institutions. Its Global Citizens program that allows 75 spaces per member higher education institution, is designed to link students from different systems to work together on major world problems as contained in the United Nations sustainable development goals.[23]

The Association of Pacific Rim Universities network of research universities lists 15 leading Chinese higher education institutions, including three from Hong Kong, and six from Australia, all from the Group of Eight (Go8) category of research-intensive universities. Other than student competitions and interactive workshops, it also offers virtual courses and certificate programs on key issues such as global health, crisis management, disaster risk reduction, e-sports, sustainability and climate change. Its early career researchers network links researchers from the region to each other, and to more experienced researchers, with the aim to introduce them to potential collaborators.[24]

---

21   Department of Foreign Affairs and Trade n.d.
22   University Mobility in Asia and the Pacific n.d.
23   Universitas 21 n.d.
24   Association of Pacific Rim Universities n.d.

The Worldwide Universities Network of 25 universities includes as members major higher education institutions in China (Renmin and Zhejiang) and Australia (Sydney and Western Australia), and with support from the United Nations, World Bank, Organisation for Economic Co-operation and Development (OECD), and World Health Organization focuses on four major global themes: climate change; public health; higher education and research; and understanding cultures. It has supported numerous research projects including some that touch on higher education internationalisation and mobility.[25]

Referencing pre-COVID-19 worldwide projections that 7.2 million students would be studying internationally by 2025, and that 1 million from APEC economies were already doing so, APEC set a goal of having 1 million studying within APEC. At the time, the fact that Australia was among the top two student destinations for APEC students, and China by far the largest source country, made such targets appear reasonable.[26] China was one of several APEC economies where more than 10 per cent of the tertiary-educated population had emigrated.[27] Researcher mobility, including shared use of research facilities, research funding and joint research publications, was also listed as being on the rise, and again, despite the absence of detailed data, both China and Australia were highlighted as growing destinations.[28]

## Bilateral student flows

The evolution of student flows between China and Australia has been shaped by a mix of history, politics and economics. The Cold War bounded student mobility: rather than the West, international students from China tended to study in the then Union of Soviet Socialist Republics (USSR), or satellite systems in Eastern Europe, although the ideological split from the USSR in the 1950s complicated relations

---

25  Worldwide Universities Network n.d.; Welch and Li 2021.
26  Australian Council for Educational Research 2014.
27  Australian Council for Educational Research 2015.
28  Australian Council for Educational Research 2014.

including international student (and staff) mobility.[29] The Cultural Revolution marked a much more hermetic era, with dire consequences for bilateral staff and student mobility, and knowledge exchange. Only with Reform and Opening, from 1978, did the outward flow of Chinese students resume. The so-called "Gang of Nine" Chinese students, who took masters' degrees in literature and linguistics at the University of Sydney from 1979, subsequently returning to China and both spreading the Systemic Functional model of linguistics throughout China and founding numerous Australian Studies Centres, were a bright example.[30] Until recent decades, international enrolments in China were relatively minor, and only the most determined Australian students were registered. But as part of the 2010 National Plan for Medium- and Long-Term Education Reform and Development, and the Study in China initiative, international student enrolments mushroomed, reaching a peak of 500,000 prior to COVID-19, albeit with a relatively small number of Australians registered in degree programs.[31]

The China–Australia Free Trade Agreement (ChAFTA), which came into force in December 2015, included provisions governing trade in the services sector, including higher education. This is important given that China's service sector now contributes more to its economy than manufacturing, while China is Australia's largest services export market, contributing $15.8 billion in 2017, or 18.7 per cent of Australia's total services exports.[32] Export of education services alone contributed $10 billion in 2017, and ChAFTA's extensive "most favoured nation" treatment provisions committed China to extend to Australia more beneficial treatment than it provided to other trade partners in a range of areas, including education. China moved to list an additional 68 private higher education institutions to the original 105 registered with the Commonwealth Register of Institutions and Courses for Overseas Students (CRICOS) on the Ministry of Education website, and memoranda of understanding were signed to boost mutual recognition

---

29   Lan and Kraus n.d.; Huang and Kim 2022.
30   Li 2021.
31   Qi 2021.
32   Department of Foreign Affairs and Trade n.d.

of higher educational qualifications, and enhance staff and student mobility.

To this date, no foreign branch campuses have been established in either country. In China, joint ventures fall under the umbrella of Sino-Foreign Cooperation in Running Schools (SFCRS).[33] Despite 25 Australian universities being reportedly rejected for a licence to operate in China in 2011, Monash University, one of the country's most international, secured a licence in 2012, and has since established a joint graduate school with Southeast University in Suzhou's Dushu Lake Education Innovation Park, in Jiangsu province. Teaching in English, and awarding joint masters' degrees, the enrolment grew to over 200, with an ultimate target of around 1,400.[34] The graduate school also featured a joint research institute established to conduct multidisciplinary research projects, in areas of strategic importance such as nanotechnology, bioinformatics, water, energy, and light metals.[35]

But a key plank of the Australian international student platform had already been set in the mid-1980s, when two government commissioned reports came to opposite conclusions regarding the small but growing international education sector. At the time, combined international enrolments at universities and colleges of advanced education (CAEs) totalled no more than 10,500. Beginning from the view that "the overseas student program has brought a great many political, economic, educational and other benefits to Australia, particularly in the context of our relations with the countries of the Asian and Pacific region", the Goldring Report rejected a user-pays basis for international education.[36] By contrast, the Jackson Report argued "Education should be regarded as an export industry" and thus the full cost of programs should ultimately be borne by international students (except for a select number of scholarship students).[37]

33  Ministry of Education 2003; Department of Education, Science and Employment n.d.
34  Monash University 2014.
35  Southeast University n.d.
36  Committee of Review of Private Overseas Student Policy 1984; Goodman 2008.
37  Committee to Review the Australian Overseas Aid Program 1984.

Ultimately, an interdepartmental committee, established to assess the two conflicting assessments, concluded in favour of a market approach – which has been widely seen and critiqued since – as a hallmark of the Australian system.[38] With the benefit of hindsight, the latter report's critique of a lack of entrepreneurial zeal in developing education as an export industry now seems somewhat quaint.

## Financial dimensions

That decision definitively shaped the export of educational services ever since. Successive ministers of education endlessly trumpet the billions in income generated by the "industry", while doing little to tackle the long-standing underfunding of higher education. Unlike other OECD peers, Australia experienced a decline in higher education funding in per-student terms from 1996 to 2004. Funding remains lower than the OECD average. The decade from 2010 showed a lift in government funding of 140 per cent overall, but a decline in per-student support in the Commonwealth Grants Scheme, a major component of overall government funding.[39] Total government higher education spending as a proportion of gross domestic product in 2015 (0.77 per cent), compared poorly to the OECD average (0.98 per cent).[40] OECD data showed that, by 2016, private expenditure on higher education in Australia had increased to 62.2 per cent of the total, almost twice the OECD average of 32 per cent.[41]

Such persistent underfunding drove universities to more than make up for any lack of entrepreneurial zeal in recruiting international students, who became the main source of revenue to substitute for declining per-student funding, and to sustain operations. The international education sector became Australia's fourth largest

---

38    Altbach and Welch 2010.
39    S&P Global 2021.
40    Terry and Jackson 2020.
41    McGowan 2018; Organisation for Economic Co-operation and Development 2019; Terry and Jackson 2020.

Table 9.1 International student enrolments, Australia, higher education, 2002–2021.

| | 2002 | 2011 | 2019 | 2021 | 2002–2019 increase (%) |
|---|---|---|---|---|---|
| Higher education | 124,992 | 241,440 | 442,219 | 363,859 | 354 |
| English-language programs (ELICOS) | 58,435 | 94,853 | 156,880 | 41,314 | 268 |
| Non-award | 23,518 | 27,568 | 48,217 | 13,392 | 204 |
| Total | 206,945 | 363,861 | 647,316 | 408,565 | 313 |

Note: Some universities maintain their own English-language training facility; others use outside organisations. Source: Department of Education, Skills and Employment 2019b, 2022.

"industry", contributing more than $40 billion to the Australian economy in 2019 and supporting 250,000 jobs.[42]

The entrepreneurial approach yielded dramatic results, with sharp increases in international student enrolments evident over ensuing decades, at least until the travel restrictions of 2020, introduced in response to the COVID-19 pandemic.

Table 9.1 charts the dramatic growth in international student enrolments from 2002 to 2019, and the subsequent decline, in response to COVID-19 and border closures. By international standards, Australia's student cohort remains highly internationalised, with around one student in four of total enrolments being international. In several universities, the ratio is much higher. A key element underpinning this dramatic growth was the prominence of mainland Chinese students, who comprised around 40 per cent of all international enrolments. As the Chinese middle class expanded, many more families could afford the substantial expenses entailed in financing overseas study for their child.[43] In turn, revenues expanded

---

42   Hurley and Van Dyke 2020; Varghese 2018; Zhou 2021a.

dramatically: some universities earned as much as $850 million per annum, or almost one-third of their budget, from international student fees, pre-COVID-19. But from 2020, commencements and enrolments of Chinese students fell steeply.

Table 9.2 Australia, commencements and enrolments, Chinese students, 2019–2022.

|  | Enrolments | Commencements |
|---|---|---|
| 2019 | 191,986 | 56,422 |
| 2020 | 176,396 | 39,406 |
| 2021 | 162,039 | 39,025 |
| 2022 | 132,997 | 28,354 |

Source: Welch 2022a.

The impact of COVID-19 on international enrolments was uneven: more prestigious Go8 institutions were able to parlay their reputation into a greater capacity to retain enrolments, especially among the reputation-sensitive Chinese students.[44] A 2022 audit of universities in New South Wales, the most populous state, revealed the extent of the ongoing dependence on China: of the 10 universities, seven featured China as the largest source of international student fees in 2021, with the proportion ranging from 24 per cent (Wollongong) to 86 per cent (Sydney, which earned $1.18 billion in international student income in 2021).[45] Of the five leading source countries comprising overall international enrolments in 2021, the proportion from China, at 30 per cent, was almost as large as the next four countries combined.[46] The state-wide New South Wales audit of university income in 2022

---

43    Goodman 2008.
44    Baker 2022.
45    Auditor General (New South Wales) 2022.
46    Department of Education, Science and Employment 2022.

found that, while overall international enrolments had fallen by 12.5 per cent from pre-pandemic levels, enrolments from China continued to increase in both 2020 and 2021.[47] The majority were studying online. Chinese students comprised more than half of all international enrolments at New South Wales public universities in 2021. Interestingly, the effects of COVID-19 and border closures were diverse. The analysis by the New South Wales auditor general showed that both the University of Sydney and University of New South Wales gained thousands of new Chinese enrolments, while other universities, including in other states, fared less well. For each university, Chinese student fees comprised the bulk of their total international student income.

Regrettably, and paralleling similar bilateral arrangements with countries in the region, Australian universities have been far less successful at inducing their own students to enrol in Chinese higher education institutions, especially in degree-level programs, or for other than short-term, or intensive language programs.[48] A 2020 survey revealed that China was the most favoured destination for Australian students abroad, largely in the form of a for-credit experience. Some 2,292 undergraduate students were enrolled in China in 2019, more than for any other country, and comprised 15 per cent of the total number of Australian students abroad. A mere 8 per cent were enrolled in semester-length exchange programs, while 51 per cent spent a total of two to four weeks in China.[49] As an example, at the University of Sydney, which enrolled some 16,000 Chinese students (before COVID-19), there were 19 students who completed a Semester Exchange program in China in 2019, of which one was enrolled for a full year. Travel restrictions imposed by each jurisdiction from 2020, in response to the pandemic, dramatically reduced bilateral student mobility. While no overall Ministry of Education data has been released, anecdotal evidence from a range of Chinese higher education institutions indicate that international enrolments were around 10 per cent of pre-COVID-19 numbers in 2022.

---

47   Auditor General (New South Wales) 2022.
48   Welch 2014.
49   Australian Universities International Directors' Forum 2020.

## Bilateral research collaboration

Worldwide, international research collaboration is fast becoming the norm.[50] A landmark Royal Society report of 2011 showed that, worldwide, publications with authors from at least two countries had doubled since 1990, rising from 26 per cent of the total in 1996 to 36 per cent in 2008.[51] In Australia, the trend was even stronger, having risen from less than 30 per cent in 1996 to 45 per cent in 2014, with China as a major knowledge partner.[52] Such internationally collaborative papers are cited more often than those from a single system, as are those by researchers at highly internationalised institutions.[53]

At 44.5 per cent, Australia's rate of international researchers was also comparatively high and, of these, a substantial proportion were Chinese.[54] China's striking scientific rise was sustained by a major boost to its research and development (R&D) investment, with spending growing by 20 per cent per year from 1999.[55] This underpinned a dramatic rise in Chinese publications, with an annual growth rate of 18 per cent over the period 1996–2007, and a doubling of Chinese publications as a proportion of worldwide output between 1999–2003 and 2004–2008, although a somewhat slower rise in internationally collaborative papers.[56] The widely-used Scopus database of research publications is overwhelmingly in English. When including non-Scopus publications, Chinese share of worldwide physics, engineering and mathematics publications account for 36 per cent of the total, or around twice the standard Scopus measure. It also equates

---

50  Adams 2013; Australian Council for Educational Research 2015; Marginson 2021.
51  Royal Society 2011; Smith et al. 2014.
52  Department of Industry, Innovation, Research and Tertiary Education 2012; Australian Council for Educational Research 2015.
53  Adams 2013.
54  Australian Council for Educational Research 2015; Franzoni et al. 2012; Yang and Welch 2010; Chief Scientist 2013; Varghese 2018; Marginson 2021.
55  Royal Society 2011; Xie and Freeman 2019; Yang 2022.
56  Royal Society 2011; Australian Council for Educational Research 2015; Marginson 2021.

to a comparable share of global citations, and more and more highly-cited papers.[57]

This made China an increasingly attractive option as a knowledge partner to Australian researchers: by 2018, a sixth of all Australian scientific publications involved a China-affiliated researcher. For both China and Australia, the other was the third-leading knowledge partner.[58] Collaboration was strongest in disciplines such as engineering, chemistry, computer science and mathematics and included a boost in leading research outputs: of the top 1 per cent of Australian publications, those including a China-affiliated researcher increased by 13 per cent in 2018 (whereas co-publications with other key international partner countries declined).[59] Overall, joint publications involving China and Australia rose from 11,722 in 2017 to 20,773 in 2021, a far larger rise in percentage terms than co-publications with researchers in the United States (from 16,581 to 23,224 over the same period).[60] For a range of reasons – in part to do with the embeddedness of social sciences "Wen Ke" (文科) in their cultural and linguistic contexts – international collaboration in the social sciences with China, by Australian (and other nations') researchers, is more complex, less prominent and less common.[61] This is despite formal changes to the Chinese constitution in 2017, to include the building of a community with a shared future for mankind (人类命运共同体). Troublingly, overall Australian Research Council Discovery Project grant applications declined steeply over the years 2020–2022, from 79 to 24, a reflection of the increasingly febrile anti-China sentiment of recent years.[62]

---

57  Xie and Freeman 2019.
58  Department of Education, Science and Employment 2019c.
59  Laurenceson and Zhou 2020; Welch 2014, 2021b, c; Chief Scientist 2013; Rapid Research Information Forum 2020; Department of Education, Science and Employment 2019a, b, c.
60  Watt 2022.
61  Marginson 2021; Xie 2022.
62  Watt 2022; Raby 2020; Laurenceson 2021; see also contributions by Raby; O'Conner, Cooper and Cox; and FitzGerald in this volume.

## Proportion of joint publications with China

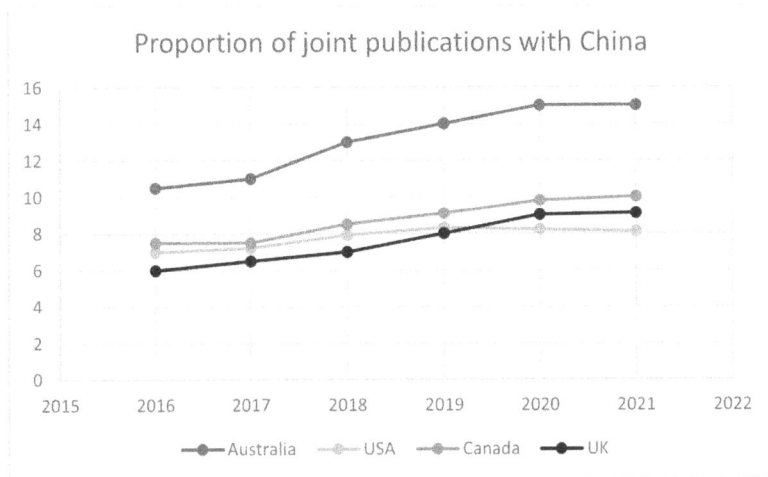

Figure 9.1 Proportion of joint publications with China, 2016–2021. Source: Watt 2022.

Notwithstanding the limits to collaboration in the social sciences and humanities, the overall importance of bilateral research collaboration and people-to-people contacts was evidently widely appreciated – the results of a 2021 poll revealed around 75 per cent of those surveyed believed "It is beneficial for Australia to work with China on global issues" and that Chinese international students "help strengthen the people-to-people links between the two countries".[63] High-skilled returnees from Australia, generically known in China as *haigui* (sea turtles), often managed to secure good, well-paid jobs in China, and contribute to domestic innovation, although anecdotal evidence suggests the return on investment may be waning somewhat in the face of increasing numbers of returnees, and rising competition from leading domestic universities.[64]

---

63   Collinson and Burke 2021, 4.
64   Welch and Hao 2015; Hao and Welch, 2012; Hao, Wen and Welch 2016.

## The Chinese knowledge diaspora

For both sides, a further advantage consists of the substantial Chinese knowledge diaspora that has been built up in the Australian research system. Over recent decades, growing numbers of mainland Chinese peopled universities and research establishments, often after first taking their doctoral degrees (PhDs) in Australia. Such highly-skilled individuals, and a broader immigration strategy that favoured the highly skilled, contributed to an OECD finding that, among member states, Australia enjoyed the highest net brain gain.[65]

Such bicultural and bilingual individuals, well connected to Chinese universities and research organisations, and with ongoing interests in boosting bilateral ties, form an important bridge between the two research systems, and are a significant source of innovation at both ends of the bridge.[66] Paralleling the proportion in the overall Australian population, scholars from Asia now constitute around 15 per cent of all academic staff, of which the mainland Chinese contingent is much the largest.[67] China-born academics employed at Australian universities increased in number from 613 to 1,733 over the decade 2005–2015.[68] Of this international contingent, more than three-quarters (76.1 per cent) had collaborated with scholars from an Asian country, and two-thirds (66.3 per cent) had worked on joint research projects. More than a third (34.6 per cent) had helped to develop exchange programs with their originating countries.

---

65 Organisation for Economic Co-operation and Development 2007.
66 Welch and Zhang 2008; Yang and Welch 2012; Welch and Hao 2015; Welch and Yang 2012.
67 Oishi 2017; Welch 2021c.
68 Oishi 2017.

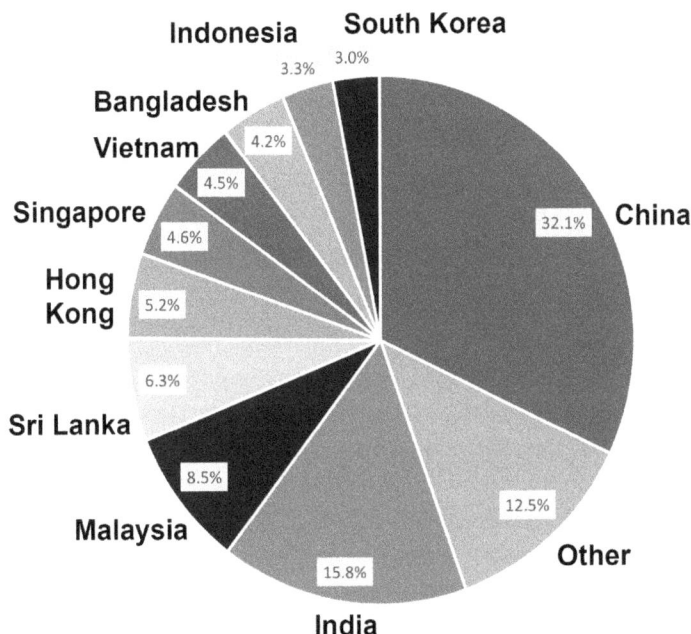

**Indonesia** **South Korea**
3.3% 3.0%

**Bangladesh**
**Vietnam** 4.2%
4.5%

**Singapore** 32.1% **China**
4.6%

**Hong**
**Kong** 5.2%

6.3%

**Sri Lanka**

8.5%

12.5%

**Malaysia**
**Other**
15.8%

**India**

Figure 9.2 Asia-born academics in Australian universities, by place of birth, 2015.
Source: Department of Education and Training data 2016, cited in Oishi 2017, 16.
Note: Hong Kong is separate in the above; if included, it would further boost the
Chinese contribution.

At the same time, interviews conducted with numerous mainland
Chinese scholars in Australian universities highlighted several limits to
bolstering bilateral engagement. At times, efforts to establish relations
with a university in China, while met with apparent initial enthusiasm,
lapsed through lack of subsequent follow-through on the Chinese side.
A second issue was a perceived lack of recognition. Several interviewees
reported that, while their disciplinary expertise was valued, the
additional work undertaken in building bilateral ties was often
undervalued.[69] As one interview lamented:

There are contributions these Chinese scholars could make for this country and for China as well. Australia is a very special western country. It is in Asia and the linkages in the future will become stronger and stronger. For example, in my field, colleagues from both China and Australia complement each other and can work together well.[70]

Disciplinary differences were also stark, with much greater representation in information technology, engineering and economics/commerce/business than in health, education or creative arts.

| | Australian-born | Asian-born | Overseas-born (non-Asia) |
|---|---|---|---|
| Creative Arts | 69.6% | 25.1% | 5.3% |
| Education | 71.8% | 22.8% | 5.3% |
| Agri & Env Studies | 62.6% | 31.8% | 5.6% |
| Sciences | 55.1% | 34.5% | 10.4% |
| Health | 63.4% | 26.2% | 10.4% |
| Society & Culture | 55.7% | 33.8% | 10.5% |
| Arch & Building | 53.0% | 33.5% | 13.3% |
| Mgt & Commerce | 47.1% | 26.3% | 26.6% |
| Engineering | 34.3% | 32.4% | 33.3% |
| IT | 38.6% | 26.8% | 34.4% |

Figure 9.3 Academics in Australian universities, by discipline and birthplace, 2015. Source: Department of Education and Training data 2016, cited in Oishi 2017, 19.

Further barriers consisted of under-representation in senior ranks of universities; and discrimination, with over 40 per cent of respondents reporting experiences of "racism, microaggressions, ethnic racial or cultural stereotyping, and marginalisation" at work.[71] As one

---

69   Welch and Yang 2012; Yang and Welch 2010.
70   Yang and Welch 2010, 604.

interviewee responded, "I often feel that I am non-existent in meetings. People don't even see my face or talk to me".[72] This pattern broadly corresponds to the experience of mainland Chinese interviewees at Australian universities, and reflects wider patterns of privilege in Australian society, which include a "bamboo ceiling".[73] As an Australian Human Rights Commission report of 2019 pointed out, Asian Australians represented around 10 per cent of the population, yet a mere 3.1 per cent of partners in law firms, 1.6 per cent of barristers and 0.8 per cent of the judiciary.[74] Of members of federal parliament, only 1.7 per cent were from an Asian cultural background.[75]

On the other side, Australian researchers form a modest cohort among international academics working in China, despite the proliferation of foreign talent schemes such as 一百计划 (One Hundred Talents), 千人计划 (One Thousand Talents), 长江学者奖励计划 (Chang Jiang Scholars Program), and 海外名师 Haiwai Mingshi (International Famous Teacher).[76] In addition, major national programs such as Project 985 (1998) selected several dozen leading universities for additional funding, including the capacity to recruit international scholars (many of whom were overseas Chinese, working in the West). The subsequent 双一流 (Double First Class) Project (2017) set targets of having 42 world-class universities and around 465 world-class disciplines, to be achieved by 2050. Despite such incentives, and the expansion of Sino-Foreign collaborative programs and universities (Zhongwai Hezuo Banxue), such as Xi'an Jiaotong-Liverpool and Nottingham Ningbo, which employ many international staff, and often teach in English, limited research shows that Australian academics form only around 5 per cent of international academics in the Chinese research system.[77] Despite current travel

---

71  Oishi 2017; Gibney 2013, 2015.
72  Oishi 2017, 37.
73  Soutphommasane 2014; Yang and Welch 2010; Welch and Yang 2012.
74  Tan 2019.
75  Australian Human Rights Commission 2018; Evans 2019; Soutphommasane 2014.
76  Welch and Cai 2010; Peters and Besley 2018.
77  Huang and Kim 2022.

restrictions introduced in response to the COVID-19 pandemic, China remains committed to attracting global talent to its national innovation system.[78]

As in other systems, including in neighbouring Korea and Japan, many international staff working in Chinese universities complain "about bureaucratic administrative procedures and difficulties in dealing with renewing visas, income taxation, and other issues that are not relevant to teaching or research activities".[79] Administrative staff, it is lamented:

> do not want to take any responsibility for handling your problem. They always ask me to go to another department of administration or just ask me to discuss with my Dean, or Director of Department of International and Foreign Affairs.[80]

## Bilateral barriers: COVID-19, culture wars, decoupling

Despite highly unequal student flows and the waxing and waning of Australian policy on regional engagement, higher education bilateral relations were, by the first decade or so of the new century, on a sound footing.[81] But major recent disruptions of recent years presented challenges to the ongoing strength of academic relations.

The first of these arose from the US–China trade war, now increasingly recognised as a technology war and even a culture war.[82] The concept of "culture war", originating in Bismarck's *Kulturkampf*, and subsequently reformulated by Gramsci to refer to the struggle for dominance in the cultural domain, certainly included education. Current understandings, developed by James Davison Hunter in the early 1990s to explain the increasing polarisation of US politics, now

78  Sun 2021.
79  Huang and Kim 2022.
80  Huang and Kim 2022, 347.
81  Walker 2019; Welch 2014, 2021b, 2022c.
82  Brophy 2021; Marginson 2019; Raby 2020 – and the contributions of Raby, and O'Connor, Cooper and Cox to this volume.

focus on a range of issues around identity, immigration, religion, health and education.[83] In this instance, increasingly rancorous and rivalrous US–China relations over recent years have tended to cleave the world into two opposing camps, and directly encroach on cultural relations, including in education.

Increasingly concerned at China's rise, including its dramatic scientific rise, several measures were successively introduced in the United States to curtail scientific collaboration. These included the National Security Review (2017), the China Initiative (2018) and the National Defense Strategy (2018). The rationale for each deemed China a strategic rival and adversary, whose further rise needed to be checked.[84] Notwithstanding the hyper-partisan nature of US politics – especially during the presidency of Donald Trump – anti-China sentiment, at times reduced to little more than slogans such as "China is eating our lunch", prevailed across the ranks of Republicans and Democrats.[85] As one critic pointedly noted, this was largely motivated by a "desire to contain China's technological rise" more generally.[86] In June 2021, the US Senate passed the *Competition and Innovation Act*, with bipartisan sponsorship. It provided approximately US$250 billion for scientific research, including US$52 billion for semiconductor research, design and manufacture (an area considered particularly vulnerable to foreign competition). Other measures expanded the list of Chinese firms subject to a black ban on US investment, banned or restricted Chinese investment in US technology firms, and encouraged US firms to move production of key technological components out of China.[87]

Specific measures restricting higher education and research collaboration included a ban on US visas for 3,000–4,000 Chinese researchers and postgraduates in key technology areas, revoking the visas of a further 1,000 researchers and students, and prosecuting 10 Chinese-American scientists.[88] On-campus Confucius Institutes

---

83  Hunter 1991; Welch 2022a.
84  Department of Defense 2018; Department of Justice 2021; Franck 2021a, b.
85  Franck 2021a, b.
86  Evans 2020, 4.
87  Evans 2020; Franck 2021b.

(China's culture and language institutions, each in the form of partnerships with a Chinese university), were threatened with closure, and Fulbright exchanges with Hong Kong and mainland China cancelled.[89] As a Chinese-American physicist from the highly regarded MIT responded, "we're all poorer for it".[90] A 2022 survey of 2,000 scientists in major US universities found racial profiling of Chinese scientists, greater difficulties in securing promotion and research grants, and reduced bilateral research collaboration.[91]

The measure was aimed squarely at countering China's technological rise, articulated in national policies such as Made in China 2025, and the subsequent 14th Five-Year Plan (2021–25) for National Economic and Social Development and the Long-Range Objectives Through the Year 2035. Each aimed to strengthen domestic scientific achievements, especially in basic research, and focused on the high-tech areas of artificial intelligence, advanced materials, new energy, aeronautics, quantum information, integrated circuits, and neuroscience. The US response was summed up by a legislator: "The Chinese Communist Party is working overtime on cyber, AI, and machine learning so that they can become the world's pre-eminent superpower. We can't let our foot off the gas".[92]

But it has been argued that at least some of these measures were too blunt: in 2022, a case brought against Anming Hu, a former professor of engineering from the University of Tennessee was dropped after the judge argued "there was no evidence presented that [the professor] ever collaborated with a Chinese university in conducting NASA-funded research."[93] Professor Hu returned to work at the university. Another case by the Department of Justice against Dr Gang Chen from MIT was dropped in 2022, after the department acknowledged it could not prove its case. In February, the Biden government shut down the China Initiative altogether, amid lingering fears by researchers of its enduring

88  Zhu 2021.
89  Redden 2019, 2020; Wang and Wen 2021; Welch 2021a; Zhu 2021.
90  Cheng 2021a, b.
91  Li and Lee 2022.
92  Franck 2021b.
93  Lillis 2022.

damage. As MIT's Chen responded, "While I am relieved that my ordeal is over, I am mindful that this terribly misguided China Initiative continues to bring unwarranted fear to the academic community and other scientists still face charges".[94]

The export of the US–China culture war was boosted by pressure on US allies to align their policies accordingly. In Australia's case, the fact that this occurred after a decade or so of worsening relations has been traced back to Prime Minister Rudd's speech to Beijing University students in 2008 and the Defence White Paper of 2009, which, among other things, helped create a climate in which a reflexive response could occur.[95] This soon became evident, amplified by a few populist politicians and elements of the media. As pointed out by a former ambassador to China: "Australia is joined to the US hip in a way that hasn't happened since the Cold War".[96] The onset of the COVID-19 pandemic, during the intense US–China culture wars, as well as the impositions of travel restrictions by Australia from early 2020, tended only to deepen the suspicions of some regarding the so-called "China threat". The resultant culture war over China's rise, including its scientific rise, resonated strongly in the higher education and research sectors. The claim made by some as to the origins of the virus in a Chinese laboratory was given credence by some conservative media outlets, while a series of reports and media interventions by a national security institute added fuel to the fire.[97] Bellicose pronouncements by some conservative politicians, including in the context of the 2022 federal election, further fanned the flames. As a 2022 reflection on the dramatic change in perceptions of threat by China in the years immediately prior concluded:

> There is little doubt that the beating of the drums of war by Australian political leaders and sensationalist reporting by the

---

94  Guo 2022, see also Lillis 2022; Jalonick 2021; Gilbert and Kozlov 2022; Associated Press 2021.
95  Wang 2021.
96  Raby 2020, and his contribution to this volume; des Garets Geddes 2020; O'Connor, Cooper and Cox in this volume.
97  Jennings 2017; Dobell 2018; Brophy 2021; Zhou 2021b.

Australian media has exacerbated the threat perception of the Australian public.[98]

The net result was a rise in anti-China and anti-Chinese sentiment in the community, a phenomenon by no means unique to Australia.[99] "The Five Eyes, the EU, Japan and India have all decided to confront China, albeit in different ways."[100] Effects on campus were soon apparent. Universities were forced to mediate competing demonstrations by pro and anti-Chinese groups, and disputes in student newspapers.[101] Responding to increasing tensions between rival groups of critics and supporters of China, the University of Queensland temporarily suspended a student activist whose outspoken criticisms of the university's China ties and of the Chinese Communist Party threatened to disrupt international fee income. At the University of Sydney, an article in the student newspaper naming two academics who allegedly failed to disclose links to Chinese foreign talent programs, such as the *Qianren Jihua* (Thousand Talents) scheme, was subsequently withdrawn. But its removal did little to defuse the resultant commotion, between critics who accused the editors of "McCarthyism 2.0", and opponents who alleged the deletion of the article amounted to capitulation to the Chinese Communist Party. A third incident at Australian National University surrounded action taken by the university's art gallery to remove a suite of works dealing with COVID-19 and the Chinese Communist Party.[102] At the University of Melbourne, allegations of racism were raised in response to an article in an unofficial magazine at its law school, urging the university to stop accepting Chinese students.[103] As in the United States and elsewhere, such on-campus disputes only served to underline how culture wars and polarisation were heightening tensions around China and Chinese students.[104]

98  Ni 2022; Kassam 2022.
99  Biddle, Gray and Lo 2019; Cheng 2021a, b; Redden 2019, 2020; Wang and Wen 2021; Zhu 2021.
100  Des Garets Geddes 2020.
101  Bonyhady 2021a, b; Kuang 2021; Welch 2022a; Xiao and Walsh 2021.
102  Bonyhady 2021a, b.
103  Kuang 2021.

Students were not the only ones affected. In 2020, two well-known Chinese academics, each of whom was a director of an Australian Studies Centres at a major Chinese university, and each with a long history of developing good relations between the two countries and promoting Australian culture in China, had their visas cancelled.[105] The thirteen Australian Confucius Institutes were also put at risk, after being subjected to the *Foreign Influence Transparency Scheme*, introduced in 2019.[106] The imposition of a new *Foreign Relations Act* clearly aimed at China, audits of universities' China links and threats to Confucius Institutes, raised fears among many Chinese scholars in Australian universities, some of whom voiced their concerns regarding effects on their work.[107] Lowy Institute surveys in 2020 and 2021 each found that "one in five Chinese-Australians (18 per cent) had been physically threatened or attacked because of their Chinese heritage".[108] The extent of concern at a rising anti-China atmosphere was underlined in the 2022 federal elections, when several parliamentary seats with high proportions of Chinese Australians turned strongly against the government.[109]

A further example of culture wars was evident in the resolute refusal of the Australian federal government to meaningfully support universities, which, experiencing a substantial loss of income from declining international enrolments, faced a looming financial crisis. The fact that Australian universities were so dependent on international student income made COVID-19 effects particularly consequential. The abrupt closing of borders in early 2020 left Australia, as an external review bluntly pointed out: "far more exposed to the unprecedented downturn in international student flows than other Anglosphere countries".[110] In part, this was due to the strongly regional character of Australia's international student intake: all top 10 source countries were East Asian, South-east Asian, or South Asian.[111] In 2018, Chinese

---

104 Jalonick 2021; Nakazawa 2020.
105 Bolton 2019; Ferguson 2021; Hurst 2020; Rubinsztein-Dunlop 2020.
106 Visentin 2021.
107 Bonyhady 2021a; Chen 2021; Hurst 2020; Visentin 2021.
108 Hsu and Kassam 2021.
109 Knott and Sakkal 2022.
110 S&P Global 2021.

students alone numbered 150,000 (Hong Kong included), or 40.5 per cent of total international higher education enrolments.[112]

COVID-19 stranded 170,000 students overseas, including tens of thousands of Chinese students who had returned home for Spring Festival.[113] Unable to return to Australia to continue their studies, estimates noted that 61 per cent of Chinese students were stuck outside Australia, a much higher proportion than students from other countries. Many were marooned in China for as long as two years, and while some transferred to online enrolment, student complaints soon emerged, along with a desire to return to on-campus learning in Australia.[114] By October 2020, an estimated 75,000 international students were no longer enrolled, including almost 8,000 Chinese students.[115] A further update showed that in November 2020, only 16,916 new students had enrolled from outside Australia, which represented 3.4 per cent of all enrolments.[116]

Recent research further highlighted the dependence of higher education institutions across the country on fees derived from international students (around 40 per cent of whom were from China): of the country's 40 universities, 12 gained at least 30 per cent of their budget from that source.[117] Overall, as a submission from Universities Australia revealed, the sector contributed $41 billion to the Australian economy, and supported 259,100 full-time jobs.[118] But, as a submission from La Trobe university argued: "Australia's university sector cannot sustain these losses without serious damage to national productivity and the country's knowledge base".[119]

Unsurprisingly, evidence soon revealed major losses: an overall A$1.8 billion in 2020, with a further A$2 billion losses for 2021. Given

111 Ferguson and Spink 2021.
112 Babones 2019; Hurley 2021a, b; Hurley and Van Dyke 2020; Ferguson and Spink 2021; Varghese 2018.
113 Hurley 2021a.
114 Gwynn 2021; ICEF Monitor 2021; Menchin 2021; Zhou 2020.
115 Hurley 2021b.
116 Hurley 2021b.
117 Yezdani 2021; Zhou 2021a.
118 Terry and Jackson 2022.
119 La Trobe University 2020; see also Universities Australia 2021.

the pipeline effect, overall losses over the years 2020–23 were estimated to be between A$10 billion and A$19 billion.[120] Estimates of job losses in the sector were over 17,000 nationally in 2020, and the same again in 2021. Yet, once again, the federal government withheld substantial support, repeatedly amending the national JobKeeper scheme, introduced to mitigate the effects of job losses in key industries, to exclude public universities although making it available to private universities. Seeking explanations for the government's steadfast refusal, one analyst found a common response among vice-chancellors, public servants and former ministers: "It's not that complicated. The government hates universities".[121] Evidently, as one China scholar pointed out: "Some industries in Australia are too important to fail, but education and tourism are not among them".[122]

Further evidence of culture wars was seen in the withholding of financial sustenance from thousands of international students, many Chinese, who became trapped in Australia due to travel restrictions, and many of whom lost their part-time jobs, amid growing unemployment nationwide.[123] Thousands struggled to maintain themselves. University food banks, set up in response, were soon swamped. But the response of the federal government remained obdurate. In contrast to the support provided to international students in Canada and the United Kingdom, the advice to international students from the Australian prime Minister was brutally simple: "Go home".

## Conclusion

Despite strikingly different higher education traditions, a legacy of Australian racism, and tensions between its history and geography that help explain the fluctuating Australian engagement with its region, by

---

120  Hurley and Van Dyke 2020; Terry and Jackson 2020; Universities Australia 2021.
121  Megalogenis 2021, 52.
122  Lester 2021; see also Brophy 2021.
123  Berg and Farbenblum 2020; Bolton 2020.

the early part of the 21st century, the basis for solid Australia–China higher education relations seemed to have been established. The wider context too, including a substantial Chinese community in Australia, also seemed unproblematic. As Prime Minister Turnbull underlined in 2018, "Modern Australia is unimaginable without the talented and dynamic contribution of Australians of Chinese descent. They are a vital thread in the fabric of Australian society". His speech went on to reference numerous examples of academic collaboration and research innovation, including from China's substantial knowledge diaspora.[124]

But worsening China–Australia relations from around 2007, a more assertive international posture by China from around 2012, the onset of the COVID-19 pandemic in 2020 within the febrile climate of the US–China culture war, and associated pressure by the United States on its allies to conform, abruptly challenged this assumption. The equally abrupt Australian border closures, which were kept in place longer than in almost any other country and led to accusations of the country becoming a "hermit kingdom", affected Chinese students particularly. As in other countries, rising anti-Chinese sentiments led to an increase in racist incidents and a climate of uncertainty and fear among some Chinese-Australian academics and Chinese international students.

Such concerns were unsurprising, given the imposition of draconian foreign interference legislation, the preference given to security over diplomacy, audits on university links with China, numerous sensationalist accounts inconservative media outlets, several accounts by a security institute stoking fears of the China threat, the signing of the AUKUS agreement between Australia, the United Kingdom and the United States in September 2021, and the closure of Confucius Classrooms throughout New South Wales schools, together with threats to university Confucius Institutes. China's rising status as a world power, and its increasing assertiveness in the region, as well as incidents such as the Dastyari affair, the detention of an Australian academic and jailing of an Australian journalist in China also heightened concerns.[125] The net effect was, as the former Chinese diplomat, and later Australian academic, Wang Yi, characterised the

---

124  Turnbull 2018.

transition: "Since the establishment of diplomatic relations in 1972, China had been a country to be worked on; however, with the adoption of the foreign interference legislation, China became a country to be guarded against".[126] From the Chinese side, this was viewed as both an affront and a betrayal: an example of what is called *si po lian,* meaning to strip away the last pretence of cordial relations.[127]

The potential impact of both reduced Chinese student mobility and scientific decoupling was more profound for the Australian higher education and research sector than elsewhere, given Australia's high dependence on Chinese enrolments, high international co-publication rates and China's growing importance as a major knowledge partner. Effects on higher education are likely to endure even after the end of the pandemic, and there is little prospect of resolving long-term underfunding to higher education (thus lessening the urge by universities to enrol ever more fee-paying international students), but it is the persistence of US–China culture wars and the resultant undifferentiated pressure for scientific decoupling that presents a clear and present danger to an important relationship in Australian higher education. The resort of some within the former Coalition federal government of 2022, supported by a climate of securitisation of policy in general, to seek domestic political advantage by deploying Culture Wars and anti-China rhetoric at the cost of more mature diplomatic approaches, gave little cause for confidence that the higher education sector can immunise itself from such effects.

While the change of government in mid-2022 signalled a more mature and nuanced approach, accompanied by some modest signs of change on the Chinese side, the febrile climate of polarisation and decoupling will take time and work to dissipate. It leaves governments on both sides with limited room to manoeuvre, and leaves universities and research collaboration still facing a somewhat uncertain future. Fortunately, notwithstanding recent restrictions, bilateral relations between universities have persisted, albeit amid greater caution and

---

125  BBC 2022; Remeikis 2017; Valencia 2022; Needham, McNeilage and Wade 2017.
126  Wang 2021, 12.
127  Wang 2021.

uncertainty. As Australia re-opened its borders, student mobility from China rose again, although student and staff mobility to China was unlikely to open again until later. The China–Australia higher education relationship will need sustained nurturing, and calm and considered responses on both sides, at both institutional and governmental levels, if it is to recover from the recent reversals of sentiment and rebuild on a more solid footing.

## References

Adams, Jonathan (2013). The fourth age of research. *Nature* 497(2013): 557–60.

Altbach, Philip and Anthony Welch (2010). Australia: the perils of commercialism. *University World News*, 22 August. https://bit.ly/44RCdYu.

Asia-Pacific Economic Cooperation (2012). APEC Economic Leaders' Declaration: annex D – promoting cross-border education cooperation. https://bit.ly/475q2bQ.

Associated Press (2021). US university reinstates Professor Hu Anming, who was acquitted of hiding China ties. *South China Morning Post*, 4 February. https://bit.ly/475q2bQ.

Association of Pacific Rim Universities n.d. Members. https://www.apru.org/members.

Auditor General, New South Wales (2022). *Universities 2021*. https://bit.ly/3Qo3UDE.

Australian Council for Educational Research (2014). Promoting regional education services integration: APEC university associations cross-border education cooperation workshop. https://bit.ly/3nTw3qs.

Australian Council for Educational Research (2015). *Researcher mobility workshop report: Researcher mobility among APEC economies.* https://bit.ly/3VUDw4Y.

Australian Human Rights Commission (2018). Leading for Change: A Blueprint for Cultural Diversity and Inclusive Leadership Revisited. https://bit.ly/3Koh0gy.

Australian Universities International Directors' Forum (2020). Learning Abroad 2019. https://bit.ly/42qySy8.

Babones, Salvatore (2019). *The China student boom and the risks it poses to Australian universities.* Analysis paper 5. Centre for Independent Studies. https://bit.ly/44QwrXj.

Baker, Jordan (2022). Sydney University records $1 billion surplus as staff demand a share. *Sydney Morning Herald*, 23 May. https://bit.ly/3VUPs6K.

BBC (2022). Cheng Lei: Australian journalist on trial in China for spy charge. *BBC News*, 31 March. https://bbc.in/3Mjutrd.

Berg, Laurie and Bassina Farbenblum (2020). *As if we weren't humans: the abandonment of temporary migrants in Australia during COVID-19*. Migrant Worker Justice Initiative. https://bit.ly/44LxuHA.

Biddle, Nicholas, Matthew Gray and Jieh-Yung Lo (2019). *Research note: Asian Australian experiences of discrimination*. ANU Centre for Social Research and Methods. https://bit.ly/41t2g5t.

Bolton, Robert (2019). Universities forced to take action over China ties. *Australian Financial Review*, 14 November. https://bit.ly/41sSctw.

Bolton, Robert (2020). Struggling international students don't get any JobSeekers. *Australian Financial Review*, 13 April. https://bit.ly/42rYVVS.

Bonyhady, Nick (2021a). Former Turnbull security adviser auditing universities' foreign interference risks. *Sydney Morning Herald*, 11 April. https://bit.ly/3W34KXq.

Bonyhady, Nick (2021b). Wrestling with free speech, racism and China on university campuses. *Sydney Morning Herald*, 11 April. https://bit.ly/3rXYt4o.

Brophy, David (2021). *China panic: Australia's alternative to paranoia and pandering*. Melbourne: LaTrobe University Press.

Chen, Minglu (2021). Teaching Chinese politics in Australia: polarised views leave academics between a rock and a hard place. *Conversation*, 20 May. https://bit.ly/44Q6xmC.

Cheng, Yangyang (2021a). The grieving and the grievable. *The China Project*, 9 April. https://bit.ly/3VYr9VR.

Cheng, Yangyang (2021b). The US is building walls around science, and we're all poorer for it. *Vice News*, 12 March. https://bit.ly/3Mjv2RR.

Chief Scientist (2013). Partners in influence: how Australia and China relate through science. https://bit.ly/3IqF41p.

Collinson, Elena and Paul Burke (2021). *UTS: ACRI/BIDA Poll 2021 Australian views on the Australia–China relationship*. https://bit.ly/3YUiVOd.

Committee of Review of Private Overseas Student Policy (1984). *Mutual advantage: report of the Committee of Review of Private Overseas Student Policy* [Goldring report]. Canberra: Australian Government Publishing Service.

Committee to Review the Australian Overseas Aid Program (1984). *Report of the committee to review the Australian Overseas Aid Program* [Jackson Report]. Canberra: Australian Government Publishing Service.

Curran, James (2022). *The costs of fear and greed: past and present in Australia's China story.* Sir Peter Cosgrove lecture in history, 21 February. Australian Catholic University. https://bit.ly/3HZ1kz5.

Department of Defense, United States government (2018). *Summary of the 2018 National Defense Strategy of the United States of America.* https://bit.ly/44UCWbK.

Department of Education, Science and Employment, Australian government n.d. Approvals processes for Sino-Foreign Joint institutions and Joint programs. https://bit.ly/3LX4qF1.

Department of Education, Science and Employment, Australian government (2019a). 2019 higher education providers finance table. https://bit.ly/3DHr40l.

Department of Education, Science and Employment, Australian government (2019b). International Student Data Monthly Summary. https://bit.ly/3Kl52nK.

Department of Education, Science and Employment, Australian government (2019c). The Australia–China education relationship: diversity, complexity and maturity. https://bit.ly/44UUOD4.

Department of Education, Science and Employment, Australian government (2022). International Student Data Monthly Summary (December 2021). https://bit.ly/41tuA7S.

Department of Foreign Affairs and Trade, Australian government n.d. About the new Colombo Plan. https://bit.ly/45dZhAr.

Department of Industry, Innovation, Research and Tertiary Education, Australian government (2012). *Science and research collaboration between Australia and China.* Canberra: DSIIRTE.

Department of Justice, United States government (2021). *Information about the Department of Justice's China Initiative and a compilation of China-related measures since 2018.* https://bit.ly/3KqcspY.

Des Garets Geddes, Thomas (2020). UK–China relations: from gold to dust. *Diplomat,* 2 October. https://bit.ly/3VURtzQ.

Dobell, Graeme (2018). China and Australia's fifth icy age. *ASPI: Australian Security Policy Institute,* 10 May. https://bit.ly/3MhwL9h.

Evans, Gareth (2019). The "bamboo ceiling" in Australia is real. *Sydney Morning Herald,* 12 September. https://bit.ly/44QHdMG.

Evans, Paul (2020). Techno-nationalism in China–US relations: implications for universities. *East Asian Policy* 12(2): 80–92. https://doi.org/10.1142/S1793930520000161.

Ferguson, Hazel and Harriet Spink (2021). Overseas students in Australian higher education: A quick guide. https://bit.ly/44TuNUP.

Ferguson, Richard (2021). Elite unis submit 4000 foreign deals for Marise Payne. *Australian*, 16 June. https://bit.ly/3NFDjPx.

Fitzsimmons, David (2023). *Australia's relations with China: the illusion of choice 1972–2022*. London: Routledge.

Franck, Thomas (2021a). Biden prohibits U.S. investment in 59 Chinese companies allegedly tied to military, surveillance. *CNBC*, 3 June. https://cnb.cx/3DDqWPu.

Franck, Thomas (2021b). Democrats, GOP team up on bill targeting China as U.S. suffers microchip shortage. *CNBC*, 25 May. https://cnb.cx/3Qo7duy.

Franzoni, Chiara, Giuseppe Scellato and Paula Stephan (2012). Foreign born scientists: mobility patterns for sixteen countries. National Bureau of Economic Research Working Paper 18067. https://bit.ly/42PxyVg.

Gibney, Elizabeth (2013). Lingering racism in British academe. *Inside Higher Education* 10 April. https://bit.ly/3okafV1.

Gibney, Elizabeth (2015). How to tackle racism in UK universities. *Nature*, 2 April. https://go.nature.com/3I3jOhS.

Gilbert, Natasha and Max Kozlov (2022). The controversial China Initiative is ending – researchers are relieved. *Nature*, 24 February, 603: 214–15. 2022. https://go.nature.com/41sAWEz.

Goodman, David (2008). *The new rich in China: future rulers, present lives.* London: Routledge.

Guo, Eileen (2022) All Charges against China Initiative defendant Gang Chen have been dismissed. *MIT Technology Review*. https://bit.ly/3OkLSBt.

Gwynn, Liz (2021). University of Tasmania joins others in ditching face-to-face lectures in favour of online learning. *ABC News*, 12 November. https://ab.co/41teL14.

Hao, Jie and Anthony Welch (2022). A tale of sea turtles: job-seeking experiences of hai gui (high-skilled returnees) in China. *Higher Education Policy*, 25(2): 243–60.

Hao, Jie, Wen Wen and Anthony Welch (2016). When sojourners return: employment opportunities and challenges facing high-skilled Chinese returnees. *Asian and Pacific Migration Journal* 25(1): 22–40.

Hartnett, Richard (2011). *The Jixia academy and the birth of higher learning in China.* New York: Edwin Mellen.

Hayhoe, Ruth (2017). *China's universities 1895–1995: a century of cultural conflict.* London: Routledge.

Holenbergh, Rosita (2005). Relations in higher education, Australia and the People's Republic of China: a study of higher education linkage with special reference to the University of Sydney, 1949–1999. PhD thesis, University of Sydney.

Hsu, Jennifer and Natasha Kassam (2021). *Being Chinese in Australia: public opinion in Chinese communities*. Lowy Institute. https://bit.ly/41sW79I.

Huang, Futao and Yangson Kim (2022). International faculty members in China, Japan, and Korea: their characteristics and the challenges facing them. In Claudia Sarrico, Maria Rosa and Teresa Carvalho (eds) *Research handbook on academic careers and managing academics*, 338–55. Cheltenham: Edward Elgar.

Hugo, Graeme (2005). Australia's international migration transformed. *Australian Mosaic* 9(1):20.

Hunter, James (1991). *Culture wars: the struggle to define America*. New York: Basic Books.

Hurley, Peter (2021a). Future Asian students vital to the health of Australian universities. *East Asia Forum*, 2 March. https://bit.ly/3DEE4Ug.

Hurley, Peter (2021b.) Stuck in transit: international student update. Mitchell Institute, Victoria University, 28 April. https://bit.ly/3I7zdxB.

Hurley, Peter and Nina Van Dyke (2020). Australian investment in education: higher education. Mitchell Institute, Victoria University, 17 April. https://bit.ly/3O27NwM.

Hurst, Daniel (2020). Chinese professor "stunned" by Australian decision to cancel his visa. *Guardian*, 10 September. https://bit.ly/47a2pPx.

ICEF Monitor (2021). Australia: Large-scale return of international students not expected until 2022. 5 May. https://bit.ly/42AmGew.

Jalonick, Mary Clare (2021). Senate OKs bill to fight hate crimes against Asian Americans. *AP News*, 23 April. https://bit.ly/3OiAcgB.

Jennings, Peter (2017). Australia needs to toughen up on China relations. *ASPI: Australian Security Policy Institute*, 28 March. https://bit.ly/44RuoCe.

Jupp, James (2002). *From White Australia to Woomera: The story of Australian immigration*. Sydney: Allen & Unwin.

Jupp, James (ed.) (2001). *The Australian people: an encyclopedia of the nation, its people and their origins* (2nd edition). Melbourne: Cambridge University Press.

Kassam, Natasha (2022). Australians worry about China and muscle-flexing over Taiwan. *Interpreter*, 30 June. https://bit.ly/3Ql2zxB.

Kendall, Timothy (2008). Chapter three: foreign policy and "identity stuff": Hu Jintao addresses the Australian Parliament. In *Within China's orbit? China through the eyes of the Australian Parliament*. Canberra: Australian Parliamentary Library.

Knott, Matthew and Paul Sakkal (2022). Chinese-Australian voters punished Coalition for hostile rhetoric. *Sydney Morning Herald*, 25 May. https://bit.ly/3MeuGfg.

Kuang, Wing (2021). Racism alleged after anonymous op-ed urges unis to ban Chinese students. *ABC News*, 1 April. https://ab.co/3YhyXD9.

La Trobe University (2020). COVID-19's impact on Australian research. https://bit.ly/3ODVuH1.

Lan, You and Charles Kraus, n.d. Caught in the split: Chinese students in the Soviet Union, 1960–1965. Wilson Centre, e-Dossier 52. https://bit.ly/3ODBPqQ.

Laurenceson, James (2021). Australia's China politics heats up. *Interpreter*. https://bit.ly/3VYwv3p.

Laurenceson, James and Michael Zhou (2020). The Australia China science boom. Australia–China Relations Institute, University of Technology Sydney. https://bit.ly/3Mkvhw7.

Lester, Amelia (2021). Australia is the new hermit kingdom: closed borders have shut out diverse citizenry. *Foreign Policy*, 11 May. https://bit.ly/42KOqws.

Lew Williams, Beth (2018). *The Chinese must go: violence, exclusion, and the making of the alien in America*. Cambridge, MA: Harvard University Press.

Li, Jianjun (2021). Forty years of Australian studies in China. *Social Alternatives* 40(1): 51–3.

Li, Xiaojie and Jenny Lee (2022). US–China geopolitical tensions: implications for universities and science. *International Higher Education* 110 (Spring).

Lillis, Katie Bo (2022). FBI investigation determined Chinese-made Huawei equipment could disrupt US nuclear arsenal communications. *CNN: Politics*, 25 July. https://cnn.it/3rR9Lat.

Luo, Michael (2021). The forgotten history of the purging of Chinese from America. *New Yorker*, 22 April. https://bit.ly/3YdCPoL.

McGowan, Michael (2018). Private education spending in Australia soars ahead of other countries. *Guardian*, 11 September. https://bit.ly/43RXvnc.

Marginson, Simon (2014). Richard A. Hartnett: the Jixia academy and the birth of higher learning in China. *Higher Education* 68(2014): 323–24.

Marginson, Simon (2019). How should universities respond to the new Cold War? *University World News*, 16 November. https://bit.ly/3KnMbZn.

Marginson, Simon (2021). National modernisation and global science in China. *International Journal of Education Development* 84(2021): 102407. https://doi.org/10.1016/j.ijedudev.2021.102407.

Megalogenis, George (2015). *Australia's second chance: what our history tells us about our future*. Melbourne: Penguin.

Megalogenis, George (2021). Exit strategy: politics after the pandemic. *Quarterly Essay*, 82. Melbourne: Black Inc.

Menchin, Jennifer (2021). Australia: challenges will "prolong" HE tuition fee revenue downturn. *The PIE: News*, 4 May. https://bit.ly/3ODdl0H.

Ministry of Education, People's Republic of China (2003). Regulations of the People's Republic of China on Chinese foreign cooperation in running schools. https://bit.ly/42Ao54M.

Monash University (2014). Monash and Southeast Universities celebrate first joint graduates. https://bit.ly/478cfkN.

Nakazawa, Katsuji (2020). China talks of US decoupling and a divided world. Former official urges citizens to prepare for the worst-case scenario. *Nikkei Asia*, 9 July. https://s.nikkei.com/43Uke26.

Needham, Kirsty, Amy McNeilage and Matt Wade (2017). UTS Professor Feng Chongyi told he is suspected of threatening state security. *Sydney Morning Herald*, 26 March. https://bit.ly/3DCfN1f.

Ni, Adam (2022). Brief #118: Australian views of China in 2022. *China Neican*, 8 July. https://bit.ly/3puXJ5o.

Oakman, Daniel (2004). *Facing Asia: a history of the Colombo Plan*. Perth: Pandanus Books.

Oishi, Nana (2017). Workforce diversity in higher education: the experiences of Asian academics in Australian universities. Asia Institute, University of Melbourne. https://bit.ly/3DC9uL5.

Organisation for Economic Co-operation and Development (2007). Education at a glance 2007. Paris: OECD.

Organisation for Economic Co-operation and Development (2019). Spending on tertiary education. https://bit.ly/3M0hpG1.

Peters, Michael A. and Tina Besley (2018). China's double first-class university strategy: 双一流. *Educational Philosophy and Theory* 50(12): 1075–79.

Pietsch, Tamson (2010). Wandering scholars? Academic mobility and the British world, 1850–1940. *Journal of Historical Geography* 36(2010): 377–87.

Pietsch, Tamson (2013). *Empire of scholars. universities, networks and the British academic world 1850–1939*. Manchester: Manchester University Press.

Qi, Jing (2021). Impact of rising international student numbers in China. *University World News*, 22 May. https://bit.ly/3VYxz7p.

Raby, Geoff (2020). *China's grand strategy and Australia's future in the new global order*. Melbourne: Melbourne University Press.

Rapid Research Information Forum (2020). *Impact of the pandemic on Australia's research workforce*. Report. https://bit.ly/45dbOnL.

Redden, Elizabeth (2019). Closing Confucius Institutes. *Inside Higher Education*, 9 January. https://bit.ly/3Km8a2E.

Redden, Elizabeth (2020). Trump targets Fulbright in China, Hong Kong. *Inside Higher Education*, 16 July. https://bit.ly/44RH9wu.

Remeikis, Amy (2017). Sam Dastyari quits as Labor senator over China connections. *Guardian*, 12 December. https://bit.ly/42rTnKJ.

Royal Society (2011). Knowledge, networks and nations: global scientific collaboration in the 21st century. Policy document. https://bit.ly/42AoGDy.

Rubinsztein-Dunlop, Sean (2020). Australia revokes Chinese scholar visas and targets media officials, prompting furious China response. *ABC News*, 9 September. https://ab.co/3MhxE2K.

S&P Global (2021). Australian university finances under COVID-19: degrees of discomfort. https://bit.ly/3qkJGjv.

Sherington, Geoffrey (1990). *Australia's immigrants 1788–1988*. Sydney: Allen & Unwin.

Sherington, Geoff (2019). *Alexander Mackie: an academic life in education*. Sydney: University of Sydney.

Smith, Matthew J., Cody Weinberger, Emilio M. Bruna and Stefano Allesina (2014). The scientific impact of nations: journal placement and citation performance. *PLOS ONE* 9(10): e109195.

Southeast University College of International Students (n.d). Programs of Southeast University–Monash University Joint Graduate School (Suzhou). https://bit.ly/45jEwnD.

Soutphommasane, Tim (2014). Are Asian Australians trapped under a bamboo ceiling? *Guardian*, 11 July. https://bit.ly/47oY9fc.

Sun, Luna (2021). China will "exhaust all means" to lure global talent, despite push for tech self-sufficiency, Xi Jinping says. *South China Morning Post*, 16 December. https://bit.ly/3QfWAtP.

Tan, Chin (2019). Diversity in the Legal Profession – William Lee Address. 5 June. https://bit.ly/3OCaTrn.

Terry, Deborah and Catriona Jackson (2020). The crucial role of universities in a coronavirus recovery. *Universities Australia*, 7 April. https://bit.ly/3Ql3tdt.

Turnbull, Malcolm (2018). Speech at the University of New South Wales, Sydney – 7 August. https://bit.ly/3QjYkSI.

University Mobility in Asia and the Pacific (n.d). Home page. https://bit.ly/3nKJMjq.

Universitas 21 (n.d). U21 Global citizens. https://bit.ly/3OcXbK1.

Universities Australia (2021). Budget 2021: unis urge national plan for safe return of international students. Media release. *Universities Australia*, 11 May. https://bit.ly/3YkVXRS.

Valencia, Mark J. (2022). What is driving China's assertiveness in the South China Sea? *South China Morning Post*, 30 May. https://bit.ly/44MEiod.

Varghese, Peter (2018). Australian universities and China. Speech to the 2018 National Conference on University Governance. Adelaide, 4 October. https://bit.ly/3rUEtPZ.

Visentin, Lisa (2021). China-backed Confucius Institutes face closure under veto laws. *Sydney Morning Herald*, 10 May. https://bit.ly/3IwMVul.

Walker, David (2019). Significant other: anxieties about Australia's Asian future. *Australian Foreign Affairs* 52: 5–28.

Wang, Lizhou and Wen Wen (2021). China–global relations: a higher education cold war? *International Higher Education* 105. https://doi.org/10.36197/IHE.2021.105.06.

Wang, Yi (2021). Australia–China relations: the larrikin and the rising giant. In Europa Publications (ed), *The Far East and Australasia 2022*, 8–14 London: Routledge.

Watt, Ian (2022). Presentation, Australia–China Business Council. Australia–China Education Symposium. Darling Harbour, May.

Welch, Anthony (1996). *Australian education: reform or crisis?* Sydney: Allen & Unwin.

Welch, Anthony (2014). Richer relations? Four decades of ASEAN–Australia relations in higher education. In Sally Wood and Baogang He (eds), *The Australia–ASEAN dialogue: tracing 40 years of partnership*, 145–66 London: Palgrave Macmillan.

Welch, Anthony (2018). Global ambitions: internationalization and China's rise as knowledge hub. *Frontiers of Education in China* 13(2018): 513–31.

Welch, Anthony (2021a). Australia's China challenge. *International Higher Education* 109: 44–5.

Welch, Anthony (2021b). Challenging times for Sino-Foreign sci-tech relations. *International Higher Education* 105: 15–17.

Welch, Anthony (2021c). International academics in Australian higher education: people, process, paradox. In Futao Huang and Anthony Welch (eds), *International faculty in Asia, Europe and the United States* (115–34). London: Bloomsbury.

Welch, Anthony (2022a). A plague on higher education? COVID, Camus and culture wars in Australian universities. *Higher Education Quarterly*, (2022): 213–29. https://doi.org/10.1111/hequ.12377.

Welch, Anthony (2022b). Cultural difference and identity, *Education, Change and Society.* Oxford: Oxford University Press.

Welch, Anthony (2022c). History v geography in an evolving national system. In Devesh Kapur, Lily Kong, Florence Lo and David Malone (eds), *Oxford handbook of higher education in the Asia–Pacific region* (735–54). Oxford: Oxford University Press.

Welch, Anthony and Hong-Xing Cai (2010). Enter the dragon: The internationalisation of China's higher education system. In J. Ryan (ed), *Chinese education* (9–33). London: Routledge.

Welch, Anthony and Jie Hao (2015). Global argonauts: returnees and diaspora as sources of innovation in China and Israel. *Globalisation, Societies and Education* 14(2): 272–97.

Welch, Anthony and Jun Li (eds) (2021). *Measuring up in higher education: how university rankings and league tables are re-shaping knowledge production in the global era.* London: Palgrave Macmillan.

Welch, Anthony and Rui Yang (2012). Belonging from afar: transnational academic mobility and the Chinese knowledge diaspora: an Australian case study. In N. Bagnall and E. Cassity (eds), *Education and belonging* (123–37). New York: Nova Science Publishers.

Welch, Anthony and Zhang Zhen (2008). Communication networks among the Chinese knowledge diaspora: a new invisible college? In R. Boden, R. Deem, D. Epstein, F. and Rizvi (eds), *Geographies of knowledge, geometries of power: higher education in the 21st century. World Yearbook of Education 2008* (338–54). London: Routledge, 2008.

White, Daniella (2022). How NSW unis bypassed "great firewall of China" to gain students mid-pandemic. *Sydney Morning Herald*, 3 July. https://bit.ly/3rNKs9b.

Wong, Jan (1996). *Red China blues: my long march from Mao to now.* New York: Bantam.

Worldwide Universities Network (n.d). https://bit.ly/3LUYgoF.

Xiao, Bang and Michael Walsh (2021). Why an Australian student who is anti-Beijing is facing expulsion from the University of Queensland. *ABC News*, 23 April. https://ab.co/3O2PxDz.

Xie, Meng (2022). *Internationalizing the social sciences in China: the disciplinary development of sociology at Tsinghua University.* Singapore: Springer.

Xie, Qingnan and Richard Freeman (2019). Bigger than you thought: China's contribution to scientific publications and its impact on the global economy. *China and World Economy* 27, 1(2019): 1–27.

Yang, Rui (2022). *The Chinese idea of a university: phoenix reborn.* Hong Kong: Hong Kong University Press.

Yang, Rui and Anthony Welch (2010). Globalisation, transnational academic mobility and the Chinese knowledge diaspora: An Australian case study. *Discourse*, 31(5): 593–607.

Yang, Rui and Anthony Welch (2012.) A world-class university in China? The case of Tsinghua. *Higher Education* 63(5): 645–66.

Yezdani, Omer (2021). Which universities are best placed financially to weather COVID? *Conversation*, 4 February. https://bit.ly/42S8HAt.

Zhou, Naaman (2020). Up to 50% of university students unhappy with online learning, regulator finds. *Guardian*, 2 December. https://bit.ly/3KlzwGa.

Zhou, Naaman (2021a). Australian universities warn of economic ripple effect if international students remain locked out. *Guardian*, 23 January. https://bit.ly/3O30JA9.

Zhou, Naaman (2021b). Death threats, distrust and racism: how anti-Chinese sentiment in Australia "seeped into the mainstream". *Guardian*, 4 March. https://bit.ly/3qgSjvq.

Zhu, Lia (2021). Chinese-American academics on edge. *China Daily*, 9 July. https://bit.ly/3W0aml1.

# 10
# Cultural diplomacy on the ground: bridging the Australia–China divide

*Ien Ang*

In the past few years, the Australia–China relationship has seen a rapid decline. Less than a decade ago, a rising China was still mostly seen as an economic boon for Australia, but today it is regularly considered as a national security threat. Under the Morrison Coalition government (2019–22) in particular, the bilateral relationship reached a toxic phase, characterised by seemingly irrefutable mutual distrust and hostility. This chapter discusses the role cultural diplomacy – broadly defined – can play to "soften" tensions in a time of hardening political antagonism by establishing modes of engagement that navigate national divides through mutually beneficial exchange and cooperation. The chapter will rely to a great extent on public opinion surveys conducted by the Lowy Institute for International Relations. Surveys can be controversial measures of people's views, as they tend to slot nuanced and complex mindsets into blunt statistical scores on pre-given multiple-choice questions. Nevertheless, the Lowy polls provide a broadbrush picture that gives us insight into some important trends that underpin the state of Australia–China relations within society at large.[1] Since 2020 the Lowy Institute has conducted a series of special surveys among the Chinese-Australian segment of the population, which was funded by the Australian Department of Home Affairs. This reflects increased

---

1   See also Bates Gill's chapter in this volume for a discussion of these polls.

government concern with the role and impact of geopolitical tensions on Chinese diaspora communities in Australia. It also illuminates why cultural diplomacy effort is now focused more strongly on these communities, as will be discussed in this chapter.

## Australia's shifting perception of China

According to the annual Lowy Institute Poll, 2021 was the first year when a majority of Australians (63 per cent) considered China "more of a security threat to Australia" than "more of an economic partner" (34 per cent). This is a significant reversal from just a year earlier, when a majority (55 per cent) still emphasised China's role as an economic partner, as opposed to those who saw it more as a security threat (41 per cent). In the preceding years (2015–18) even larger majorities were positive about the economic relationship with China, with persistently more than three-quarters of Australians expressing the view that China was more of an economic partner than a security or military threat (a view persistently held by only 15 per cent or fewer).[2] These statistics are a clear indication of a major shift in Australian public opinion in relation to China, which has turned decidedly sour after years of relatively rosy perceptions, primarily associated with China's contribution to Australia's economic prosperity. In 2021, China was also the least-trusted country for Australians: only 16 per cent said that they trust China to act responsibly in the world, a 7-point decline from 2020.[3] By 2022, Russia displaced China as the least-trusted country for Australians as a consequence of Russia's invasion of Ukraine, but trust in China remained very low, with only 12 per cent of Australians saying they trusted China somewhat or a great deal.[4]

Further evidence of this decline in public sentiment is provided by the Lowy Institute's "feelings thermometer", which measures Australians' feelings about countries on a scale of 0° (coldest feelings) to 100° (warmest feelings). Since this annual measurement was first taken

---

2    Kassam 2021.
3    Kassam 2021, 6.
4    Kassam 2021, 6.

in 2005, Australians have routinely expressed their warmest feelings to fellow white settler Anglophone countries such as New Zealand and Canada (around 80°). China, on the other hand, has never invoked very warm feelings in Australians: the warmest was in 2005, when China rated 69°, with a gradual cooling ever since then. By 2014, the temperature had declined to 60° and it continued to decline to 49° in 2019.[5] In 2021, China slipped to the bottom of the Lowy Institute feelings thermometer scale, a place held by Saudi Arabia and Iran a year earlier, registering a very cool 32°.[6] Not surprisingly, a year later the coldest feelings were reserved for Russia, which saw a 22° drop in a single year (to an icy 19°), but feelings towards China remained persistently cool in 2022 (33°).[7]

It is clear, then, that escalating governmental tensions between China and Australia have had a consequential impact on how ordinary Australians perceive and relate to China. China's poor international image has been reinforced by the Chinese government's handling of COVID-19, the crackdown on Uyghurs in Xinjiang and the repression of the democracy movement in Hong Kong. Moreover, China's persistent refusal to condemn Russia for its invasion of Ukraine – it claims to be ambiguously "neutral" – has further damaged its reputation as a responsible global power, at least in the West. These circumstances have led to much discussion about the emergence of a new cold war, where the Western world, led by the United States, is pitted not just against Russia but, more importantly, against China. As China under President Xi Jinping has become an increasingly assertive global power, the narrative of a new cold war between China and the West has steadily gained prominence.[8] For example, in a 2019 essay entitled "A new cold war has begun", American foreign affairs expert Robert Kaplan argues "because the U.S.–China relationship is the world's most crucial ... a cold war between the two is becoming the negative organizing principle of geopolitics".[9] This overshadows

5    Munro 2019.
6    Kassam 2021, 22.
7    Kassam 2022, 31.
8    Brands and Gaddis 2021.
9    Kaplan 2019.

any positive assessment of China, including its enormous economic capacity, which has rapidly descended into escalating international trade tensions. As Kaplan argues, "[w]ith the waning of the liberal world order, a more normal historical era of geopolitical rivalry has commenced, and trade tensions are merely accompaniments to such rivalry".[10] In this context, Kaplan continues, trade tensions cannot be separated from security tensions. Indeed, the fact that China has been Australia's largest trading partner for years now tends to be seen more darkly as a liability than as an economic bonus. The reversal could not have been more stark: in less than a decade, China went from being embraced as a "land of opportunity", the source of wealth and prosperity, to being shunned overwhelmingly as a global "threat".[11] The Lowy Institute Poll data confirms this: while in 2016 a large majority of Australians (75 per cent) found that China's economic growth had a positive influence on their overall view of China, by 2021 50 per cent of Australians judged China's economic growth negatively.[12] Thus, China's economic clout is now deeply implicated in the calculated dangers of the new cold war.

In Australia, the spectre of this new cold war has percolated deeply in the government's national security rhetoric, especially under the Coalition government until it lost power in 2022. Former Prime Minister Scott Morrison, following US President Joe Biden, described the current world (dis)order in terms of an ideological battle between democracy and autocracy, with former Defence Minister Peter Dutton (later the Opposition leader) stressing the prospect of war with China over Taiwan.[13] Describing the relationship with China in terms of such a binary contest draws a sharp national antagonism between Australia and China – one in which, from Australia's point of view, China is resolutely positioned as the hostile Other. This absolutist suspicion of China has major implications for the future of Australia–China relations, not just strategically, but across the economy and society.

---

10 Kaplan 2019.
11 The bifurcated pendulum of "opportunity" versus "threat" in Western knowing of China has been criticised by Pan 2012.
12 Kassam 2022, 18.
13 Kelly 2021.

There has been much talk of an economic "decoupling" between the two countries, evidenced for example by the many Australia companies divesting from China, on the one hand, and a major decline in Chinese investments in Australia in the past few years, on the other.[14] This mutual withdrawal has been underpinned by a crippling of trust and goodwill on both sides. If this rise of distrust and loss of goodwill is not kept in check, it will reinforce a fraying international political landscape characterised by a nationalist turn against mutual understanding and reciprocal cooperation, which may result in a generalised "decoupled" future where China and Australia may, once again, be poles apart on a shared planet. Some commentators have even warned of the possibility of the new cold war evolving into a hot war – a dismal prospect that would be devastating for humanity, especially in a time when the world requires a concerted approach to tackle some urgent global challenges, such as climate change. It remains to be seen to what extent the apparent thawing of bilateral relations under the Labor government, especially since the first meeting of Prime Minister Anthony Albanese with President Xi Jinping in November 2022, may ease tensions in the years to come, although Australia's decision to sign the AUKUS nuclear submarine deal with the United States and the United Kingdom in March 2023 clearly shows that the force of the threat narrative regarding China has continued unabated.

With a population of more than 1.4 billion people, China represents almost one-fifth of humanity. Its spectacular economic rise has turned China into a formidable global superpower, challenging the long-standing hegemony of the United States. In short, China is simply too big and too powerful to ignore. Australian policymakers do generally recognise this reality, with politicians from both major parties arguing that it would be an act of "national self-sabotage" if Australia were to try to untangle itself from its economic reliance on China.[15] They understand the continuing importance of nurturing Australia–China relations, even in a time of rising mistrust and turbulence in the relationship. The Albanese government, which came to power in May 2022, has therefore begun to bring the bilateral

---

14    Hu 2022.
15    Hurst 2020a.

relationship on a more even keel. Fundamentally though, Australia's attitude towards China remains framed by a profound ambivalence, driven by a sometimes grudging acknowledgement that China cannot be dispensed with.[16]

## Cultural diplomacy to the rescue?

To be sure, a wholesale severing of ties between Australia and China seems improbable in a world that has become so thoroughly intertwined due to globalisation in the past few decades. While during the Mao years (1949–76) relations between China and the West were almost entirely halted, leading to almost complete separation, today too many interconnections and interdependencies have grown over time that won't be easily undone, preventing total disconnection. These linkages go beyond the strictly economic and business sphere, where relationships tend to be more pragmatic and transactional. Government plays an active role in fostering deeper mutual connections through broad cultural exchange in the context of various forms of cultural and public diplomacy. Cultural diplomacy does not often feature centrally in foreign policy debates, but it is an important – though often overlooked – dimension in the governmental management of international relations.

In broad terms, cultural diplomacy refers to a policy field in which states seek to mobilise their cultural resources to achieve foreign policy goals. But the nature of those goals and of the cultural resources mobilised to achieve them can vary, and there is a lack of clarity – both in the scholarly literature and among practitioners – on what cultural diplomacy "is".[17] This uncertainty is expressed in the following much-cited definition of cultural diplomacy by Milton Cummings:

> The concept of "cultural diplomacy," refers to the exchange of ideas, information, art, and other aspects of culture among nations and their peoples in order to foster mutual understanding.

---

16   Davis 2020.
17   Clarke 2020.

But "cultural diplomacy" can also be more of a one-way street than a two-way exchange, as when one nation concentrates its efforts on promoting the national language, explaining its policies and point of view, or "telling its story" to the rest of the world.[18]

In other words, cultural diplomacy can range from an open-ended pursuit of international cultural exchange to a more instrumental use of "culture" (however defined) to enhance a nation's "soft power".[19] Moreover, many forms of "culture" can be deployed in the context of cultural diplomacy, not just the arts but also the media, sports, language education and people-to-people exchanges, among others. In this regard, cultural diplomacy can be seen as a facet of the broader field of public diplomacy.[20] In all these instances, it is important to underscore that the purpose of cultural diplomacy, as supported by governments, is categorically to advance the national interest: it involves the deployment of cultural displays and exchanges to enhance national security and prosperity, and to promote the nation's international standing.[21] A US State Department report, published in 2005 in the aftermath of the disastrous Iraq war, stated that "cultural diplomacy can enhance our national security in subtle, wide-ranging and sustainable ways" by creating a "foundation of trust" between peoples and serving as "a flexible, universally acceptable vehicle for rapprochement with countries where diplomatic relations have been strained or absent".[22] Cultural diplomacy, in other words, is seen as a soft way of overcoming or alleviating tensions or stresses in the more hard-nosed dimensions of international relations such as security and trade. In today's climate of rising geopolitical hostility it may therefore be of particular importance to navigate the tensions in the China–Australia relationship through cultural means. It may contribute, modestly but significantly, to preventing the relationship from collapsing altogether.

18   Cummings 2003, 1.
19   Nye 2004.
20   Cull 2008.
21   Ang, Isar and Mar 2015.
22   Department of State 2005.

The importance of cultural diplomacy was underlined by Stephen FitzGerald, Australia's first ambassador to China, as early as in 1976, when he stated:

> there is a very specific Australian interest in the promotion of what is broadly described in China as cultural exchange. Without this, our relations with China will never be more than superficial, and we will be damagingly ill-equipped to adjust to a China dominant in the region.[23]

FitzGerald's advocacy led to the establishment of the Australia–China Council (ACC) in 1978, which was given the brief and the funding to deepen and broaden Australia's engagement with China by promoting mutual understanding, co-operation and people-to-people relations between the two countries.[24] For more than 40 years the ACC, which was based at the Department of Foreign Affairs and Trade, provided grants for hundreds of projects and programs in science, education and the arts to help advance and strengthen the bilateral relationship.[25] A flagship program nurtured by the ACC was the establishment of an Australian Studies in China program, which has built a vibrant community of researchers, teachers and students in China who are interested in the study and research of Australian literature, culture and society.[26] An important priority of the ACC has also been the showcasing of Australian arts and creative industries to Chinese audiences and to build closer and broader cultural and artistic partnerships. At the same time, the ACC sought to support practical and effective solutions to enhance China literacy in Australia and to improve the capability of Australian institutions and people to engage effectively with China.[27]

---

23  FitzGerald, letter to Foreign Affairs Minister Andrew Peacock, 11 May 1976, quoted by Smith 2015.
24  Chey 1982.
25  Farrelly 2018.
26  Carter 2015.
27  See Department of Foreign Affairs and Trade n.d.

There is no question that the ACC has done much important work to familiarise the two countries to each other and to strengthen the connectivity between them. Some have argued that the overall impact of this work has remained limited, not least because its budget was so small that it could only fund relatively small-scale projects whose lasting effects were restricted.[28] Reflecting on the 40th anniversary of the ACC in 2018, FitzGerald noted that much remained to be done, pointing to deficiencies in knowledge and awareness of China and its culture, language, norms and values within Australia's political class. He also bemoaned the lack of a critical mass of China literacy among a broad spectrum of Australians – a goal that, he observed, remains elusive.[29] This is not surprising because, as FitzGerald argued more than 40 years earlier, "China is not a habit of mind for Australians".

To change a habit, of course, requires enormous transformative work, which arguably cannot be done quickly and with limited resources. Cultural diplomacy to nurture bilateral relations, in short, requires patient, long-term, painstaking investment throughout the society. In this regard, ACC funding has certainly contributed to long-term cultural change, even though this is not widely acknowledged. This is especially the case where projects go beyond just showcasing and involve sustained people-to-people cultural co-operation. For example, Carillo Gantner, a veteran theatre director who was cultural counsellor at the Australian embassy in Beijing in the 1980s, describes how ACC funds helped him organise a series of visits to Australia by members of the Nanjing Acrobatic Troupe to train young Australian artists in acrobatic and circus skills (in which the Chinese excelled). Over time, this has resulted in the national and international success of Australian physical theatre companies such as Circus Oz and the Flying Fruit Flies, epitomising "an exciting new hybrid, a recognisably Australian style now celebrated around the world", which, Gantner says, can be seen as "a very rich legacy of deep Australia–China cultural sharing and exchange".[30]

---

28    Comment made by John Yu, one of the ACC's former chairpersons, at a China Matters event: Yu 2022.
29    Stephen FitzGerald, "Thoughts on the Australia-China Council's 40th anniversary and its future," in Farrelly 2018 (43.1).

In 2019, as diplomatic tensions with China were rapidly worsening, the ACC was abruptly disbanded and replaced with fanfare by a new National Foundation for Australia–China Relations. In a media release the Foreign Minister, Marise Payne, announced the new organisation "to turbo-charge our national effort in engaging China". The timing of the establishment of the foundation appeared to reflect the government's wish to reset the parameters of the bilateral relationship, mindful of the need to continue "a constructive relationship with China, founded on shared interests, mutual benefit and mutual respect" in a time of rising enmity and mistrust. The new body would have substantially more funding than the ACC, "enabling it to engage on a much broader scale than the Council" and moving "beyond the latter's focus on education, culture and the arts, to also promote Australian excellence in areas such as agriculture, infrastructure, health and ageing and the environment and energy".[31] Here, then, the ambit of cultural diplomacy is broadened across a wide range of sectors across civil society, exceeding the field of "culture" in a narrower sense.

The foundation was meant to be "an important demonstration of the Government's commitment to invest in people-to-people ties and practical cooperation between Australia and China".[32] But its start was "tortured and unspectacular", according to its inaugural chair of the board, Warwick Smith, who resigned from the position after less than a year. Smith, who also served as the last chair of the ACC, protested that the operations of the new entity were fully controlled by the Department of Foreign Affairs and Trade, and that members of the board were appointed directly by the minister, suggesting a lack of arm's-length management as was the case with the ACC.[33] Moreover, the board's composition was subjected to criticism for its lack of mainland Chinese representation: although the membership included several Chinese Australians, they tended to have strong links with Hong Kong or South-east Asia, not the People's Republic of China (PRC). Some members also have strong public records as hawkish

---

30   Gantner 2022.
31   Payne 2019.
32   Payne 2021.
33   Hui and Cohen 2020.

critics of the PRC, such as Maree Ma, manager of the virulently anti-China Chinese-language newspaper *Vision China Times*, raising concerns that the foundation would underscore the government's "tough line" against China rather than working towards "dialogue and breakthroughs that may lead to resolution of differences".[34] By December 2021, the foundation had a newly-appointed CEO in Peter Cai, a China-born expert of China's business and political economy, researcher, journalist and historian. With the coming to power of a new Australian government in May 2022 and a possible stabilisation of the bilateral relationship, the hope is that the National Foundation for Australia–China Relations will work to transcend politics in the coming years and become "a platform for ongoing soft diplomacy, quietly maintaining people-to-people ties, ready for when official ties may improve".[35]

## Diaspora engagement

One explicit priority of the National Foundation for Australia–China Relations is to step up engagement with diasporic Chinese communities in Australia. Indeed, one reason that ties between Australia and China can no longer be entirely severed is the critical mass of Chinese people now living, working, visiting or studying in Australia. Precisely the expansion of Australia–China relations since the 1970s has led to an exponential increase of linkages, especially through people-to-people exchanges that will continue to leave a mark, especially in Australia. For example, people-oriented industries such as tourism and international education have been particularly lucrative for Australia during the boom years of China–Australia economic relations, as thousands of tourists and students from China landed on Australian shores, necessitating tourist operators and educational institutions alike to cater to the needs of their Chinese customers. More importantly, the opening up of China after Mao and Australia's reliance on high levels of immigration as a means of economically

---

34  Chey 2020.
35  Korporaal 2021.

beneficial population growth have led to a rapid increase in immigrants from the PRC, especially in the first two decades of this century. For example, at the end of June 2019, 677,240 China-born people were living in Australia, twice the number (344,980) 10 years earlier. PRC immigrants were the second-largest immigrant community in Australia in 2019, after only those from the United Kingdom, equivalent to 9 per cent of Australia's overseas-born population and 2.7 per cent of Australia's total population.[36] There is now a critical mass of Chinese residents from the PRC in the country to suggest that "China" is no longer out there, but here, inside Australia. Engaging with this diaspora community as a matter of priority thus makes sense: its presence in Australia represents a clear instance where international relations and domestic social tensions intersect, spawning an increasingly thorny clash between perceptions of national security and national cohesion.

Unfortunately, the deterioration of diplomatic relations between the two countries has had a detrimental social impact on people of Chinese descent in Australia. Increasingly strident anti-China rhetoric by political leaders and in the media has created a murky atmosphere of suspicion, distrust and general Sinophobia affecting Chinese Australians whose belonging to Australia is being questioned. This came into sharp focus in the context of the heated debate on " foreign interference", which solidified Australia's new political consensus view of China as an "enemy state".[37] Public alarm over undue Chinese meddling in Australian political processes and other domestic affairs exploded with the publication of Clive Hamilton's book *Silent invasion: China's influence in Australia* in early 2018. In a sensationalist narrative tone, Hamilton asserted, without much evidence, that advocates of the Chinese Communist Party have made an "almost complete takeover" of Chinese community groups in Australia, such as social organisations, student groups, professional bodies and Chinese-language media.[38] The spectre was thus raised that the whole Australian-Chinese diaspora should be put under suspicion. In a session during the Senate inquiry into issues facing diaspora communities in Australia in 2020, Liberal

---

36  Department of Home Affairs 2022.
37  For an incisive critical analysis of this "debate", see Brophy 2021.
38  Hamilton 2018.

senator Eric Abetz demanded that three Chinese-Australian witnesses – Osmond Chiu, Wesa Chau and Yun Jiang – "publicly and unconditionally condemn the Chinese Communist party dictatorship". All three refused to comply with this demand, arguing that Abetz's interrogation was akin to a McCarthyist "loyalty test".[39] In an opinion piece for the Sydney Morning Herald, Chiu, who is a research fellow at the progressive think tank Per Capita, pointed out that Abetz's line of questioning implied he had "divided allegiances" by virtue of his ethnicity. As he insisted: "I may have Chinese heritage but I'm Australian. I was born here and my family has been here for half a century. This is my home, the only home I have ever known."[40]

This incident clarifies a number of issues facing Australia's Chinese diasporas. First, there is a persistent tendency in the Australian imagination to homogenise all people of Chinese background, ignoring or overlooking the diversity of their origins, identities and histories as they are commonly racialised as "Chinese" – a tendency of essentialised othering with a deep history going back to the invention of the Yellow Peril in the early days of the White Australia policy. The example of Australian-born Osmond Chiu is a case in point: his Chinese heritage condemned him to be treated as an outsider like any Chinese immigrant, whether from Hong Kong, Singapore or the PRC. Chinese Australians of all stripes have been subjected to this blanket anti-Chinese racism, which has seen a worrisome spike in the past few years, as anti-China sentiment has mounted. The Lowy Institute's 2021 *Being Chinese in Australia* survey found that one in five Chinese Australians had been physically attacked or threatened because of their Chinese heritage, while 34 per cent said they were treated "differently or less favourably because [they] are of Chinese heritage", and 25 per cent said they "have been called offensive names because [they] are of Chinese heritage".[41]

A homogenised understanding of "the Chinese" obscures the fact that there is no singular "Chinese diaspora community", which is too easily assumed in the oft-repeated statistic of 1.2 million people of

---

39    Hurst 2020b.
40    Chiu 2020.
41    Hsu and Kassam 2022, 10.

Chinese ancestry now living in Australia, as counted in the 2016 census.[42] By far the largest cohort (41 per cent) were born in China, far ahead of those hailing from Malaysia (8 per cent) and Hong Kong (6.5 per cent). Australian-born Chinese, including the descendants of early Southern Chinese immigrants who came to Australia during the gold rushes, now make up only 25 per cent of people with Chinese ancestry. Nearly half speak Mandarin at home (46 per cent), having overtaken Cantonese (22 per cent) and English (18 per cent).[43] COVID-19 caused a sharp decline in overseas immigration, particularly from China. The onset of COVID-19 in Wuhan, China, in early 2020 led to the imposition of strict border closures, which made immigration almost impossible, causing a net loss of 50,000 in the China-born population from China in the 2020–21 financial year.[44] Although it is unclear whether high immigration numbers will resume, what is significant is that Mandarin-speaking immigrants from the PRC, most of whom arrived in the course of the 21st century, now make up at least half of all Chinese Australians.

It is these so-called "new Chinese immigrants" (*xin yimin*), in themselves a highly diverse and by no means monolithic group, who are particularly caught in the middle in the tensions between Australia and China.[45] Having mostly grown up after the communist revolution in China, they tend to have personal experience of life in the People's Republic, for better or worse. Many of them still have strong family, friendship or business connections in China.[46] It is therefore not surprising that they have a dual sense of belonging to both Australia and China, as has been borne out in Lowy's *Being Chinese in Australia* surveys. It found that in 2021, 62 per cent expressed a great or moderate sense of belonging to China, only slightly less than in 2020 (65 per cent). But there has been a significant decline in those stating a sense of belonging to Australia, from 71 per cent in 2020 to 54 per cent in 2021,

---

42  According to the 2021 Census, there were 1,390,639 people of Chinese ancestry in Australia, or 5.5% of the total population. This is an increase of more than 250,000 compared with 2016. Australian Bureau of Statistics n.d.
43  Australian Bureau of Statistics 2018.
44  Australian Bureau of Statistics 2021.
45  Sun 2020.
46  Li 2017.

with only 17 per cent expressing a great sense of belonging to Australia. Moreover, Chinese Australians who arrived in the 1980s expressed a greater sense of belonging to Australia and their local community than those who arrived more recently (between 2010 and 2019).[47] While the latter is understandable as it takes time for immigrants to feel at home in their new country, the sharp decline in sense of belonging to Australia in just one year may indicate the increasingly inhospitable political climate within which Chinese immigrants from the PRC now have to live. They are most likely to be subjected to suspicion, even by non-mainland Chinese who, to avoid being tarred by the same brush, sometimes feel compelled to stress their dissociation from mainlanders and to highlight that they are bona fide Australians. Feeding into the concern with divided allegiance is an anxiety about the role played by Chinese diaspora community organisations, which the Lowy Institute has also put under examination.[48] The report observes that while older organisations were mostly focused on local welfare delivery such as aged care, childcare and language education for ethnic Chinese immigrants, newer organisations – established mostly after 2000 by PRC immigrants – were focused less on service delivery and more on cultivating business and economic ties with China.[49] It is these organisations that have now come under suspicion of being potential vehicles for Chinese Communist Party influence and interference. While there is often little known evidence for such accusations, it explains efforts to counter possible overtures from Beijing through the foreign interference laws. Ironically, however, these efforts can be counterproductive, as the authors of the Lowy report conclude: the atmosphere of suspicion created, amplified by the occurrence of anti-Chinese racism, "has alienated Chinese-Australians and in some cases made them more receptive to messages critical of Australia", such as those pushed by the Chinese Communist Party.[50] As Wanning Sun has pointed out, "anyone with a mainland background runs the risk of

---

47  Hsu and Kassam 2022, 10.
48  Hsu, McGregor and Kassam 2021.
49  Hsu, McGregor and Kassam 2021, 9.
50  Hsu, McGregor and Kassam 2021, 2.

being suspected of, or insinuated as 'having links' to or being 'associated with' the CCP [Chinese Communist Party]".[51]

The idea of divided allegiance that is central to such suspicions highlights these people's purported lack of loyalty to Australia. This may be reinforced by survey data that found that there is a growing gulf between Chinese Australians and the broader Australian population in their views on key China-related issues. As mentioned earlier, Australians now overwhelmingly view China as a threat to national security, with even its economic growth seen increasingly negatively. By contrast, a large majority of Chinese Australians (72 per cent) continued to see China more as an economic partner than as a security threat in 2021. They also had much more favourable views of China's environmental policies, military activities and system of government – all issues perceived very negatively by Australians in general. A large majority of Chinese Australians (74 per cent) believed that in the event of a military conflict between China and the United States, Australia should remain neutral, while this applies to only 57 per cent in the broader Australian population. Some 41 per cent of Australians in general opined that Australia should support the United States, while only 1 per cent thought Australia should support China. Among Chinese Australians, there was a more even spread of views, with 11 per cent favouring support for the United States and 14 per cent favouring support for China.[52] Similarly, on the question of who was more to blame for the tensions in the Australia–China relationship, only 4 per cent of the Australian population said that Australia is more to blame, with 56 per cent saying China is to blame, while among Chinese Australians 40 per cent blamed Australia more compared with 19 per cent who blamed China more. About 40 per cent in both groups blamed Australia and China equally.[53]

We should be careful in interpreting such statistics, especially in the current highly strained geopolitical context. One could suggest that there is a strong pro-China predisposition among Chinese Australians, but one could equally observe that the fervent anti-China bias across

51    Sun 2020, 10.
52    Hsu and Kassam 2022, 30.
53    Hsu and Kassam 2022, 45.

the Australian population as a whole is now extreme, falling in line with the vehement shrillness of the dominant anti-China discourse that often comes from government circles and the media in Australia today.[54] In this regard, Chinese Australians on the whole seem to be less willing to be drawn into the polarising cold war rhetoric that relegates China to the realm of evil otherness. This is not a sign of disloyalty to Australia, but of real reticence and uncertainty. As Sun observes, there is a high level of ambivalence on the part of many mainland Chinese immigrants about their identity and sense of belonging. Most of them don't want to be put in either the "pro-China" or the "anti-China" camp; they refuse the absolutist binary choice for Australia over China that nationalistic demands for loyalty impose.[55]

In this light, one rationale for soft power diplomacy to target diaspora communities would be to counter the disaffection Chinese Australians may feel as a result of the anti-China and anti-Chinese environment they now live in, and to steer their affection towards Australia. As Jason Yat-Sen Li has argued, "the most powerful defence against any appeal by the CCP [Chinese Communist Party] to a Chinese Australian's sense of cultural heritage" is "to have them feel they are trusted, empowered and valued by Australia and their fellow Australians".[56] This aligns with the National Foundation's objective of greater diaspora engagement, as put in its strategic plan: "Recognising the contributions of Chinese-Australian communities to Australian society, and the important role they play as advocates and stakeholders in our international relationships".[57] That said, only a few grants have been awarded to Chinese-Australian community groups in the first two years of the foundation's grant rounds (most of the grants were awarded to large-scale organisations such as universities and arts companies for medical, scientific or artistic collaboration with partners in China). A $300,000 grant was awarded for the establishment of a new Museum

---

54 A particularly pernicious example is the alarmist "Red Alert" series of articles in the *Sydney Morning Herald* and the *Age* in March 2023, which asserted that "Australia faces the threat of war with China within three years – and we're not ready" (Hartcher and Knott 2023).
55 Sun 2020, 10.
56 Li 2019.
57 National Foundation for Australia–China Relations n.d.a.

of Chinese in Australia in Sydney, which will feature the contribution of Chinese Australians to the Australian story.[58] This is a worthwhile project that seeks to positively inscribe the Chinese within Australia's multicultural national identity, but it focuses primarily on the history of older-generation immigrants and its key organisers are long-time Chinese-Australian community leaders. More direct engagement with contemporary PRC immigrants is a project run by the Chinese Australian Forum, of which Yat-Sen Li has been the president. Funded with an $80,000 grant, it aims to provide civics education workshops for Chinese-Australian communities, focusing on Australia's parliamentary democracy.[59] The pedagogic aim of this project is clearly to educate recent immigrants on Australian political values. Such initiatives are examples of diaspora diplomacy to bind Chinese immigrants more to the Australian nation, to bolster their "loyalty".

### From loyalty to conviviality: bridging the China–Australia divide

As an important focus of current diaspora diplomacy, loyalty enhancement is clearly seen as in the national interest. But exclusive consideration of the goal of national allegiance yields an inward-looking nationalistic perspective that discounts the more cosmopolitan, transnational resources that diaspora communities can provide. While less than a decade ago, talk was still about the potential of harnessing Australia's "diaspora advantage",[60] today's Australia-centric anti-China obsession risks treating all diasporic connections with China as potential national security hazards. This threatens to delegitimise all links that immigrants from China may wish to nurture with their homeland and denigrates their senses of multiple belonging, which has been so central to the experience of all immigrants in multicultural Australia and has benefited Australia's transnational connectivity. It also overlooks the most tangible

---

58   National Foundation for Australia–China Relations n.d.b.
59   National Foundation for Australia–China Relations n.d.c.
60   Rizvi, Louie and Evans 2016.

opportunity Australia has in fostering people-to-people links with Chinese at the everyday level.

Until quite recently, Australia keenly welcomed thousands of Chinese business immigrants for their input into the national economy. Research has shown that many of them have emigrated to Australia with typical middle-class aspirations for a better quality of life and better education and future for their children, and used conducting business as a means of achieving permanent residency in Australia. A sense of "dual embeddedness", including the freedom to travel back to China when it suits them, has been essential for them for business and family reasons. But this transnational flexibility has been up-ended by COVID-19 and by the wider disruption of bilateral relations between the two countries, while their settlement in Australia has often been hindered by a lack of language skills and familiarity with local culture and society. When interviewed, many of them were also critical of Australia's transactional approach to business immigration, which they thought was overwhelmingly focused on the intake of capital and disregarded settlement challenges.[61]

Contemplating the plight of immigrants like these points to the limitations of diaspora engagement if it is pursued purely through a negative national security lens: it focuses on correcting the (alleged) loyalty deficit of PRC immigrants, not on assisting their social integration into Australian life. For the latter to happen, we need to recommit to Australia's vision of multicultural togetherness and embrace more expansive, less oppositional and less mutually exclusive understandings of national belonging. In short, I suggest that to ease the damaging impact of toxic geopolitics on Chinese Australians, we need a more positive diaspora diplomacy, one that moves from loyalty concerns to advancing conviviality. One interesting finding from the Lowy surveys actually supports this aim. Although, as discussed, most Australians now see China in an overwhelmingly negative light, a very large majority of them, 76 per cent in 2021, said that for them personally, "Chinese people they have met" have had a positive influence on their overall view of China. For 68 per cent, "Chinese culture and history" has had a positive influence.[62] This means that

---

61   Colic-Peisker and Deng 2019.

Australians make a clear distinction between Chinese people and culture, on the one hand, and geopolitical, economic and security concerns, on the other, in their opinion of China. It reinforces the importance of enhancing mundane people-to-people links, developing convivial relationships that are removed from politically sensitive contexts.

Ample opportunities for conviviality exist, but they need to be seized. For example, in many neighbourhoods of Australia's cities, immigrants from China now make up a significant proportion of the population, such as in Sydney's Hurstville, where 37 per cent of the population were born in China.[63] But it has only been quite recently that the Georges River Council, of which Hurstville is a part, has actively stepped up its engagement with this constituency through forms of local cultural diplomacy that recognise these immigrants as full participants in local society. For example, the local library has recently appointed a diversity librarian who has made it his mission for the library to recognise that serving Mandarin-speaking library users should not be an afterthought, but integral to the library's service provision. He worked on signage in the library, replacing a drab A4 sign with "Chinese collection" in Roman English with an appropriate bilingual sign to make the library a more inclusive space. One of the fundamental challenges, in his experience, is to educate immigrants from various countries that the public library is there for everybody, not just the white Anglo community.[64] Similarly, in 2022 the Hurstville Museum and Gallery has for the first time developed a special exhibition on the long history of ongoing Chinese settlement in the area, entitled *Our Journeys/Our Stories*, which also features commissioned works by six well-known contemporary Sydney Chinese artists.[65] The exhibition received a small grant from the National

62   Kassam 2021, 14. But it is concerning that these good percentages were even higher in 2016, suggesting a decline overall in positive views of China in the last five years even in relation to people and culture.
63   .idcommunity: demographic resources n.d.
64   Ang and Wong 2022a.
65   Georges River Council n.d.

Foundation of Australia–China Relations and CEO Peter Cai delivered a speech at the opening of the exhibit.

At the same time, Chinese artists in the local Georges River area are active in their own grassroots forms of cultural diplomacy. One of them is Ginger Li, a woman from Jinan, Shandong Province, who came to live in Sydney in the mid-2000s. An experienced book designer and publisher, she has had a successful business producing artistic catalogues for various museums and institutions in Australia, using her contacts in China to print the books economically. She also organised some artist exchanges between Australia and China, working with Chinese local government departments and cultural institutions. Much of this work dried up even before COVID-19, she said. She has now established an art society, the Australian Chinese Heritage Paper Arts Club, bringing together a group of PRC Chinese immigrants who are amateur artists in the Georges River area, and organising collective painting sessions and exhibitions, some in their home garages, to which all neighbours are invited. The purpose, she says, is to make connections, "getting to know Australian people", developing more understanding of each other in an atmosphere of conviviality and friendship. The general motto here is that art can bridge cultural differences despite the difficult relations between Australia and China.[66]

Such local civic initiatives may fly under the radar of the more ambitious cultural and public diplomacy programs at the national and international level. They are modest, grassroots and perhaps too small scale to be recognised by the National Foundation of Australia–China Relations. But they involve real people working to transcend the China–Australia divide from the ground up.

## Conclusion

As many chapters of this book have highlighted, Australia's relationship with China has suffered serious deterioration in the past decade for a range of reasons after a substantial period of relative improvement since China's opening up in the 1980s. As Wanning Sun shows in her

---

66    Ang and Wong 2022b.

chapter, the worsening of diplomatic relations has been amplified by an exceedingly hostile mainstream media, which has tended to portray China as Australia's enemy state. As a consequence, Australian public opinion of China has also seen a sharp decline, with a significant majority of Australians now seeing China as a major threat to national security. Nevertheless, concrete Australia–China links that have been built up over decades, through business and economic ties as well as social and cultural exchange, will not simply disappear. In particular, Australia itself now has hundreds of thousands of China-born people in its midst, whose role in changing Australia's social fabric is undeniable, but who may also potentially suffer most from the tensions between the two countries. It is in this complex and contradictory context that practices of cultural diplomacy, discussed in this chapter, can help "soften" relations – reduce blanket hostility and mutual alienation – through efforts of cultural exchange and cooperation. But such efforts cannot be a quick fix, nor are they a simple counterbalance to the governmental exigencies of "hard" diplomacy and strategic geopolitics. The work of cultural diplomacy occurs across society at large, at local, national and transnational levels, in various sectors, and ranges from ambitious, large-scale government-funded projects to small-scale grassroots initiatives involving numerous ordinary people. Above all, the work of cultural diplomacy – in its role of bridging differences and facilitating mutual understanding – is an ongoing task that will never be done, requiring ongoing nurturing and resourcing.

## References

Ang, Ien, Yudhisthir Raj Isar and Phillip Mar (2015). Cultural diplomacy: beyond the national interest? *International Journal of Cultural Policy* 20(4): 365–81. https://bit.ly/3VSXXPX.

Ang, Ien and Alexandra Wong (2022a). Unpublished interview with Court Wright, diversity librarian, Georges River Council libraries, 24 February. Interview in the context of ARC Discovery project Civic Sinoburbia: new Chinese migrants and everyday citizenship in Sydney (DP200102072).

Ang, Ien and Alexandra Wong (2022). Unpublished interview with Ginger Jingzhe Li, 28 March. Interview in the context of ARC Discovery project Civic

Sinoburbia: new Chinese migrants and everyday citizenship in Sydney (DP200102072).

Australian Bureau of Statistics n.d. *Australia 2021 Census All persons QuickStats.* https://bit.ly/42S951T.

Australian Bureau of Statistics (2018). ABS reveals insights into Australia's Chinese population on Chinese New Year. Media release, 16 February. https://bit.ly/3VVRqUt.

Australian Bureau of Statistics (2021). Overseas migration. Statistics on Australia's international immigration and emigration, by state and territory, country of birth, visa, age and sex. Reference period 2020–21 financial year. https://bit.ly/47a9QzR.

Brands, Hal and John Lewis Haddis (2021)."A new Cold War: America, China and the echoes of history. *Foreign Affairs* 10(1): 10–20.

Brophy, David (2021). *China panic: Australia's alternative to paranoia and pandering.* Melbourne: La Trobe University Press.

Carter, David (2015). Living with instrumentalism: The academic commitment to cultural diplomacy. *International Journal of Cultural Policy* 21(4): 478–93. https://bit.ly/42GedWQ.

Chey, Jocelyn (1982). Australia–China Council retrospective. *Australian Journal of Chinese Affairs* 7: 137–40.

Chey, Jocelyn (2020). Turbo Charge or Tough It Out? The New Board for the Foundation for Australia-China Relations, *Pearls and Irritations*, March 4. https://bit.ly/3ObfOOy.

Chiu, Osmond (2020). I was born in Australia. Why do I need to renounce the Chinese Communist Party? *Sydney Morning Herald*, 14 October. https://bit.ly/3O9bBuM.

Clarke, David (2020). Cultural diplomacy. *Oxford research encyclopedia of international studies*, 19 November. https://doi.org/10.1093/acrefore/9780190846626.013.543.

Colic-Peisker, Val and Ling Deng (2019). Chinese business migrants in Australia: middle-class transnationalism and "dual embeddedness". *Journal of Sociology* 55(2): 234–51. https://bit.ly/42Q0Jrd.

Cull, Nicholas (2008). Public diplomacy: taxonomies and histories. *Annals of the American Academy of Political and Social Science* 616(1): 31–54. https://bit.ly/3BfXkGG.

Cummings, Milton (2003). *Cultural diplomacy and the United States government: a survey.* Washington, DC: Center for Arts and Culture.

Davis, Michael J. (2020). Australia and China: framing an ambivalent relationship. *Asian Studies Review* 44(2): 278–96. https://doi.org/10.1080/10357823.2019.1698006.

Department of Foreign Affairs and Trade, Australian government n.d. Australia–China Council (decommissioned). https://bit.ly/3qfcASk.

Department of Home Affairs (2022). Country profile – People's Republic of China. https://bit.ly/41pgxjD.

Department of State, United States government (2005). *Cultural diplomacy: the linchpin of public diplomacy*. Report of the Advisory Committee on Cultural Diplomacy. https://bit.ly/44Wf3Rc.

Farrelly, Paul (2018). *The Australia–China Council: the first forty years*. Canberra: Department of Foreign Affairs and Trade and Australian Centre on China in the World.

Gantner, Carillo (2022). *Dismal diplomacy, disposable sovereignty: our problem with China and America*. Melbourne: Monash University Publishing.

Georges River Council (n.d.). Our journeys/our stories. https://bit.ly/3KlOxIf.

Hamilton, Clive (2018). *Silent invasion: China's influence in Australia*. Melbourne: Hardie Grant Publishing.

Hartcher, Peter and Matthew Knott (2023) . Australia faces the threat off war with China within three years – and we're not ready. *Sydney Morning Herald*, 7 March. https://bit.ly/42SuKqF.

Hsu, Jennifer and Natasha Kassam (2022). *Being Chinese in Australia: public opinion in Chinese communities*, Lowy Institute. https://bit.ly/41sW79I.

Hsu, Jennifer, Richard McGregor and Natasha Kassam (2021), *Lines blurred: Chinese community organisations in Australia*. Lowy Institute, November. https://bit.ly/45aAZXI.

Hu, Dan (Diane) (2022). China and Australia: economic decoupling? *Melbourne Asia Review* 9. https://bit.ly/42v1u9F.

Hui, Echo and Hagar Cohen (2020). Government body meant to boost relations with China has been "tortured and unspectacular", according to former chair. *ABC News*, 4 August. https://ab.co/3o1zs6t.

Hurst, Daniel (2020a). Economic decoupling from China would be "act of national self-sabotage", Labor and Liberal MPs agree. *Guardian*, 8 December. https://bit.ly/3MhaBFd.

Hurst, Daniel (2020b). Eric Abetz refuses to apologise for demanding Chinese-Australians denounce Communist party. *Guardian*, 16 October. https://bit.ly/44TUy75.

.idcommunity: demographic resources (n.d.). Georges River Council: community profile, Hurstville (total). https://bit.ly/3I5uz3k.

Kaplan, Robert (2019). A new Cold War has begun. *Foreign Policy* 7 January. https://bit.ly/44OyF9i.

Kassam, Natasha (2021). Lowy Institute Poll 2021. https://bit.ly/450Zbfu.

Kassam, Natasha (2022). Lowy Institute Poll 2022. https://bit.ly/44Nmutr.

Kelly, Lidia (2021). Chance of China–Taiwan conflict should not be discounted – Australian defence minister. *Reuters*, 25 April. https://reut.rs/450ZgzO.

Korporaal, Glenda (2021). Transcending politics. *Australian*, 21 April. https://bit.ly/42rY9In.

Li, Barry (2017). *The new Chinese: how they are changing Australia*. Brisbane: Wiley.

Li, Jason Yat-Sen (2019). Trusting Chinese Australians as partners in managing a rising superpower. *Disruptive Asia* 3. https://bit.ly/44V46iq.

Munro, Kelsey (2019). Poll: Australians sour on China. *Diplomat*, 26 June. https://bit.ly/3nRRxE2.

National Foundation for Australia–China Relations n.d.a. Strategic plan 2020–21. https://bit.ly/3BmhHC5.

National Foundation for Australia–China Relations n.d.b. 2020–2021 grant round. https://bit.ly/3Ykful9.

National Foundation for Australia–China Relations n.d.c. 2021–22 grant round. https://bit.ly/3nUnMT6.

Nye, Joseph (2004). *Soft power: the means of success in world politics*. New York: Public Affairs.

Pan, Changing (2012). *Knowledge, desire and power in global politics: Western representations of China's rise*. Cheltenham, UK: Edward Elgar.

Payne, Marise (2019). Strengthening the future of the Australia–China relationship. Media release. 29 March. https://bit.ly/3DCeUWr.

Payne, Marise (2021). National Foundation for Australia–China Relations chief executive officer appointment. Media release, 1 December. https://bit.ly/3MjWSNS.

Rizvi, Fatal, Kam Louie and Julia Evans (2016). Australia's diaspora advantage: realising the potential for building transnational business networks with Asia. Report for the Australian Council of Learned Academies. Canberra: ACOLA.

Smith, Warwick (2015). Building engagement with China. *Public Administration Today* 42, 35–38. https://bit.ly/3rUL6ll.

Sun, Wanning (2020). Henry Chan lecture: multicultural citizenship re-imagined: engaging migrants from China. University of Technology Sydney, Australia–China Relations Institute, 25 November. https://bit.ly/3Qlyr5g.

Yu, John (2022). Rethinking China. In conversation with Lisa Murray, 16 March. Sydney lecture series. China Matters. https://bit.ly/3pEgxyY.

# 11
# China and the opening of the Australian mind

*Stephen FitzGerald*

This chapter is a perspective on Australia's relations with China, in which I have been involved, at times deeply, over the decades since before diplomatic recognition in 1972. It is not intended as a distillation of the chapters that have gone before, nor is it the product of new research. It is my perspective on how Australia's attitudes to China have evolved from the time of recognition, and why relations reached such a low point over the prime ministerships of Abbott, Turnbull and Morrison.

In the 1970s, although I anticipated the rise of China as a resurgent Great Power, economic giant and dominant force in our region and the huge challenge that would present for us – and predicted so from the embassy in Beijing – I could not have imagined that Australia's relations with China would reach the nadir we had by the last days of the Morrison government, with talking at senior level frozen, the official relationship going nowhere and no apparent inclination on the part of the government to move it forward. It is true that with the ascension of Xi Jinping, China had become more assertive than it once was, exerting more forcefully its economic and political influence in and beyond our region, militarily exerting influence in the South China Sea and challenging the supremacy of the United States in Asia and the Pacific. But our government was out in front of all other countries, including the United States, in refusing even back-channel communication and in verbal confrontation and gratuitous vilification of China. And publicly beat its breast in self-congratulation for doing so.

This requires explanation. Other countries in the region have been able to maintain dialogue and ministerial relations even where they have more significant differences with China than we do: for example, Japan. Understanding why the Australian response to China was so singular is needed if we are to understand how, or even whether, it will be possible to resume some kind of effective working relationship, which is demonstrably in our national interest. I'd suggest the explanation lies deeper than the simplifications of the dominant public discourse would have it.

When Whitlam went to China in 1971, although change was underway in Australian society – for example, in the burgeoning women's movement, the student movement across the nation's universities and the mass popular movement against the Vietnam War – this initiative was still against the dominant narrative of the Coalition government and conservative voices in both the major political parties and much of the Australian establishment. This narrative held to an Anglo-centric view of Australia, its education and cultural inspiration and horizons European, ignorant of our First Peoples' history and what they had suffered, and fearful yet patronising of Asian countries and people.

Whitlam's visit punctured that in a dramatic way and ushered in an entirely new way of thinking about China in Australia. It both represented and became an important ingredient in a wider historic shift in the Australian imagination, an opening of the Australian mind. While no single event can be claimed as the catalyst for this opening of the mind, Whitlam's China démarche in mid-1971 certainly had an immediate and powerful effect. The reports from the Australian media accompanying him in China presented for the first time an image of China that was real and of Chinese people as not some kind of demonic undifferentiated "Reds", but of people who could be civilised, sophisticated, personable and prepared to engage in a frank and open way. When the Whitlam delegation returned to Australia at the end of that visit, there was an almost complete turnaround in public attitudes to China. For months thereafter, and on to the election in December 1972, members of the delegation were besieged by requests for speaking engagements across the country, and found an immense new interest, not about their visit so much as about China itself. It was no longer an audience wanting to hear worst fears and prejudices confirmed, but people coming with an intense curiosity, a desire to learn, to engage, an interest in visiting this recently forbidden land.

And this was at a time when China was still in the latter stages of the violence, havoc and near anarchy of the Cultural Revolution. It showed a remarkable capacity for a more open, mature and forward-thinking Australia.

This change in turn helped stimulate change in how we thought about other Asian countries and the idea of Asia in general, and also fed into ongoing change in the way we thought about ourselves: for example, accepting the idea of Australia as a multicultural society, of welcoming Vietnamese refugees and immigration from Asia more generally, of opening the horizons of our education and our minds to knowing more about our neighbourhood through the study of its languages and societies, and beyond that, of becoming "enmeshed" with Asia (Hawke), of finding our security *in* not *from* Asia ( Keating), of the whole idea of Australia being a part of Asia. New Asian courses and centres sprang up across the universities, and businesses joined in this opening of the mind and jostled for places in courses on working in unfamiliar cultures.

This more open-minded and sophisticated Australia meant that, by the time of the Tiananmen Square massacre in 1989, on the one hand we were prepared to condemn that action and grant residence to a very large number of Chinese students already in the country, but, on the other, we were able to recognise that there was more to be gained from keeping relations going and communications open than in closing them off.

These changes were a product of leadership from the top combined with a popular and spontaneous readiness for change in society at large. And they were merged in a wider opening of the mind in our own literature and creative and performing arts, and in international scientific engagement and collaboration.

By the mid-1990s, Australia had become a very exciting place in which to live, with ever-broadening horizons. In a book finished just before the change of government in 1996, I wrote of a vision I had for the 2020s, drawing from the example of cases in history (I had in mind Tang Dynasty China or the renaissance states of the Italian peninsula):

> of small societies open to people from outside and welcoming to political and intellectual and economic refugees, and open domestically to talent and ideas, which [became] havens for people of talent, and nurtured that talent into major creativity and great contribution to the advancement of civilisation. They have been trading societies, and they have also been societies in which many foreign languages have been spoken. We have the elements of such a society in embryo.[1]

That was indeed over-optimistic. Because, when we actually did arrive in the 2020s, we had once more a closed door on China; in the ruling Coalition, in parts of the Australian Labor Party, and in the general public discourse – and we were not even speaking at ministerial level. But there was a broader and more fundamental context. No one in politics and few elsewhere talked any more of expanding our intellectual horizons or our world view; almost no one talked of being part of Asia, let alone enmeshed, and the study of Asian languages had been in decline for many years. We were again inward-looking, frightened, starting at shadows, stricken with what Allan Gyngell has called "fear of abandonment" by the United States, a return to the mentality of Fortress Australia.[2]

It was a closing once more of the Australian mind. How did we get here? There are many factors, domestic and foreign, but one that I would suggest is a pretty substantial drag on changing back to a more imaginative and constructive relationship with China and must be considered if we are to do so, is this closing of the Australian mind, epitomised in the re-legitimisation of race in political and public discourse.

Race had of course been part of the Australian narrative on China since the 19th century, and confronting our racist foreign policy had been an essential prerequisite to a modern relationship with China.

---

1    FitzGerald 1997.
2    Gyngell 2021.

Whitlam was not alone in challenging it, or the first. In the late 1950s and '60s the Coalition government had initiated moves to dismantle the White Australia policy, and Whitlam sealed these moves with a legislated end to the policy in 1973. It didn't, of course, mean an end to racism. But the rejection of racism as a prominent and in some respects determining factor in our external relations was critical to opening our minds to China and to other Asian countries, and to the way we related to them and to the wider world. The policy of multiculturalism, drawing as it did on non-discriminatory immigration and sustained positive messaging from the top, also had a sublimating effect on this racist strand in domestic Australian society.

Yet from the second half of the 1990s, there was a slow closing of the Australian mind as we became less idealistic and more materialistic, led with a different messaging from the top about Asia and our place in it, and about immigration and race. Soon after he was elected, John Howard, on a visit to Indonesia, in just three speeches said no less than 16 times that Australia was not part of Asia, thereby reinstating an unequivocal demarcation between us and "them". Shortly after that trip he gave tacit endorsement to the racist views of Senator Pauline Hanson, proclaimed in the national parliament.

It was the introduction of race as a calculated political weapon, which began in earnest with the since discredited "children overboard" affair in 2001 (where Coalition ministers and the prime minister claimed that refugees had deliberately thrown their children into the ocean to be rescued by Australian defence forces), that became the hallmark of where Howard and his government stood on this issue. It was often a dog whistle rather than explicit, but it roused and encouraged the dormant Australian racism, and it persisted throughout Howard's time as prime minister, with the demonisation of refugees and asylum seekers, who were of course brown-skinned and mostly Muslim. Although his government fell in 2007, the effect of dog-whistle politics on race is that it legitimises racist attitudes and behaviour in society, even if the politician who whistles denies it, or has moved on.

The Labor governments that followed Howard either did not recognise its insidious effects or did not want to, and in any event did not confront it head on. Indeed, their policies on offshore detention can only have given comfort to the xenophobia and racism that were by now in much of the public discourse. With the arrival of the Abbott government there was a distinct turning of Australia inward. Julia Gillard's *Asian Century* White Paper, her attempt to redirect the public narrative, was ditched, along with the whole idea that had informed it, and the strategic partnership she had established with China lost all momentum and interest on the Australian side. When Abbott told German Chancellor Angela Merkel in 2015 that Australia's policies towards China were driven by fear and greed, he spoke a truth about the deep-seated attitudes of his government and his leadership. The negative messaging about refugees and particular ethnic groups became more pointed. There was no longer a reaching for new horizons in foreign affairs, and enthusiasm for close engagement with Asian countries, particularly the Association of Southeast Asian Nations (ASEAN), all but disappeared from both policy and the dominant narrative. This continued more intensely under Turnbull, and then was pursued in full force under Morrison. It became clear that the government and the foreign policy community in Canberra did not want and was not going to court the kind of enmeshment with Asian countries we had sought from the mid-1970s to the mid-1990s.

It was over this period that the strategic environment for Australia changed very substantially, with China's more assertive foreign policy under Xi Jinping, the sharpening contest between the United States and China as the USA strove to preserve its hegemony and deny China an equal place in the region, and then the maverick behaviour of Donald Trump thrown into the mix. These certainly warranted a deep strategic reassessment on our part. But they still do not adequately explain the extreme reaction to China of the Coalition government, or why it was prepared to put itself out in front even of the United States in hairy-chested challenging of China, eschewing dialogue and diplomacy, and even seeming to welcome the freeze in relations that ensued. It is due in part to the fact that over this same period the voice of the Department of Foreign Affairs and Trade was totally sidelined in Canberra, losing out to the weight of advice and opinion from the intelligence and security agencies. These agencies, known to harbour nationalistic and xenophobic views, have been driving the policy and the narrative of the politicians and also the public narrative through briefings and leaks to favoured and pliant journalists, and through their favoured publicity vehicle, the Australian Strategic Policy Institute in Canberra.

In late 2018, one of the most senior and deeply experienced heads of department in Canberra confirmed this to me in a private comment in the wings of a discussion on China: "What we have now in Canberra is the complete securitisation [using security as the central aspect] of all aspects of government policy".

How did this become so? In research over several months in 2021, veteran newspaper editor and investigative journalist Max Suich set out to explore why and how Australia did what he calls a U-turn on China policy. He talked to many with firsthand knowledge of the inside of government over recent years including, importantly, serving and retired senior officers of the security and intelligence agencies. The conclusion was:

> while we dramatically changed our approach, we did not define a policy objective for the new relationship with China or a strategy to achieve it. Nor did we thoroughly review alternative options. We elevated anger about Chinese activities in Australia and latent ministerial hostility towards China, turning threadbare slogans into policy.

He found that this approach originated from:

> informal discussions between staffers in ministerial offices, backbench hawks and key figures in the security and intelligence agencies, designed to provide an encouraging environment for agency arguments to the NSC (National Security Council). Thus, their proposals came to the NSC pre-endorsed by the security hawks of the backbench and ministerial advisers in key departments.

One official observed to him "the close relationship between the right wing of the Coalition and the intelligence agencies and their co-ordinating influence in establishing the 'don't argue' climate among policy makers was disturbing then and continues."[3]

---

3    Suich 2021.

What is significant about this is that an extreme anti-China positioning found such ready and enthusiastic adoption and promotion by ministers. It seems that it resonated with views and fears that in most cases they already held about China as China, as distinct from China as the Chinese Communist Party: "A majority of ministers were quickly persuaded *their long-held antipathy to China* had been justified".[4]

The deeper reason for the extremity and obduracy of the Australian anti-China stand, therefore, lies not so much in the behaviour of the People's Republic of China (PRC) but here, in Australia, in the mindset and the attitudes and prejudices of those directing foreign policy and of the politicians they advised.

One manifestation of this was government messaging relating to Chinese Australians, often by implication but sometimes openly and directly, which impugned their loyalty, lumped them together and indiscriminately scapegoated them as somehow disloyal or complicit in PRC "interference" in Australia, and in some cases alleged or implied they are agents of the Chinese Communist Party working for the overthrow of our democracy. Even in instances where this may not have been intentional, there was little apparent regard for the impact on Chinese Australians of the government's public rhetoric on China and the Australia–China relationship.

A Lowy Institute survey, in its annual update released in April 2022, reported that of the 1.2 million Chinese Australians, almost one in five (18 per cent) said they had been physically threatened or attacked because of their Chinese heritage, around one-third (34 per cent) said they had been treated differently or less favourably because they are of Chinese heritage, and 25 per cent said they had been called offensive names because they are of Chinese heritage.[5]

This is tragic for Chinese Australians, deeply divisive for Australia's social cohesion, and devastating for a country that once embraced multiculturalism as an Australian value and public good. But on the opportunity to redress this, which could have been done with unremitting strong, positive public messaging, the Coalition government passed.

---

4   Suich 2021, my emphasis.
5   Hsu and Kassam 2022.

Instead, it continued to feed the negative messaging with drops and leaks and dog whistles, and the pursuit and harassment of particular individuals. One of the early, dramatic and more egregious examples of the latter was the leaking and briefing against major philanthropist Dr Chau Chak Wing, implying he was working for Chinese Communist Party interests, to an ABC *Four Corners* program in 2017 made jointly with the Nine Network as it is now. Dr Chau sued them all and in his court cases was cleared and vindicated and awarded damages, against both of these media organisations and against at least one individual who contributed to the program. But the event still served the purpose of intimidation of Chinese Australians and anyone else who might be of a mind to have normal and non-political relations with PRC officialdom.

These policies and attitudes on China reflect a turning inward, increasingly pronounced since 2017. They are known to have been driven strongly by certain advisers who harboured profound personal animosity to China and all things Chinese. It didn't help that no one in the leadership of government was known for having knowledge or understanding of international affairs or was intellectually equipped to interrogate the advice they received from the intelligence and security community, even if they had a mind to, which clearly they didn't.

Australia under these governments had reverted to old attitudes of race fear, fear not only of China but of Chinese people, fear of a dominant influence in our region that is Chinese not Anglo, of a China and a Chinese society that most in our political elites in government and elsewhere do not know and do not understand, whose language they cannot speak, whose political system is a mystery to them, a country where in the upper levels of power they have no friends or even acquaintances, and of which our government and its ministers, with rare exceptions, could not even name their PRC counterparts.

This fear drove an apparent phobia that to even speak formally to the PRC at high level was to be avoided. Witness the extraordinary statement by Morrison in 2022 that for him even to receive the newly arrived PRC Ambassador to Australia – a normal courtesy even between countries with strained relations – would be a sign of weakness. So much for the uses of diplomacy. There were in fact many indications of signals from Beijing of an interest in talking with

Australia at a senior level, including through private channels, but none of these was taken up.

A closing of the mind against the unknown and the "other", race fear and prejudice, and paranoia about China, became and are still widely apparent in the media and in public attitudes and opinion surveys, and they are there because the political leadership and its advisers legitimised them, both tacitly in the case of race; directly and openly in the case of China; and in important respects in the case also of Chinese Australians. The trend has been across the spectrum of our political elites and not only in the Coalition. It is also present in the Labor Party, which did nothing of consequence or impact to challenge this race fear and stand up for Chinese Australians.

All this means that to resume some kind of effective working relationship with China is not going to be easy. When Morrison stopped briefly in Singapore on his way to a meeting of international leaders in Cornwall in June 2021, Singapore Prime Minister Lee Hsien Loong, when asked by the media how Australia should handle its relations with China, offered this advice:

> You need to work with the country. It is going to be there, it is going to be a substantial presence ... You don't have to become like them, neither can you hope to make them become like you ... You have to be able to work on that basis, that this is a big world in which there are different countries, and work with others who are not completely like-minded but with whom you have many issues, where your interests do align ... There will be rough spots ... and you have to deal with that. But deal with them as issues in a partnership which you want to keep going and not issues which add up to an adversary which you are trying to suppress ... that's from Singapore's point of view how you have the best chance of developing a constructive relationship *and avoiding very bad outcomes.* (my italics)[6]

---

6    Barrett 2021.

For Morrison, that seemed to have been as "wind past the ears", which is only consistent with his government's general attitude to the countries and leaders of South-east Asia.

If Australia is to live securely and constructively with a dominant China in its region, it would need to work its way back to that Singapore-kind of thinking on dealing with China. The election of a Labor government in May 2022 presented an opportunity, and from very early in the life of this government there was a willingness, on both sides, to engage, and ministerial contact was resumed. It became apparent that the government was developing a two-pronged approach to China, although not explicitly stated as such: the public rhetoric of the previous government continued, in lower key, presumably to forestall Opposition attempts to make China a destructive and divisive public issue, while at the same time they moved quietly behind the scenes to "stabilise the relationship", an expression used by both countries after Labor assumed office. There was constructive private messaging between the two, discussion between Foreign Minister Penny Wong and her Chinese counterpart Wang Yi, and then an important breakthrough meeting between Anthony Albanese and Xi Jinping during the G20 in Bali in November 2022.

It was also evident, from Foreign Minister Penny Wong's immediate appointment of a China-experienced senior career diplomat to head the Department of Foreign Affairs and Trade and a motivational speech she gave to the entire staff of the department that she was intent on restoring the pre-eminence of the Department of Foreign Affairs and Trade as the primary authoritative foreign policy agency and voice in Canberra. This would be a necessary prerequisite to any attempt to contain or balance the role and influence of the security and intelligence agencies.

But it was obvious that most of those same individuals in the security and intelligence community were still in positions of influence; they were not known to have shed their views on China and race; and their influence could be detected in some of the Labor government's rhetoric and positioning. Choosing to make a joint statement with Japan and the United States on the PRC firing of missiles in the wake of the visit to Taiwan by the US Speaker of the House, Nancy Pelosi, might be one example, and certainly not the brightest or most effective diplomacy in any attempt to influence Beijing towards restraint and moderation.

There are risks in maintaining the Morrison rhetoric, even if more muted and measured. It is not conducive to working towards a more stable and constructive relationship with China and could easily be misconstrued in Beijing. Fundamentally for Australia, it does not deal with, indeed it encourages, the underlying racism against China and the concomitant stigmatising of Chinese Australians. The dog whistle is embedded in this rhetoric, and will remain unless consciously and definitively confronted.

What Australia needs, for the good of our society and social cohesion, is for the Labor government to find a dramatic circuit-breaker, comparable in effect to Whitlam's in 1971, to open our minds, jolt us out of our complacency and self-referencing, confront our attitudes to race and demonstrate the great contribution of Chinese Australians to the Australian story in our history and today, and the benefits of talking seriously and productively with China.

That doesn't mean surrender to China or capitulation or weakness. We must be sceptics: China sceptics *and* US sceptics. This will require strength of mind and intellectual capacity, a knowledge of international politics and a grasp of the dynamics of diplomacy, and courage and fortitude against opponents in their own party and in the face of the now well-established countervailing discourse. Foreign Minister Wong has shown that she does have such attributes, and the potential to deliver.

If a stabilised relationship with China could also go hand in hand with a government policy to renew support and funding and encouragement for a nationwide effort to know China, to learn its language, to want to understand how the PRC works, what younger generations aspire to, what they are fearful of and how they see the international environment, this can only enhance the Australian capacity to deal with China and the Chinese-influenced world in which we now live.

# References

Barrett, Chris (2021). 'Don't have to become like them': Singapore advises Australia to work with China. *Sydney Morning Herald*, 10 June. https://bit.ly/41u2Ujl.
FitzGerald, Stephen (1997). *Is Australia an Asian country?* Sydney: Allen & Unwin.
Gyngell, Allan (2021). *Fear of abandonment. Australia in the world since 1942.* Melbourne: Black Inc.
Hsu, Jennifer and Natasha Kassam (2022). Being Chinese in Australia: public opinion in Chinese communities, Lowy Institute. https://bit.ly/41yjSgm.
Suich, Max (2021). How Australia got badly out in front on China. *Australian Financial Review*, 17, 18 and 19 May. https://bit.ly/3VUsVXY.

# Contributors

**Ien Ang** is Distinguished Professor of Cultural Studies at Western Sydney University, where she was the founding director of the Institute for Culture and Society. Her work has focused on cultural diversity and globalisation, Asia–Australia relations, immigration and urban change, and the politics of media and cultural institutions. An important strand of her work engages with the complexities of Chinese diaspora and identity. She is the author of several books, including *On not speaking Chinese: living between Asia and the West* (Routledge, 2001) and, most recently, the co-authored *Chinatown unbound: trans-Asian urbanism in the age of China* (Rowman and Littlefield, 2019).

**Danny Cooper** is a researcher and tutor at the University of Sydney. He is the author of *Neoconservatism and American foreign policy: a critical analysis* (Routledge, 2011). He also published "Lessons from Iraq: the agony and ambivalence of an American liberal" in the *Australian Journal of International Affairs* (May 2014), and, with Brendon O'Connor, "Ideology and the foreign policy of Barack Obama: A liberal-realist approach to international affairs", *Presidential Studies Quarterly* (July 2021).

**Lloyd Cox** is a senior lecturer in Politics and International Relations at Macquarie University, Sydney. He is the author of *Nationalism: themes, theories and controversy* (Palgrave, 2021) and co-author of *Australian* *politics in the twenty-first century: old institutions, new challenges* (Cambridge University Press, 2018). In recent years his work has focused on international relations, emotions, and the US–Australia alliance, with work published in *Political Science Quarterly*, *Review of International Studies* and the *Australian Journal of International Affairs*.

**Stephen FitzGerald AO** is chairman of the board of the Museum of Chinese in Australia; Adjunct Professor at the Institute for Australian and Chinese Arts and Culture, and Distinguished Fellow at the Whitlam Institute, both at Western Sydney University; board member of China Matters; and fellow of the Australian Institute for International Affairs. He was the first Australian ambassador to the People's Republic of China. He has been the chair of the Asian Studies Council, of the Committee to Advise on Australia's Immigration Policies, of the Griffith Asia Institute and founder and chair of the Asia–Australia Institute at the University of New South Wales. He has held professorial positions relating to China and Asia in four Australian universities.

**Bates Gill** is Executive Director of the Center for China Analysis with the Asia Society Policy Institute and an honorary professor with Macquarie University. He is also a Senior Associate Fellow with the Royal United Services Institute. Previously he was Professor of Asia–Pacific Security Studies and head of the Department of Security Studies and Criminology at Macquarie University, CEO of the United States Studies Centre at the University of Sydney (2012–15), director of the Stockholm International Peace Research Institute (2007–12), and the Freeman Chair in China Studies at the Center for Strategic and International Studies (2002–07). His most recent book is *Daring to struggle: China's global ambitions under Xi Jinping* (Oxford University Press, 2022).

**Hans Hendrischke** is Professor of Chinese Business and Management at the University of Sydney Business School. He leads the school's China Research Network and chairs the Business and Economics cluster of the University's China Studies Centre. Educated at universities in Germany, Taiwan and Japan, Hans did his postgraduate research at the Contemporary China Institute at the School of Oriental and African Studies, University of London. He speaks and writes fluent Chinese and is a frequent commentator on China business and Australia–China business relations in national and international media. His team's reports with KPMG on *Demystifying Chinese investment in Australia* receive wide international coverage. Hans lived in China from 1979, working for the diplomatic service and in the finance industry. In his academic career he was director of the Centre for Chinese Political Economy at Macquarie University, co-director of the University of New South Wales – University of Technology Sydney Centre for Research on Provincial China and head of school at University of New South Wales, and director of the University of Sydney Confucius Institute.

**Glenda Korporaal OAM** is a Sydney-based writer and journalist. She has been visiting China since 1978 when she went on a "farm study tour". She has worked as a correspondent for the *Australian Financial Review* in London, Washington and New York, returning to Sydney as the first woman deputy editor of the paper. She has worked in Hong Kong and Singapore and was the China correspondent for the *Australian* in 2018 and 2019. She has worked as a journalist for the *Sydney Morning Herald*, the *Australian Financial Review*, the *Bulletin* magazine and the *Australian* newspaper, where her roles have included editing the paper's monthly business magazine, *The Deal*, and becoming associate editor (business). The author of several books, she is now a columnist for the paper and an industry fellow at the Australia–China Relations Institute at the University of Technology Sydney. She was awarded an OAM for her contribution to newspaper journalism in 2019.

**James Laurenceson** is director of the Australia–China Relations Institute at the University of Technology Sydney. He has previously held appointments at the University of Queensland (Australia) and Shandong University (China). His academic research focuses on the Chinese economy and the Australia–China economic and broader relationship, and has been published in leading journals such as *China Economic Review* and *China Economic Journal*. Professor Laurenceson also provides regular commentary on contemporary developments in these areas in outlets such as the *Australian Financial Review* and *South China Morning Post*.

**Wei Li** is a Lecturer in International Business at the University of Sydney Business School. Dr Li is a core member of the KPMG/Business

School research team and leads the Chinese outbound investors' survey project. She co-developed the KPMG/University of Sydney database on Chinese outbound direct investment in Australia. She previously held the Australian-Chinese Chamber of Commerce and Industries research fellowship. She has worked as a researcher on water conservation and renewable energy for the World Bank, the Chinese Ministry of Environmental Protection and Renmin University of China. She has published articles on green innovation and solar energy, environmental impact assessment, governance of water resources, small- and medium-enterprise finance, and Chinese investment in Australia.

**Brendon O'Connor** is a professor in the Department of Government and International Relations and in the United States Studies Centre at the University of Sydney. He has authored two books, co-authored two books, edited nine books and numerous articles on anti-Americanism, US foreign relations, and US welfare policy. His most recent books are *Ideologies of American foreign policy* (Routledge, 2019, co-authored with John Callaghan and Mark Phythian) and *Anti-Americanism and American exceptionalism: prejudice and pride about the USA* (Routledge, 2020). He has an article on US alliances in the Fall 2020 edition of *Political Science Quarterly*.

**Geoff Raby AO** was Australia's ambassador to China from 2007 to 2011. Between 2002 and 2006, he was Deputy Secretary in the Department of Foreign Affairs and Trade, with responsibilities for north-east Asia and international trade negotiations. He has held a number of other senior positions in the department, including APEC ambassador (2002–04); first assistant secretary, International Organisations and Legal Division (2001–02); ambassador and permanent representative to the World Trade Organization, Geneva (1998–01); and first assistant secretary, Trade Negotiations Division (1995–98). He has published numerous academic articles and is the author of three books, the latest being *China's grand strategy and Australia's future in the new world order* (Melbourne University Publishing 2020). In recognition of his contributions to advancing relations between Australia and China and his contribution to multilateral trade diplomacy, Dr Raby was awarded the Order of Australia in June 2019.

**Jamie Reilly** is an associate professor in the Department of Government and International Relations at the University of Sydney. He has been a Jean Monnet Fellow at the European University Institute in Florence, Italy, and a post-doctoral research fellow at the University of Oxford. He also served as the East Asia Representative of the American Friends Service Committee in China from 2001 to 2008. His articles have also appeared in numerous edited volumes and academic journals. He is the author of *Strong society, smart state: the rise of public opinion in China's Japan policy* (Columbia, 2012) and the co-editor of *Australia and China at 40* (NewSouth Books, 2012). His most recent book is *Orchestration: China's economic statecraft across Asia and Europe* (Oxford, 2021).

**Wanning Sun** is Professor of Media and Communication at University of Technology Sydney. She is a specialist in a number of areas, including Chinese media and cultural studies; rural-to-urban emigration and social change in contemporary China; and soft power, public diplomacy and diasporic Chinese media. She is the author of three monographs: *Leaving China: media, migration, and transnational imagination* (Rowman & Littlefield, 2002); *Maid in China: media, morality, and the cultural politics of boundaries* (Routledge, 2009); and *Subaltern China: rural migrants, media, and cultural practices* (Rowman & Littlefield, 2014). Two of her edited volumes – *Media and the Chinese diaspora: community, communication and commerce* (Routledge, 2006) and *Media and communication in the Chinese diaspora: rethinking transnationalism* (Routledge, 2016) – document the history and development of Chinese language media in Australia, North America, Europe, Africa, South America and South-east Asia.

**Anthony Welch** is Professor of Education at the University of Sydney. Numerous of his publications address education reforms, principally within Australia and the Asia–Pacific, mainly on higher education. He has advised state, national and international agencies, governments, institutions and foundations in Australia, the United States, Europe and East, Central and South-east Asia. His work appears in numerous European and Asian languages, and he has been a Visiting Professor in the United States, United Kingdom, Germany, France, Japan, Malaysia, Turkey, Sweden and Hong Kong. He has been a Fulbright Scholar,

DAAD Scholar, Carnegie Foundation, INRP and Tübitak awardee, among others. His recent books include *Measuring up in higher education* (Palgrave, 2021) and *International faculty in Asia in comparative global perspective* (Springer, 2021).

**Jingdong Yuan** is Associate Professor at the Centre for International Security Studies, University of Sydney, and an Associate Senior Fellow at Stockholm International Peace Research Institute. Dr Yuan's research focuses on Indo–Pacific security, Chinese foreign policy, Sino–Indian relations, China–European Union relations, and nuclear arms control and nonproliferation. He has held visiting appointments at the National University of Singapore, University of Macau, East–West Center, National Chengchi University, Mercator Institute for China Studies, Fudan University, Berlin Social Sciences Centre (WZB) and the United Nations Institute for Disarmament Research (UNIDIR). He is the co-author of *Chinese cruise missiles: a quiet force-multiplier* (National Defense University, 2014) and *China and India: cooperation or conflict?* (Lynne Rienner, 2003), and co-editor of *Trump's America and international relations in the Indo–Pacific* (Springer, 2021) and *Australia and China at 40* (NewSouth Books, 2012). His publications have appeared in numerous journals and edited volumes. He is currently completing a book manuscript on China–South Asian relations.

**Weihuan Zhou** is Associate Professor, Director of Research and an inaugural member of the Herbert Smith Freehills China International Business and Economic Law (CIBEL) Centre, Faculty of Law and Justice, University of New South Wales. His research explores the most current and controversial issues in the field of international economic law, particularly the nexus between international trade law and China. His work has appeared in all top journals in the field and has been cited widely. Dr Zhou is co-secretary of the Society of International Economic Law (SIEL) and a member of the editorial board of the *Journal of International Trade Law and Policy*.

# Index

# Index